THE ANGER CONTROL WORKBOOK

Matthew McKay, Ph.D.
& Peter Rogers, Ph.D.

New Harbinger Publications, Inc.

Publisher's Note

This publication is designed to provide accurate and authoritative information in regard to the subject matter covered. It is sold with the understanding that the publisher is not engaged in rendering psychological, financial, legal, or other professional services. If expert assistance or counseling is needed, the services of a competent professional should be sought.

Distributed in the U.S.A. by Publishers Group West; in Canada by Raincoast Books; in Great Britain by Airlift Book Company, Ltd.; in South Africa by Real Books, Ltd.; in Australia by Boobook; and in New Zealand by Tandem Press.

Copyright © 2000 by Matthew McKay and Peter D. Rogers
      New Harbinger Publications, Inc.
      5674 Shattuck Avenue
      Oakland, CA 94609

Cover design by Lightbourne Images
Edited by Heather Garnos
Text design by Michele Waters

Library of Congress number: 00-134871
ISBN 1-57224-220-5 Paperback

Printed in the United States of America

New Harbinger Publications' Web site address: www.newharbinger.com

02   01   00

10   9   8   7   6   5   4   3   2   1

First printing

This book is dedicated to all the people I've ever loved. And especially those who have loved me back.

—P.D.R.

For Noah Landis and Wendy Millstine, who've shown me a lot about having a passion for life.

—M.M.

CONTENTS

Acknowledgment

We wish to acknowledge the extraordinary body of research by Jerry L. Deffenbacher, Ph.D., which has greatly advanced our knowledge of anger and its treatment, and is the basis of the core anger management program presented in this book.

INTRODUCTION

As psychologists with a combined fifty-two years in practice, we've come to some conclusions about the problem of anger:

1. For most people, chronic anger covers incredible pain. And while anger often feels like a release at the moment, it inevitably makes the underlying pain worse.

2. Of those people who suffered the greatest damage in childhood, most were harmed by repeated exposure to anger. The majority of chronically angry people were also damaged by anger as children.

3. People struggling with chronic anger suffer long-term consequences in both work and personal relationships. They tend to feel more alone, more disappointed by life, and less nourished by their relationships.

4. The greatest predictor of satisfaction in marriage is how people learn to handle conflict and anger.

5. Anger is a learned response, and the anger response can be *unlearned* with commitment and effort.

Anger is ubiquitous in our society, from road rage to the soaring incidence of child physical abuse. Everyone is touched by it. Over the years, and tens of thousands of hours of therapy, we have seen what it costs our clients—both those who struggle with overwhelming bouts of anger, and those who are its victims. The regret, the loss, the hurt and fear leave deep scars on everyone.

Because we've seen so much pain associated with anger, we wrote, in 1989, a book called *When Anger Hurts*. The response to this book has shown us just how important the issue of anger has become. More than 200,000 copies are now in print. The book has been used as a text in anger management courses at Kaiser Permanente and the Nursing Education of America, as well as clinics and adult education programs all over North America. Hundreds of therapists regularly assign the book as homework for clients with anger problems. Many dozens of readers have contacted us to express their appreciation, and sometimes to offer suggestions for future publications.

One of the most frequent suggestions we've gotten regards the need for a step-by-step workbook that teaches anger management through a series of structured exercises. "Less theory and more practice," someone said. Another reader asked for "a sequence of skill-building exercises that teach what you need to know in the order you need to learn it."

The Anger Control Workbook has grown from these requests. This book is all about acquiring, in a step-by-step format, the skills you need to better manage anger. There are no fancy explanations, no wasted words. Just key information, along with exercises that will give you greater control over your anger response. The techniques you will learn here are proven. In study after study, relaxation techniques combined with cognitive restructuring and anger inoculation have helped to lower the frequency and intensity of anger. They will work for you too—if you commit the time and effort to actually do the exercises in this book.

The Anger Control Workbook is, unfortunately, work. It takes practice to master anger control skills. Reading won't be enough. Hoping to change won't be enough. You've already done that, and you now know that wishes and hopes are forgotten with the next outburst. You need to turn hope into action—a commitment to work your way, stepwise, through each chapter in the workbook, and to practice the new skills until they start to become second nature.

While the work won't be easy, we promise you that the reading will be. Everything you need to do is carefully and clearly explained. There are lots of examples. Worksheets help you organize your efforts, and learning is broken into small steps so nothing feels overwhelming. You will find that each chapter is set up to help you change in increments, and from the very beginning you will be given new tools to start acting differently.

Everything you need to know to overcome anger is here. Just keep reading. And working. We'll be there to help you every step of the way.

Matthew McKay
Peter D. Rogers
Calistoga, California
April 2000

CHAPTER 1

GETTING STARTED: EMERGENCY ANGER CONTROL

You're reading this book because you want to change. Chances are you're been struggling with anger for a long time, and you don't like how it affects you and those you love. Looking back, you can remember plenty of situations where you said or did things out of anger that you later wished deeply you could undo. And you've probably resolved—many times—to speak more calmly or gently, to be more understanding and less blaming, or simply to keep the lid on.

It hasn't worked. You remembered for a few hours or a few days. Then something pushed your buttons and before you knew it, all your best intentions were swept away. You may have felt guilty and bad—disgusted with yourself that your reactions seemed so automatic, so difficult to control. Perhaps you have felt helpless, watching yet another wave of anger sweep over you. It wells up in your stomach, flooding you with the need to shout and blame.

For some people, anger feels more like a cold rage, deep and poisonous. It leaks out a little at a time but never resolves, never heals. Something is terribly wrong or unfair; you feel trapped and in pain. Nothing you do seems to make it better, so the anger sets up housekeeping in your gut.

Anger isn't always about the current annoyance—this nitwit who can't take a message, or the person who cut in front of you at the toll plaza. Often the roots of anger can be traced back to earlier times when you were hurt, abused, or neglected in your family of origin. The pain was something you carried, year after year. It may have left scars so that now it's hard to feel safe or loved or truly worthy. Sometimes it doesn't take much of a provocation to trigger those feelings of being unloved, unworthy, or unsafe—and the anger rises up right alongside that old pain.

From the very start, it's important to get one thing straight. You aren't to blame because you struggle with anger. You are not a bad person because you've forgotten—perhaps repeatedly—all your resolutions to be cool and calm. Rather, you are a person in pain. Whether the pain is occasional or chronic, when it hits, it feels overwhelming. It's a wave that drives you into a state of mind where nothing matters but expressing what you feel. You shout it out. No matter who gets hurt or whatever the consequences.

Anger is a way of coping. It helps, temporarily, to overcome the hurt and helplessness. For a moment you feel back in control, and that's exactly why anger is so hard to manage. If you try to put a cork in your anger, you may feel acutely the pain that triggered it.

So now is the time to stop kicking yourself. It doesn't help. In fact, blaming yourself for your anger simply creates more pain—bad, unworthy feelings—and the pain triggers more anger. It's a self-perpetuating cycle. If you're going to get off this merry-go-round, you'll need another way to view your anger problem. Your anger is:

- A response you learned early in life to cope with pain.

- A way, however temporary, to overcome feelings of helplessness and lack of control.

- A habit that, up till now, you've lacked the tools to break.

This book will give you what you've needed but never before possessed. You will learn (1) effective, proven strategies to control angry feelings, and (2) ways to manage stress and solve problems that often fuel your anger.

Acquiring new anger management tools will take time, probably two to four months. That's the bad news. But the good news is that you *can* learn them and, in doing so, change your life. They're right here—keep reading, and keep doing the exercises. And there's more good news. While it will take time to learn your new anger management skills, there's something you can do about your anger right now—today.

Twenty-Four-Hour Commitment to Act Calm

Notice it isn't a commitment to *be* calm, just to *act* that way. Effective anger management starts with a specific, time-limited decision. You need to commit to yourself and to key people in your life that you are going to behave in a calm, nonaggressive way. Not forever. That's impossible; no one could promise such a thing. Not even for a week. That's far too long, given how strong and habitual your anger response is. Your commitment is just for a single twenty-four-hour day.

Here's how you make it work:

1. Tell people. Share with every significant person in your life that you are absolutely committed to behaving in a calm way between _____ and _____. Explain that this means you won't shout at, swear at, hit, blame, attack, or denigrate *anyone*. Absolutely. No exceptions or excuses. Let them know that you're going to be vigilant and on guard for aggressive behavior throughout the designated time period.

2. Ask for help. There's a good chance—especially if you experience frequent, unpredictable anger—that this won't be easy. So you need real help, not just people's good wishes. Give family and friends a nonverbal signal they can use to let you know if you're looking or sounding angry. Something like a referee's time-out sign, or the gesture an umpire uses when a player slides in safe, or just a slowly descending hand that means "relax, calm down." Whatever signal you want to use, write it in the space below and tell people how it works.

_____

Prepare yourself in advance, that whenever you see the signal you will stop talking until you can once again appear calm. Remember, you don't have to *be* calm, just *act* calm.

3. Sign a contract. Have one close person sign as witness to the contract below.

Twenty-Four-Hour Commitment

I, _____ , between _____ o'clock on _____ ,

                                                                    (date)

and _____ o'clock on _____ , promise to behave

                                 (date)

in a calm, nonaggressive manner. I will act calmly no matter what stress or provocation may occur.

_____

Your signature

_____

Witness signature

---

4. See the benefit. What's the number one thing you want to achieve through anger management? A better relationship with your spouse, your kids, your friends? A chance to heal old wounds with your family? A better shot at rewards and promotions at work? A renewed feeling of pride and self-worth? An end to dangerous or costly behavior? Whatever is your biggest and best reason for acting calm, write it in the space below:

_____

_____

5. Plan for provocations. Assume that during the twenty-four hours, things will happen to upset you. A few of them you can probably even anticipate. Write below at least four provoking events that could threaten your commitment to calm behavior.

    a. _____

    b. _____

    c. _____

    d. _____

To face these or similar anger triggers, you'll need a few simple strategies.

What to Do When You Get Angry

First, and most important, stop. Don't do or say anything. Don't act on the angry feelings. This is just an emotion. It's a strong one, but you can feel it without turning it into behavior.

Try to step back from the feeling and label it. Notice its strength: be aware of how it pushes you toward action. Accept it. There's nothing inherently wrong with anger. It's just a signal that you're in pain. The only problem is when you act on anger to hurt others or yourself.

Don't push the feeling away, but don't try to hold onto it either. It will come like a wave—building, cresting, then slowly receding. Let it come, and then let it go. Watch how it grows and diminishes, as if you were a scientist observing some interesting phenomenon. Take care not to do anything to amplify your anger. Don't dwell on the unfairness of the situation.

Don't review past failings of the offending individual. Don't rehearse in your mind the events leading to your anger. Just notice and accept the feeling, watching as it gradually diminishes.

Act the Opposite

One of the quickest ways to change a painful feeling is to act the opposite. During your twenty-four-hour commitment to calm behavior, anger can be a signal to put a very different face on your emotions.

- Smile instead of frown. The very act of smiling when angry tends to diminish the strength of your upset feelings.

- Speak softly rather than loudly. Go overboard on this. Make your voice lower and gentler than usual; try to make it soothing.

- Relax instead of tighten. Let your arms hang loose. Take a breath. Lean against something in a casual way or sit with your legs crossed comfortably. Look calm, even if you don't feel it.

- Disengage rather than attack. You may want to get right in the other person's face. You may want to shake them—emotionally if not physically. Instead, look or walk away. Make no comment about the provoking situation. Save it for another time. You'll only blow up if you try to deal with this now.

- Empathize rather than judge. Say something mildly supportive, such as, "This is a difficult situation for you," or "I can see why you're concerned (upset, overwhelmed, dismayed, etc.)." It's okay if you don't feel supportive and the words seem phony. You can have a strong desire to take a two-by-four to the other person. But just *behave* as if you can appreciate their point of view.

   "You rammed the car into the garage door? (gritting your teeth) When you're rushed, it's easy to get rattled." "You got a D+ on your math test? (rapidly growing knot in your stomach) You've been distracted, I think, but we can get back on track."

Beyond the First Twenty-four Hours

When you've gotten through the first twenty-four-hours, you have a choice. Make additional twenty-four-hour commitments (blank contracts are at the end of the chapter), or monitor your anger (using forms found in chapter 3). In either case, start working through the book to build your new anger management skills.

   Notice the word "working" in the last sentence. Simply reading this book isn't enough. It will take a real effort to change such a powerful response habit. You'll need to actually complete the worksheets, exercises, and monitoring activities. And you'll need to practice your new skills every day. It's going to take time and energy, but the benefits you'll achieve by changing your angry behavior will be more than worth it.

Twenty-Four-Hour Commitment

I, _____, between _____ o'clock on _____,
                                                                (date)
and _____ o'clock on _____, promise to behave
                              (date)
in a calm, nonaggressive manner. I will act calmly no matter what stress or provocation may occur.

_____
Your signature

_____
Witness signature

Twenty-Four-Hour Commitment

I, _____, between _____ o'clock on _____,
                                                                (date)
and _____ o'clock on _____, promise to behave
                              (date)
in a calm, nonaggressive manner. I will act calmly no matter what stress or provocation may occur.

_____
Your signature

_____
Witness signature

Twenty-Four-Hour Commitment

I, _____, between _____ o'clock on _____,
                                                                (date)
and _____ o'clock on _____, promise to behave
                              (date)
in a calm, nonaggressive manner. I will act calmly no matter what stress or provocation may occur.

_____
Your signature

_____
Witness signature

CHAPTER 2

THE COSTS OF ANGER

It's Thursday morning. George has been working on the Whitehorse account all week when his boss calls him into the office and tells him to drop everything and start working on the Twingle project. George feels victimized. The Twingle project is much less prestigious than the Whitehorse account. It's not fair—he was just starting to get into it, and now he's out. He's upset, and tells his boss so in no uncertain terms, storming out of the office.

On the face of it, George's anger in this situation seems justified. And his display of strong feelings might even serve to let his boss know about his degree of commitment. Perhaps the boss will realize that his decision was unfair, and change his mind.

Perhaps. But let's look at more of George's behavior to get a better perspective. This is not the first time that he's blown up at work. In fact, there have been three other episodes in the past thirty days alone. First, there was the incident with the equipment supplier, who admittedly was two days late delivering a part that George needed. Then there was the angry exchange with a coworker about who had priority using the copy machine. Worst of all was that misunderstanding with a customer who had complained to his boss. Maybe the customer was being unreasonable, his boss had said, but that was no excuse for George to be sarcastic and rude.

On further analysis, it turns out that George has lost two previous jobs because of conflicts at work, and he's received low performance evaluations for poor people skills. But the picture is even worse in his personal life. His wife filed for divorce eighteen months ago saying she couldn't stand living with him anymore. He's also been estranged from his sixteen-year-old daughter ever since he blew up and made a scene at her birthday party. And even his brother won't talk to him anymore after that incident at the bowling alley. To top it off, a recent physical found that George has high blood pressure.

Taken one at a time, each of the events referred to above might be justified or understandable. But added together, they point to a chronic anger pattern that is emotionally and physiologically damaging.

Physiological Costs of Anger

There's nothing wrong with occasional, moderate anger. It creates no lasting harm. But chronic, sustained anger can be a serious problem. By keeping the body in a constant state of emergency, chronic anger can contribute to hypertension, heart disease, and increased mortality from *all* causes. This chapter will begin by exploring what we know about how anger impacts your health. Later we'll look at the emotional and interpersonal costs of chronic anger.

Anger and Hypertension

"High" blood pressure can be understood by thinking about garden hoses. Let's say that you have two garden hoses, one a half-inch in diameter and the other a quarter-inch in diameter. If you attach the half-inch hose to the faucet and turn the valve all the way you will get a steady stream of water. However, if you attach the quarter-inch hose to the same faucet, and turn the valve all the way as before, you will get a much stronger stream. Anger is associated with high levels of norepinephrine, which tends to constrict blood vessels. This raises blood pressure as surely as if you had switched to a smaller diameter hose.

The idea that unexpressed anger (anger-in) could lead to high blood pressure has been circulating for more than half a century. In 1939, Franz Alexander suspected that his hypertensive patients were having trouble with feelings of anger and an inability to express them. This failure to express angry feelings, he argued, could lead to chronic activation of the sympathetic nervous system, and high blood pressure. Research as early as 1942, by Hamilton, confirmed that unexpressed anger was inextricably linked to hypertension. In 1982, Diamond reviewed four decades of research involving the role of anger and hostility in essential hypertension and coronary heart disease. He described the hypertensive individual as someone "ridden with hostility and constantly guarding against impulse expression." In the same year, Gentry studied the effects of habitual anger coping styles on over a thousand subjects. With this larger sample, he showed categorically that chronic suppressed anger increased the risk for hypertension.

Research by Dimsdale and associates (1986) once again confirmed that higher blood pressure is significantly related to suppressed anger. In fact, "normotensives" were twice as likely as "hypertensives" to be free of suppressed anger. All in all, there are dozens of studies linking anger-in with hypertension. You will find the most significant of these listed in the appendix.

It's clear from the research literature that the inability (or unwillingness) to express anger contributes to the development of hypertension for many susceptible people. But that's only half the story. As it turns out, people who tend to show more hostility and act more aggressively towards others (anger-out) also have higher blood pressure rates than normal.

In a 1979 study, Harburg and his associates asked people how they would deal with an angry and arbitrary boss. People's responses were categorized into three different coping strategies. The first, walking away from the situation (anger-in), was associated with people who had high blood pressure readings. The second strategy, protestation (anger-out), included behaviors such as confronting the boss or reporting him to the union. This strategy was associated with people whose blood pressure was even higher than those using the walk-away coping style. A third group used a style dubbed "reflection." These people, who said that they would try to talk to the boss later, after he had cooled down, were found to have the lowest blood pressure rates.

A host of other studies (see the Appendix for a sampling) all confirm the basic hypothesis that chronically expressed anger is associated with high blood pressure and hypertension. So it doesn't matter whether anger is suppressed or allowed to blow. Either way, your blood pressure tends to go up. It's the anger itself that's harmful, not the choice to express it or hold it back.

Anger, Hostility, and Cardiovascular Disease

In the 1950s, San Francisco cardiologists Meyer Friedman and Ray Rosenman began their seminal work on the psychosocial risk factors that underlie blocked arteries, angina pains, and heart attacks. Eventually they were able to identify a cluster of personality traits that appeared to be linked to coronary heart disease. Using the nonpejorative term "type A," they described someone who had the traits of time urgency (always in a hurry) and competitiveness. In addition, this person was highly ambitious, hyperaggressive, and experienced free-floating hostility. The type A person can be seen as someone seething with anger, always ready to boil over.

In the 1960s Friedman and Rosenman (as reported in the classic, *Type A Behavior and Your Heart,* 1974) conducted the massive Western Collaborative Group Study on 3,500 healthy men. Eighty percent of those men who had heart disease could be classified as "type A." Over the eight-and-a-half-year course of the study, type A men were twice as likely to have heart attacks as type Bs. Rosenman (1985), in his reanalysis of the Western Collaborative Group Study data, found that the anger-hostility dimension proved to be crucial. It was, in Rosenman's words, "the dominant characteristic among the coronary prone type A behaviors."

Evidence from the Western Electric Study, done by Shekelle and associates in 1983, tends to corroborate Rosenman's findings. Of the 1,877 men studied in Chicago, those who scored high on a hostility scale were one and a half times more likely to have a heart attack than men who had lower hostility scores. Further corroboration comes from a follow-up study of 255 male physicians who completed the Hostility Scale while in medical school. Men who scored at the median or below in hostility had one-sixth the incidence of coronary heart disease twenty-five years later, compared to those who had scored higher on the scale (Barefoot et al. 1983).

Heart disease starts early for those who are chronically angry. Grunnbaum and his research group (1997) studied the association between anger or hostility and coronary heart disease in children and adolescents. Their review of epidemiological studies uncovered a strong connection between anger and pathologic changes in the arteries of young school-age children. For additional research on the relationship between hostility and coronary heart disease, see the appendix.

So far we've described research showing that the *feeling* of hostility is related to heart disease. But there is also abundant evidence that *expressed* hostility is strongly associated with coronary artery disease—*for people of all ages.* Kawachi and associates (1996) conducted a seven-year follow-up study of 1,305 men. They concluded that high levels of expressed anger are a risk factor for cardiac heart disease among older men. Siegman and associates (1987) found that expressed hostility was related to the severity of coronary artery disease in patients 60 years or younger.

The evidence is clear and overwhelming. Chronic anger and hostility can cause serious damage to your heart and arteries.

Anger, Hostility, and Death from All Causes

In 1989, the *New York Times* carried an article reporting on the results of a twenty-five-year follow-up study of law students. Among other health evaluations, the law students had taken a test measuring hostility. A striking fact emerged from this study. Twenty percent of those who had scored in the top quarter on the hostility scale were dead. This was compared to a death rate of only 5 percent for those students who had scored in the lowest quarter on the same test.

Similar results were found by Shekelle and associates in 1983. A twenty-year follow-up study of nearly two thousand initially disease-free employees of the Western Electric Company showed that high hostility scores were related to increased mortality *from all causes.*

The Finnish Twin Cohort study (Koskenvuo, et al. 1988) provides corroborating evidence from a different culture. Using a simple three-item hostility measure and a sample of 3,750 men, they found that high self-ratings of hostility were associated with increased all-cause mortality over a three-year follow-up period.

Clearly, the evidence overwhelmingly suggests that chronic anger and hostility can lead to overall poorer health, and even a likelihood of premature death.

Emotional and Interpersonal Costs of Anger and Hostility

While the physiological effects of anger, such as hypertension and artery disease, can become dramatically obvious, the emotional and interpersonal effects are more subtle. It may simply be a lonely feeling as friendships drift away. Or a sense of isolation at work because colleagues avoid making contact. Or a lack of intimacy in personal relationships as your partner becomes more guarded.

A host of studies (see the appendix) have found that high scores on hostility are associated with fewer and less satisfactory social supports. Greenglass (1996), for example, studied a sample of 252 male and 65 female managers in Canada. Those with high scores on anger-in reported receiving less support from family members. They also reported less trust in their close relationships.

Jerry Deffenbacher and his colleagues (see the appendix for a full list of research articles) have done the most extensive research on how chronic anger affects personal and work relationships. For example, Hazaleus and Deffenbacher (1986) found that 45 percent of angry males in their sample had suffered a terminated or damaged relationship during the previous year. Among other results, Deffenbacher (1992) found that angry individuals suffer significant disruptions in work or school performance, and that high anger people drink more alcohol and get drunk more often. Houston and Kelley (1989) also reported a strong relationship between anger scores and overall levels of conflict in both the family of origin and current marriages.

In 1981, Jones and his associates, found a significant relationship between hostility and loneliness. Angry people end up feeling painfully disconnected from others. When Hansson and associates reviewed the research on loneliness in 1984, they found that anger cuts people off from social support in two ways. Angry people have cynical attitudes toward others, and are therefore unable to recognize support when it's available. Similarly, their unrealistic and overly demanding expectations make the available support seem not "good enough." No matter how sincerely interested others may be in helping, the angry person is unable to experience or appreciate that support.

It's clear that angry people keep others at arm's length. In so doing, they experience less support and a greater sense of loneliness than their less hostile peers.

Assessing the Cost of Anger for You

Using the worksheets on the next page, we want you to make an honest assessment of all the ways in which anger has had a negative impact on your life. Once you have completed the exercise, it may become much clearer exactly how much anger has cost you personally. You will be ready to move on to the next chapter, which will help you to understand your anger.

PERSONAL COSTS OF ANGER—Worksheet

In the spaces provided below, write brief descriptions of how anger has affected you in each area. Put an asterisk by any numbered item that feels like a crucial reason for you to learn more about anger management.

1. How anger has affected my work relationships (include jobs lost or jeopardized):

_____

_____

2. How anger has affected the relationships to my family of origin (including parents, siblings, and extended family):

_____

_____

3. How anger has affected my marriage or intimate/romantic relationships:

_____

_____

4. How anger has affected my children:

_____

_____

5. How anger has affected my friendships (including lost friends and strained relationships):

_____

_____

6. How my anger has harmed people who aren't family or friends (including the names of all the people my anger has hurt—on a separate sheet if necessary):

_____

_____

7. How my anger has affected my health and physical well-being (including stress-related illnesses/problems and physical discomfort from anger reactions):

_____

_____

8. How anger has endangered me (including reckless driving, physical fights, hurting myself by hitting things, legal problems, etc.):

_____

_____

continued on next page

PERSONAL COSTS OF ANGER—Worksheet cont.

9. How anger has affected me financially (include bad decisions made in anger as well as material things broken or damaged):

_____

_____

10. How anger has affected me spiritually (including bad behavior that goes against my personal code of ethics or sense of right and wrong):

_____

_____

CHAPTER 3

UNDERSTANDING YOUR ANGER

You're reading this workbook because you're concerned about your anger. It's affecting important relationships and hurting those you care about. Perhaps it's getting you in trouble at work, while driving, or with store clerks. Maybe you're breaking things. Or it may even be affecting your health. With all the negatives associated with anger, why are you still blowing up? Why does anger remain such a powerful force in your life? Why, even when you resolve to control it, does your anger still flare up? In this chapter you'll find answers to these questions. A good place to start is understanding the five short-term payoffs that anger can provide.

Anger Payoffs

1. Anger reduces stress. Stress can come from a lot of sources—worry, frustration, unmet needs, physical pain or discomfort, rushing against deadlines, and so on. You don't need this book to tell you about your stress. What's important is the link between stress and anger. Stress creates physiological arousal—tension. The greater the stress, and the number of stressors, the more unpleasant is the arousal you feel.

    Anger discharges arousal, but only temporarily. Right after a blowup, people often feel oddly relaxed, like a weight has been lifted off their shoulders. It seems like they can breathe again. Even though these effects are brief, and tension soon returns, the anger discharge can be highly reinforcing. You get a break from everything that frustrates and overwhelms you.

    But there's a downside to using anger for stress reduction. The stress comes back with a vengeance. Studies show that anger creates more anger. Blowing up makes it more likely that you'll blow up again soon. Each time you indulge in anger to cope with stress, the next outburst becomes that much easier and stronger—and harder to control.

    Not only does your anger get worse, but so does the anger of those around you. They get hurt and defensive. They counterattack. And they harden, becoming less and less concerned about your needs and feelings.

Short-term, then, anger is a good strategy for discharging stress arousal. But it tends to boomerang. Later, you pay dearly in the coin of broken relationships.

2. Anger hides emotional pain. Anger is a good defense against fear, loss, guilt, shame, and feelings of rejection or failure. It puts a tight lid on painful emotions, locking most of the feelings out of awareness. Growing up in dysfunctional families, we watch Dad push away his shame with rage. Or Mom cope with her depression by yelling at the kids. We learn that we can stop virtually any painful feeling if we can just get mad enough.

But once again, the short-term payoff has long-term consequences. First of all, you don't let yourself experience feelings that may be important signals, offering guidance for what you need to do or stop doing in your life. Maybe there's a good reason you feel guilt, and you need to face it and do something about it. Maybe you need to face your depression, taking responsibility to make key changes in your life.

The second problem with using anger to defend against your feelings is that the feelings often get worse over time. You're not only guilty for some past failure—now you feel guilty for the new damage your anger has done. Or the depression worsens because your anger is turning people off and isolating you. Now you have to crank up your anger even more to block these higher levels of guilt or sadness.

The third problem with using anger as a defense is that it becomes habitual. The anger reflex seems to go off at the slightest criticism or hurt, or the slightest anxiety. Say you're a little worried while trying to figure out the bills. Boom! It's a lot easier to blow up because your partner bought a sixty-dollar espresso maker than to feel uncertainty about your finances.

3. Anger gets you attention. Sometimes it seems that no one listens to you unless you're yelling. Anger does grab people's attention. They get alarmed and sometimes they'll try to placate you. But once again, the immediate payoff has long-term outcomes that hurt you. First, a certain percentage of people don't respond to anger with attentive listening. They get immediately defensive and tune you out. They start avoiding you or, worse, they hold it against you. The problem is that you've chosen a strategy that makes some people sit up and listen, and some people run.

The second problem with using anger to get attention is that the people who responded initially get inured and hardened over time. They stop being alarmed by your anger and start being disgusted by it. Instead of listening, they resent you and shut down.

4. Anger may be used for punishment and revenge. Someone really lets you down. They screw up because they're lazy or stupid or don't care about you. Inside is this huge wave of rage. You want to punish them and teach them a lesson. You want them to feel as much pain as you do. God, it feels good. This righteousness, this will to harm, is so powerful that it's all you care about. You hunger for the opportunity to get back at them—whether it's a screamed insult or a carefully planned revenge.

The trouble is, each time you act on these impulses, you make enemies, and the enemies often end up being the people you love and need most. Naturally, your enemies want to punish *you*. The world becomes a stage for bitter struggles, where old hurts and grudges push each of you to new excesses of rage and aggression.

5. Anger helps you change others. In dysfunctional families, we learn to use anger to extort things from others. We coerce them with blowups, or the fear of blowups, into complying with our demands. It's tempting to use anger as a club because, at least in the short term, people often give you what you want.

In the long run, of course, they turn off and turn away from you. They resent being controlled by fear. But worst of all is what it does to you. Using your anger to change others leaves you feeling helpless. When you're in pain, when something hurts, it always seems like the other person has to fix it. You feel powerless to overcome the problem yourself. And all you know how to do is try to coerce the other person into corrective action.

By placing the responsibility to change a painful situation outside yourself, you are starting down the royal slippery slope toward helplessness and depression. You're leaving others in charge of your pain and your life.

Exercise: What Are Your Anger Payoffs?

In this exercise you'll identify which of the five anger payoffs are influencing you. Don't be surprised if all or most are playing a part in your anger. For each anger payoff listed below, do a mental inventory of relationships and situations in your life (e.g., anger with family, friends, kids, coworkers, boss, clerks, receptionists; road anger; anger at objects, etc.). See if that payoff is in any way influencing or reinforcing your anger. If so, select a typical example and write it in the space provided.

1. Reduce stress—using anger to discharge stress-related arousal.

   _____

   _____

   _____

   _____

2. Hide emotional pain—using anger to defend against shame, guilt, depression, anxiety, and so on.

   _____

   _____

   _____

   _____

3. Get attention—using anger to alarm people so they'll listen to you.

   _____

   _____

   _____

   _____

4. Punishment and revenge—using anger to make people feel as much pain as you do.

   _____

   _____

   _____

   _____

5. Change the behavior of others—using anger to coerce people to do what you want.

_____

_____

_____

_____

You're now aware of some of the key factors that reinforce your anger and why anger has such powerful short-term effects. But there's more you need to know. To have a better chance at managing your anger, you'll need to understand the psychological mechanisms that create it. What follows is an explanation of the components of the anger response.

How You Get Angry

Anger is a two-step process. It starts with the experience of pain. The pain can be physical or emotional—it could be a stomachache or fatigue, feelings of rejection or loss. The pain can be something that frustrates your needs or threatens your safety. The particular kind of pain doesn't matter. What's important is that the pain by definition is unpleasant and makes you want to put an end to it. The second component of the anger response is trigger thoughts. These are interpretations, assumptions, and evaluations of a situation that make you feel victimized and deliberately harmed by others. Trigger thoughts blame and condemn others for the painful experience you've suffered.

You might think of emotional or physical pain as the fuel of anger. It's like a can of gasoline, and your trigger thoughts are the match. Either of the anger components alone is harmless. Pain by itself doesn't ignite rage, and trigger thoughts without pain are like a match without fuel.

Pain _plus_ trigger thoughts equals anger. It's a simple formula. Imagine that you have a headache and your fourteen-year-old starts nagging you about going to a party that will involve drinking. She keeps pushing, and your head keeps pounding. Her pressure and the pain in your head aren't enough to get angry. You need a match—a trigger thought that says she's an inconsiderate kid who doesn't give a damn about how tired you are. Now the anger catches fire. You're hurting, and you have someone to blame. You've decided who's responsible for your pain. The next words out of your mouth are loud and attacking. Your daughter stares at you like you just went nuts, but in reality it was a simple matter of putting the fuel and match together.

Once you get angry, trigger thoughts can also make it worse. They can escalate your upset by continually painting the other person as bad and wrong and deliberately out to harm you. Each new trigger thought pushes your anger a notch higher, until you end up saying and doing very damaging things. Pain begets trigger thoughts, which beget anger, more trigger thoughts, more anger, and so on. Your thoughts and angry feelings become a self-perpetuating feedback loop.

Exercise: The Anger Log

The Anger Log is a tool that provides an opportunity to learn more about the components of your anger response. The log is divided into seven columns. The first column is labeled Pain/Stress; there you record the emotional and physical pain that existed before your anger. It might be a headache or anxiety about your marriage. It might be a frustrated need, or pressure to get a job done. The stress or pain might have gone on for hours preceding your anger, or it might be a direct outgrowth of the provocative situation. Try to include here every stressful or painful experience you can think of that might be influencing your anger response.

The next column is labeled Provocative Situation. Here you briefly note the upsetting event that preceded your anger. The third column, Trigger Thoughts, is where you write down what you're thinking while getting angry. These thoughts tend to label the provoking person as wrong, or bad, or harming you in some way. The fourth column is Anger Rating. Here you'll write in a number, from 0 to 100, that reflects how angry you felt. Zero would indicate no anger, whereas 100 is the highest level of rage you can imagine experiencing. When you rate each anger experience, you make a subjective judgment about where your anger falls on the continuum between those two extremes. The fifth column is labeled Behavior. Here you record what you actually *did* in response to your anger. Did you yell or speak sharply? Did you curse or call the other person names? Did you say something attacking or belittling? Were you in any way physically aggressive—shoving, shaking, hitting?

The last two columns are labeled Outcome. Here you'll note the effect of your anger on yourself and others. First of all, rate the impact from a -10 to +10 in terms of how you felt and what happened to you subsequent to your anger. Write a brief description of the emotional and objective consequences of your anger. Did you feel sad, relieved, scared? Did anything change in terms of your relationships to others? Were there consequences that you regret and that impacted you negatively? Now go through the same process in terms of how your anger may have impacted others. If you have any sense of how your anger affected them, rate it on the same -10 to +10 scale. Also note anything they said or did that appeared related to your anger.

What follows are two examples of actual Anger Logs filled out by Ginny and Ralph. Ginny is a thirty-seven-year-old X-ray technician. She's married to Bob and has a twelve-year-old son, Barry. Ralph is a fifty-one-year-old flight instructor who has a rocky relationship with his girlfriend, Laura.

Ginny's Anger Log

Pain/Stress	Provocative Situation	Trigger Thoughts	Anger Rating 0–100	Behavior	Outcomes -10 to +10 Self	Others
1. Feeling frustrated and hurt.	Barry refuses to finish cleaning up living room during Saturday morning family work time.	He's defying me, trying to upset me. I've had enough of his lazy shit.	75	Yelled and physically pulled him back to living room.	-7 I was disgusted with myself for losing it.	-7 He pouted the rest of the day.
2. Have a headache; feeling frustrated	Ordered clothes from a catalog that came in the wrong size.	Stupid, careless people.	60	Yelled at order clerk; called her a jackass.	-2 Felt better for a moment, then depressed about how easily I lose control.	?
3. Anxious about next day dental visit for root canal; very tired	Helping Barry do homework he put off till late at night.	Same old last-minute lazy shit. He puts everything off and just assumes I'll do it.	50	Told Barry in a harsh voice that he's driving me crazy; gave him silent treatment after that.	+1 For some reason I felt like I got through to him.	-5 Barry cried.
4. Stress from deadline at work; sadness and anxiety re Bob's recent complaints about marriage.	Bob asked me to pick up some barbecue briquettes.	He knows red meat is no good for me. He doesn't give a damn about my health.	80	Told him he doesn't give a rat's ass about anything but himself.	-9 I felt very depressed.	-8 Bob stormed out to get briquettes and was yelling about divorce.
5. Sadness about state of marriage; frustrated because I wanted to go to movies but couldn't because of pain from root canal.	Bob asked about Barry's C- in English.	He leaves me with all the responsibility for Barry's schoolwork. He pays no attention.	55	Got really sharp and told him it was his own fault for ignoring the problem.	-5 Felt more depressed.	-7 Bob got really upset and left. Barry overheard and started crying. Had to comfort him.

Ralph's Anger Log

Pain/Stress	Provocative Situation	Trigger Thoughts	Anger Rating 0–100	Behavior	Outcomes -10 to +10 Self	Others
1. Tired from party last night. Anxious because boss gets irritated when I'm late.	Someone cut in front of me at the bridge toll plaza.	Asshole thinks he owns the road. He needs a lesson in courtesy.	70	Shouted out the window and kept honking the horn.	-3 Felt upset and couldn't calm down.	?
2. Feel invisible, like I don't count. Old feeling from growing up.	Laura gets reservation at an Indian restaurant. Indian food burns my stomach.	It's all about her; it's all what she wants.	75	Told her to cancel reservation. Refused to go; acted very cold.	-7 Depressed, lonely. Destroying the relationship.	-5 She left in a huff, hasn't called.
3. Shame, feeling forced to do something. Also worried about money because fewer people call for flying lessons.	Mother calls from a bar drunk and wants me to drive her home.	She doesn't give a shit. She's been doing this to me too long.	90	Told her to f.o. and hung up.	+5 Felt kind of relieved and relaxed.	-3 Called her later—she hardly remembered.
4. Feeling pressured, worried about money.	Frequent flying student demands that I lower my rates.	Cheap bastard, he's got the money, he's just trying to screw me.	70	Raised my voice and told him to go find another flight instructor.	-9 Lost a student and needed income.	?
5. Feeling lonely, worried about money, kind of a hunger headache.	Laura calls last minute to say she has to work late and let's skip dinner tonight.	Doesn't give a shit about me. Just kisses up to her boss; probably doesn't have to stay. She wants to.	80	Raised voice on phone. Told her she should think about me once in a while instead of kissing up to everyone else.	-8 Very lonely and depressed.	? She laughed and said she wouldn't come home at all; hung up on me.

Now it's time to get some practice filling out your own log. On the blank Anger Log provided, fill in all the anger experiences you've had from the past week that you'd rate above 40 on the scale. If it's under 40 don't include it. Make sure you fill out the log for at least five experiences. If there weren't five in the last week, keep looking back to previous weeks until you're able to list the minimum five experiences.

As you fill out the log, be careful to differentiate between pain/stress and the provocative situation. Remember, pain/stress is what you felt physically or emotionally *before* getting angry that may have contributed to your anger response. The provocative situation is the actual event your anger focused on. Try to write down as many key trigger thoughts as possible. Later, after filling out a number of Anger Logs, you'll be able to identify themes in your trigger thoughts. When you recognize and understand the kinds of thoughts that most upset you, you'll have taken a first major step toward changing these anger triggers.

Right now, go ahead and fill in the blank Anger Log based on upsets from the past week.

Anger Log

Pain/Stress	Provocative Situation	Trigger Thoughts	Anger Rating 0–100	Behavior	Outcomes -10 to +10 Self	Others

Now that you've recorded at least five significant anger episodes from the past week, there are several important questions you should consider:

- What types of stresses or pain typically foreshadow high anger episodes? Are any of these stresses preventable? Could they be calmed or coped with in ways other than anger?

- What types of provocative situations are typically associated with high anger episodes? Is there a common theme or dynamic to high anger situations?

- What category of trigger thought most angers you (i.e., feeling treated unjustly, not being cared about, being ignored, blaming others, negative labels like stupid or selfish, assuming ill will, etc.)?

- Do you behave differently in response to moderate (50–60) anger as opposed to high (75–85) anger experiences? How would you like to change the way you express your anger?

- Are the outcomes more negative for high (75–85) as opposed to moderate (50–60) anger experiences?

- Are the outcomes from your anger experiences more often positive or negative? If negative, are the outcomes affecting you temporarily or also in the long term?

- Is your anger affecting others in ways that concern you?

- Are there specific trigger thoughts or trigger thought themes that seem to generate the most negative outcomes?

- Are there particular behaviors that seem to trigger more negative outcomes, either for yourself or others?

You'll return to these questions again after completing Anger Logs for the next several weeks. However, it's good to start asking them now, because careful observation of your anger helps to build motivation to complete the anger control program.

Exercise: Monitoring Your Anger

Using the blank Anger Log on the next page and making as many copies as you need, record all anger experiences over 40 on the scale during the coming week. Review your day at a consistent point each evening (for example, right at bedtime) and fill in all seven columns for all significant anger episodes. This is important work; that's why it's necessary to make a strong commitment to see it through. If you suspect you'll have difficulty maintaining the log, make a contract with a friend, and ask him or her to check in with you about your progress with the log.

Anger Log

Pain/Stress	Provocative Situation	Trigger Thoughts	Anger Rating 0–100	Behavior	Outcomes −10 to +10	
					Self	Others

CHAPTER 4

RELAXATION SKILLS I

Learning to relax is an essential element in achieving anger management. Remember, getting angry is a two-step process. First, physical tension or stress has to exist in the body, then it requires anger-triggering thoughts to complete the picture. Half the anger battle can be won by simply learning to relax the physical tension that develops in provocative situations. It's a proven fact that if you can relax your body, and keep it relaxed, it's almost impossible to get angry. Combating stress using the skills you're about to learn can help you calm down, think clearly, and handle any situation in an effective, positive way. The eventual goal is to become so good at relaxing that you can let go of tension any time, anywhere, in thirty seconds or less.

The first step to effective relaxation is a technique called *progressive relaxation training*. It's been around since the 1920s in one form or another, and is generally regarded as the keystone to successful stress release. Keep in mind the technique described below is not as easy as it sounds. It requires practice and a commitment to follow through. But the results are well worth the effort, paying off big dividends in anger management.

Progressive Relaxation Training:

The basic principle is to first increase the tension in your muscles, hold it for five to seven seconds, and then *relax*. Remember to focus on one set of muscles at a time. Repeat each procedure as many times as necessary to achieve the desired effect. (*Caveat:* Do not tense areas of physical pain, injury, or recent surgery. And remove contact lenses.)

1. Get into a comfortable seated position and give your body a chance to relax. Allow yourself to experience a comfortable feeling of heaviness. Now, start at the bottom and, stretching your legs out, point your toes (like a *ballerina*) away from your body, noting the tension in your ankles. Now point your *toes to head*, creating tension in your calves. Let your feet fall to the floor, take a deep breath, and relax.

2. Now tighten your buttocks (remember *tight bottom*), and then your thighs by pressing down on your heels as hard as you can. Hold the tension (five to seven seconds), then let go, take a deep breath, and relax.

3. Take a deep breath, filling up your lungs completely, and flex your chest muscles. Now tighten your stomach muscles, creating, in effect, a *coat of armor*. Hold, then exhale, and relax.

4. Now arch your back, as though it were a bow (remember *bow and arrow*). Avoid straining and keep the rest of your body as relaxed as possible. Notice the tension beginning down at your coccyx (tailbone), and moving all the way up your spine to your neck. Hold as long as possible, then slump forward, take a deep breath, and relax.

5. Bend your elbows and tense your forearms and biceps in the classic *Charles Atlas* pose. Clench your fists at the same time. Tense these muscles until they feel taut. Then, straighten out your arms, shake out your hands, take a deep breath, and relax.

6. Now hunch your shoulders and pull your head in like a *turtle*. Press your chin against your chest, tightening your throat. Experience this uncomfortable sensation, then drop your shoulders and allow your head to fall forward. Now, slowly and carefully, roll your head to the side and back of your neck. Reverse direction and roll your head the other way. Take a deep breath, and allow your neck and shoulders to relax.

7. Continue to move your attention upwards toward your head and face. First, make a frown by wrinkling up your forehead (like a *walnut*) as tightly as you can. Next, scrunch up your eyes, flare your nostrils, clench your jaw (not so hard that you'll crack a tooth). Finally, compress your lips into a tight O. Pull your lips as tight as a *miser's purse strings*. In short, make an *ugly face*. Hold it, tighter and tighter. Then relax and let go. Now, take a deep breath, relax your lips, and blow out forcefully.

8. Now go back mentally over the entire procedure, and feel the relaxation in your feet, ankles, calves, back, and chest. As you let go, more and more, the relaxation deepens in your neck, shoulders, arms, and hands. Go deeper and deeper into being relaxed. Finally, feel the relaxation extend to your head and face, your jaw hanging loose and your lips slightly parted.

9. If some tension persists in a specific part of your body, simply return your focus to that spot. Increase the tension, hold it, take a deep breath, and then relax. And let go.

In order to achieve deep muscle relaxation quickly, remember *key words* in the list below. Tense muscle groups for five to seven seconds, then relax for fifteen seconds.

Key Words

- Toes like a ballerina
- Toes to head
- Tight bottom
- Coat of armor
- Bow and arrow
- Charles Atlas
- Turtle
- Walnut
- Miser's purse
- Ugly face

What Does Relaxation Feel Like?

A feeling of deep relaxation can be experienced in lots of different ways. Most people describe tingling sensations, heat, or a pleasant warmth moving through their body. Others focus on feelings of heaviness or general lassitude. For some, their muscles feel like a stick of butter slowly melting in a skillet, or maple syrup spreading over a pile of pancakes. Everyone experiences relaxation in a unique way.

Exercise: How Relaxation Feels to You

Go back to the box (above) containing the key words for progressive relaxation training. As you go through the relaxation process again, notice the specific relaxation sensations that you feel for each muscle group. Now write those down next to the key words. This will serve to reinforce, and deepen, the relaxation you already experience.

Relaxation Imagery

Another very valuable tool in combating stress is the ability to call up, at a moment's notice, a peaceful, relaxing scene. Eventually, with enough practice, you will be able to conjure this scene as an automatic reflex, and it will help you to achieve better control when faced with a stressful situation.

It's best to begin using *relaxation imagery* right after having practiced the progressive relaxation procedure. This allows you to capitalize on the good feelings that you have already created.

The idea is to think about, and visualize in detail, a time and place where you have felt especially safe, secure, and perfectly at peace. It sometimes helps to begin the process by imagining that you are walking down a path through the woods, with many trees on the left and right. Eventually you see a light at the end of the path, and come to a meadow. Here is a peaceful clearing, where the sun is always shining, warming your skin, and the grass smells lush. You can hear the tinkling of a brook nearby.

Perhaps it's just this meadow that you were looking for, or maybe you'll want to follow the road leading to the beach, where the waves come and go, caressing the white sand. The salty smell in the air clears your mind, and the sound of the waves lulls you into a peaceful, almost hypnotic state.

Or, you can see in the distance a cottage tucked into the side of a hill, with smoke lazily rising from the chimney. It's cozy in front of the fireplace. The smell of your favorite soup wafts from the kitchen and permeates the air, bringing back warm, nurturing memories.

Now it's time to create your own personal relaxation image. Perhaps one of the scenarios above triggered a memory for you. Or maybe a childhood scene, a time of innocence, will work for you.

Begin creating your scene slowly, with your eyes closed, sketching it in broad strokes like an artist preparing a major canvas. Visualize the scene and then anchor it to a specific time and place (e.g., 3 P.M. on a lazy afternoon on August 20th, 1985, in the Catskills mountains). Now start to fill in the details. Shapes and colors, the quality of light and shadow.

Next, add the dimension of sound: blackbirds cawing as they fly overhead, or waves washing up on shore. Perhaps you can hear a faint melody, a long-forgotten tune. . . .

Now, explore the tactile qualities of this place. Become aware of the temperature, whether it's warmth on your skin or a pleasant cool breeze. If you're lying on the grass, notice the tickling sensation as the blades brush your ear when you turn your head. And remember the unique smells associated with this time and place. Fresh mown grass, bread just out of the oven, or honeysuckle on the vine . . .

Finally, pay attention to the emotional "feel" of this place. Become aware of ripples of calmness, the reassuring feeling of safety and security. A sense of peace and tranquility pervades the entire scene.

When you have finished creating this peaceful scene, stop for a minute and savor the experience. Just drink it in, memorizing all the components. Let all the sights, sounds, smells, and feelings sink into your awareness. Now anchor the scene with a *key word* like "Catskills" or "Mariposa."

Open your eyes and look around. Notice where you are in the real world. Now go back to the relaxation image. Use your key word. Allow yourself to become fully immersed in the scene. See it, hear it, smell it, feel it. Notice the accompanying sense of security, peace, and relaxation. Now come back to the room again.

Use the form on the next page to record your relaxation scene. Put in as much detail as posible.

In order to help you achieve the transition from the here and now to your relaxation scene as quickly as possible, it's sometimes useful to imagine a *Magic Door*. Science fiction fans will be familiar with this concept as "teleportation," in which you are literally transported from one place to another, instantaneously. Face the nearest blank wall and picture a door with a brass knob and a brass plaque. The plaque has your key word inscribed on it. When you turn the knob and open the door, you will find, to your surprise, that your relaxation scene is already fully prepared on the other side. All you have to do is cross the threshold and there you are, safe and secure.

With a little bit of practice, you are now ready to use this relaxation scene any time there is tension, or when a situation arises that is potentially disturbing or distressing.

Summary

The two relaxation skills that you've learned in this chapter, combined with what you will learn in the next chapter, can have a major impact on your experience of anger. Progressive relaxation training, if practiced daily, can reduce overall tension. And the relaxation imagery you've created can help you face specific situations that threaten your sense of calm.

Homework

1. Using the Anger Log, continue your daily monitoring of situations that elicit anger, and be sure to note trigger thoughts. As before, all angry reactions greater than 40 (on a 100-point scale of anger arousal) are to be recorded.

2. You may photocopy the progressive relaxation training procedure and your relaxation scene in order to facilitate daily practice. Be sure to practice the relaxation training and the relaxation scene at least five times during the next week. Record all practice in the Relaxation Log.

PERSONAL RELAXATION SCENE—Worksheet

Describe time and place (where and when):

Visual components (everything that you can see):

Auditory components (everything that you hear):

Tactile components (things that you touch or feel on your skin):

Olfactory components (what you smell):

Emotional components (feelings like safety or calmness):

Anger Log

Pain/Stress	Provocative Situation	Trigger Thoughts	Anger Rating 0–100	Behavior	Outcomes -10 to +10 Self	Others

Relaxation Log

Date	Progressive Relaxation Training	Relaxation Scene

INSTRUCTIONS: Put a check mark under the relaxation exercises completed on each date.

CHAPTER 5

ADVANCED RELAXATION SKILLS

Before we move on to the next set of relaxation techniques, it's useful to review the progress that you've made so far. By now you should be able to reliably relax, using the key words to follow the memorized sequence of the progressive relaxation technique. You should also be able to produce your relaxation image quickly, and in substantial detail, using all your senses. If you don't feel completely sure of yourself, practice a few more times. Then you can begin using this chapter with a sense of confidence and mastery.

At this point you may have questions about just how useful relaxation really is, especially when you find yourself in the middle of a fight with your spouse. The answer is that if you do the relaxation exercises every day, as part of your daily routine, you will notice a marked reduction in your overall tension. You'll also be less irritable. That's because relaxation has become an automatic part of your life. But this isn't enough. You need some more tools to help you relax during a period of actual upset, and that's just what this chapter is all about.

Breathing

A proper breathing technique is the next step on the relaxation agenda. Even though we've been breathing all our lives, most of us have forgotten how to breathe properly. For a quick refresher course, go find the nearest baby. Notice her little tummy rise and fall with each breath. This is called diaphragmatic, or "deep," breathing.

You can start by putting one hand on your chest and the other over your abdomen, just above the belt line. Now take a deep breath and push it all the way down into your belly. It helps to imagine filling a canteen with water. The canteen fills from the bottom up, just like the air in your belly. As you breathe in, the hand over your abdomen will rise, while the hand on your chest hardly moves at all. Focus all your attention on your belly, and send your breath down, down, down to fill your belly. Allow your breath to slightly stretch and relax your abdomen. As you take each breath, noticing your belly rise and fall, you experience a sense of calm. By doing this exercise, you are automatically sending a message to your brain that all is well. Just like a peacefully sleeping baby.

If you're having trouble pushing the air into your belly, it might be helpful to press down on your abdomen with both hands or place a moderately heavy telephone book on your abdomen. Both of these methods will not only increase your awareness, but will also force you to use your abdominal muscles.

Exercise: Deep Breathing during Stress

In order to practice *deep breathing* during stressful situations, use the outline provided on the next page. For this practice exercise, you'll need to prepare two scenes where stress can lead to a moderate anger response (but not a nuclear meltdown). Create one scene using your work environment and one scene using your home environment. Break down each situation into at least three segments. At the end of each segment is a cue to remind you to take a "deep breath." Now practice your deep breathing technique by visualizing the scenes, one segment at a time, taking a deep diaphragmatic breath at the end of each segment. Notice how the deep breath affects your tension level while you're imagining the scene.

Practice your first moderate stress scene two or three times. When you move on to the second scene, visualize it once without taking your deep breaths. Really get into it; try to make it as real as possible. Notice your stress level when you're finished. Visualize the scene at least two more times, but now taking a deep breath as you finish each segment. Chances are, you'll see that your stress level goes down when you include deep breaths during the scene.

To give you an idea of how to structure your stressful scenes on the worksheet, we've included an example worksheet with two scenes created by a forty-three-year-old insurance adjuster.

When she did this exercise, she experimented with different strategies. First she went through each scene and just thought about how it made her feel. Then she went through each scene again and did some deep breathing, as recommended. She was amazed to find how much her tension level actually went down at the end of the exercise.

Exercise: Relaxation without Tension

Up to now you've practiced the progressive relaxation technique (PRT) by increasing tension, but now it's time to eliminate that tension as well, using a technique called *relaxation without tension*. Once again, go through the PRT sequence. But this time, as you scan each muscle group, simply *notice* any tension in that part of your body, take a deep breath, and as you exhale, *relax away* and let go of all that tension.

- Start at the bottom just as before, and point your toes, then gently reverse, toes to head. Notice any tension, take a deep breath, and on the exhale, relax away the tension.

- Now focus on your buttocks. Again, just notice tension (if you find any), then take a deep breath, and on the exhale, relax.

- Next, your chest and stomach muscles. Notice, breath, exhale, relax.

- Arch your back, and, without straining, notice any tension. Then, take a deep breath, and relax away the stress.

- Focusing on your arms and biceps, simply notice any tension you may feel there. Now, take a deep breath, and on the exhale, relax the tension. Just let it go.

- Check out your neck and shoulders. Notice, breathe, exhale, relax away the tension.

DEEP BREATHING DURING STRESS—Worksheet

Instructions: In the spaces provided below, create two scenes that are stressful and would lead to a moderate anger response. Break each scene down into at least three segments. Fill in enough detail to allow you to fully imagine each scene. Be sure to take a deep breath at the end of each segment.

Scene 1:
(work)

_____

_____

_____ (deep breath)

_____

_____

_____ (deep breath)

_____

_____

_____ (deep breath)

_____

_____

_____ (deep breath)

Scene 2:
(home)

_____

_____

_____ (deep breath)

_____

_____

_____ (deep breath)

_____

_____

_____ (deep breath)

_____

_____

_____ (deep breath)

DEEP BREATHING DURING STRESS—Worksheet Example

Instructions: In the spaces provided below, create two scenes that are stressful and would lead to a moderate anger response. Break each scene down into at least three segments. Fill in enough detail to allow you to fully imagine each scene. Be sure to take a deep breath at the end of each segment.

Scene 1:
(work)

I'm in the car on my way to work and it's hot. The traffic is slowing down to a crawl.

(deep breath)

Now I'm literally stopped. All the windows are open, but not the hint of a breeze. A car pushes into my lane.

(deep breath)

It's a souped-up station wagon with flames painted on the side. The kid is practically hitting my fender.

(deep breath)

Heavy metal blares from his window. Now he's honking and gesturing to let him in. I won't. He keeps inching his bumper closer to my car. (deep breath)

Scene 2:
(home)

My mother calls. High creaky vocie. Complains bitterly about life in the same house with my aunt. Suddenly she says she wants to visit. (deep breath)

She has the tickets already—arriving June 4. Right in the middle of finals. I tell her no way. She starts sounding irritated. Talking fast. (deep breath)

She says the tickets aren't refundable. Accuses me of not wanting to see her, and not answering the phone when she calls. I feel hot/perspiring. (deep breath)

She's talking really fast. I interrupt, I say my grades will suffer if she comes. She says I ought to loosen up and enjoy life; and stop bringing everyone down. (deep breath)

- Now turn your attention to your forehead and notice any tension you may find. Move your focus to the rest of your face, and mouth. Notice any tension there, take a deep breath, and relax on the exhale.

Practice this at least five times before going on to the next section, and be sure to keep track by using the Relaxation Log at the end of this chapter.

Cue-Controlled Relaxation

Now it's time to choose your personal *cue word*, a two-syllable word or phrase. This will enable you to enter into a state of deep, *cue-controlled relaxation* each time you repeat it. You don't have to say it out loud. Just saying it under your breath, or even thinking it, will work just fine. Choose something like "relax," "let go," "release," or "okay." You might prefer a color, such as "deep blue," or a feeling, such as "true love." A phrase that evokes a personal memory of peace and contentment often works best.

Keeping your cue word (phrase) in mind, return your attention once again to your deep, diaphragmatic breathing. Now, each time you exhale, say your cue word (phrase) out loud or to yourself. Try to relax your entire body as you exhale, and think (or say) your cue word. Make your whole body feel as relaxed as it was when you had just finished the relaxation without tension exercise. Do this ten times in a row, to set up an automatic response pattern. Write your cue word (phrase) in the space below as a reminder:

Exercise: Cue-Controlled Relaxation during Stress

In order to practice this new skill, go back to the scenes you developed earlier for the deep breathing exercise. You can use the same worksheet as before—just replace the deep breathing prompt with your cue word (phrase). This will help you learn to relax by triggering the cue-controlled relaxation response, using your cue word (phrase).

Be sure to practice relaxation without tension and cue-controlled relaxation daily for the next week to ten days. Note all practice times in the Relaxation Log provided at the end of the chapter.

Combined Relaxation Skills

Once you have learned all of the essential elements of relaxation, it's time to practice them by quickly switching them on and off. For practice, do the following combinations: First, do the relaxation imagery for two minutes, followed by relaxation without tension for five minutes, and finally, cue-controlled relaxation (using deep, diaphragmatic breathing) for two minutes. Next, do the relaxation imagery again, cue-controlled relaxation, relaxation without tension, and a final round of relaxation imagery. All in all, this combined relaxation exercise will probably take no more than fifteen minutes. Practice this combined relaxation exercise at least three times in the next week (in addition to the separate relaxation without tension and cue-controlled relaxation described above). Be sure to note all practice times in the Relaxation Log. You can photocopy the sample provided to make as many sheets as you need.

Coping When You're Stressed

Everything that you've done so far is to prepare you for the "real thing." Inevitably, you'll be faced with a provocative situation in real life that challenges your resolve and threatens to blow your composure. That's why it's so important to be really comfortable with brief stress reduction strategies for anger management. This next exercise will allow you to find out for yourself exactly which strategy is most comfortable and effective for you.

Exercise: What Works for You

For this last exercise, write out another provocative scene on the worksheet provided on the next page. Be generous in your attention to detail. This will allow you to fully visualize and experience the scene so that you can *notice* where tension is concentrated in your body. Be sure to insert breathing and relaxation cues. In this exercise, relaxation without tension should focus only on the most tense part of your body. First, do a run-through of each scene without any relaxation, to determine where in your body most of the tension accumulates. Then, during relaxation without tension, you can focus only on those specific muscle groups. Alternate cue-controlled relaxation and relaxation without tension exercises. See which works best for you.

That's it. You have now learned all the key relaxation skills necessary to help control your anger and make your life less stressful. Progressive relaxation and relaxation imagery should become part of your daily routine, because they lower your overall stress and arousal level. Deep breathing, relaxation without tension, and cue-controlled relaxation can be used any time that you are faced with a provocative situation.

The key to success (How do you get to Carnegie Hall?) is practice, practice, practice. Over time these skills will become automatic, just like riding a bicycle or driving a car.

Homework

1. Continue using your Anger Log to record anger situations greater than 40 on the scale.

2. Use Relaxation Log II to note dates you practiced relaxation imagery, cue-controlled relaxation, and relaxation without tension. Plan to practice all three relaxation skills at least five out of seven days in the next week.

COPING WHEN STRESSED—Worksheet

Instructions: In the spaces provided below fill in the details of a provocative scene which is stressful and would lead to a moderate anger response. Break the scene down into 6 segments. Fill in enough detail to allow you to fully imagine the scene. Alternate deep breathing, relaxation without tension (rwt), or cue-controlled relaxation (using your cue word), at the end of each segment.

Provocative Scene:

_____

_____

_____

_____ (deep breath)

_____

_____

_____ (deep breath)

_____

_____

_____ (deep breath)

_____

_____

_____ (deep breath)

_____

_____

_____ (deep breath)

_____

_____

_____ (deep breath)

_____

_____ (deep breath)

Anger Log

Pain/Stress	Provocative Situation	Trigger Thoughts	Anger Rating 0–100	Behavior	Outcomes -10 to +10 Self	Others

Relaxation Log II

Date	Relaxation Imagery	Cue-Controlled Relaxation	Relaxation without Tension

INSTRUCTIONS: Put a check mark under the relaxation exercises completed on each date.

CHAPTER 6

TRIGGER THOUGHTS

Imagine that you're in an office where several coworkers like to listen to radio talk shows at their desks. The sound isn't terribly loud, but you find yourself distracted by the constant prattle. It continues all day long. Just visualize the scene for a moment. Now imagine that you're saying to yourself, "How inconsiderate they are, how selfish, how unaware of the needs of others." Imagine yourself getting a bit worked up, thinking that they're doing this to you deliberately because they simply don't give a damn about anybody but themselves. Take a moment to notice what you are feeling.

Now imagine the scene with a little twist. Your coworkers are listening to the same distracting talk shows. This time you say to yourself, "I can't think, I can't concentrate, I'm never going to get my work done. I'm never going to get this in on time. I'm not going to be able to function here. How can I keep my job if I can't do a simple task like this when there's a little noise?" Pause a moment to notice what you're feeling.

Now imagine one last version of this scenario. Same office, same coworkers, same radio noise. On this occasion you think to yourself, "I never fit in anywhere. Things always bother me. They'll be resentful if I ask them to turn off the radio. This is the story of my life—I'm the weird one. I'm so rattle-brained that I can't even think with a little background jabber. I can't handle the slightest stress or problem." Now pause and notice what you feel with the situation framed in this way.

In the first scenario, there's a good chance that you felt a little angry. Thoughts that label others as selfish or inconsiderate, blaming them for your discomfort, tend to trigger angry feelings. The second scenario had very different thoughts. When you perceive the situation as dangerous ("I'm not going to be able to function . . . how can I keep my job?"), your emotional reaction is likely to be anxiety. In the last scene, thoughts focus on self-criticism; the problems are all your fault. Your emotional response is likely to be sadness.

As you learned in chapter 2, trigger thoughts have a major impact on your anger. But anger isn't the only emotion that your thoughts influence. The above visualization suggests that thoughts can create anxiety and sadness as well. In fact, how you frame and interpret your experience has far more influence on your feelings than actual events. Your assumptions and beliefs about reality are more powerful than reality itself.

The suggestion that our own thinking might be responsible for some of our most painful emotions runs contrary to conventional wisdom. Normally, we tend to see events as the cause of our feelings, and this conception is embedded in our language. "You made me angry." "This makes me sad." "The situation scares me." But in between the event and the emotion lies your prefrontal cortex—the place in your brain where you interpret experience. It's not what actually happens that you react to, but the conclusions you draw and the assumptions you make.

Sensory Input Versus Assumptions

One way to understand the role of trigger thoughts in our emotions is to look at the distinction between sensory input (what eyes, ears, and touch tell us) and the *meanings* we create out of sensory information. In truth, we are entirely cut off from direct experience of reality. What we "see" is an internal computer screen created by our conclusions and evaluations, not a picture of the actual event.

Consider this example. Sensory input tells you a friend is frowning, her eyes are narrowing, and her voice is getting higher. She is saying something about having to rush. Because you are late for a lunch appointment, your evaluation is that she must be angry at you. That's the conclusion on your internal screen, so you begin to react defensively, perhaps even picking a fight. Only later do you learn that she was late too, had rushed to meet you, and was relieved that she hadn't kept you waiting. Here's what's important: The assumptions on your screen had almost nothing to do with reality. You'd taken a frown, narrow eyes, and an ambiguous comment and created a completely distorted picture out of them. We do this all the time. We make assumptions about the motives and feelings of others—often very wrong—and get enraged by them.

Exercise: What's on Her Screen?

The following is a transcript of a woman describing, in a psychotherapy session, a recent anger episode with her invalid mother. Read it and underline every statement that is sensory input only; then put a wavy line under every statement that comes from her screen (assumptions, conclusions, beliefs, and meanings drawn from the situation). Here's the transcript:

"She was looking at me with wide open, 'help me, help me' eyes, like she didn't care that I'd already been over there three times that week. So I said, 'What is it, Mom?' And she just sits there and doesn't say anything. She's really still. Like it's beneath her to speak the obvious, that I was put on this earth to take care of her. And I'm screwing it up. I can tell she's just disgusted with me. Finally she says, 'How about some music,' and puts on this hideous Lawrence Welk record. Which she knows I hate, and only plays when she's annoyed with me. My mother lives in passive-aggressive-ville.

"And she lies. If she says A, assume she means B. While the record is on, she says, 'All I really want is to get along with you, Carol.' But I know that's code for 'What's wrong with you, Carol, that you don't get along with me?' It's disguised criticism. That's the way she works. Then she kisses me and says all the hassling is wearing her out and she's going to take a nap before dinner. And she sort of shuffles off like I've destroyed her or something."

If you've finished doing the underlining, look ahead to see what in the transcript is sensory input, and what comes from Carol's "screen."

Sensory Input

She was looking at me with wide open eyes, so I said, "What is it, Mom?" And she just sits there and doesn't say anything. She's really still. Finally she says, "How about some music?" and puts on this Lawrence Welk record. While the record is on she says, "All I really want is to get along with you, Carol." Then she kisses me and says all the hassling is wearing her out and she's going to take a nap before dinner. She sort of shuffles off.

What's on Carol's Screen?

(She was looking at me with) "help me, help me" eyes. Like she didn't care I'd already been over there three times that week . . . (She's really still) like it's beneath her to speak the obvious, that I was put on this earth to take care of her. And I'm screwing it up. I can tell she's just disgusted with me . . . (she puts on) this hideous Lawrence Welk record. Which she knows I hate, and only plays when she's annoyed with me. My mother lives in passive-aggressive-ville.

And she lies. If she says A, assume she means B . . . I know it's code for "What's wrong with you, Carol, that you don't get along with me?" It's disguised criticism. That's the way she works . . . (she shuffles) like I've destroyed her or something.

When you separate the sensory data from the conclusions on the screen, it seems like two almost totally different experiences. In particular, the assumption, "She's just disgusted with me," appears very disconnected from what was actually said and done. In our normal thinking, sensory input and screen conclusions get folded together. The belief, "She's disgusted with me," seems every bit as real as what we actually see and hear. The trouble is that distorted conclusions on our screen often trigger big anger reactions, and we have no idea how far the assumptions on our screen are from reality.

To help distinguish sensory input from screen conclusions, you'll use a slightly modified anger log during the next week. It can be found at the end of the chapter, and it's labeled Anger Log II. It's very important, as you work toward improved anger control, to separate your thoughts (the screen) from the objective facts of a situation. Exaggeration and negative labeling are major sources of anger, and using Anger Log II will ultimately help you do less of both.

Recognizing Trigger Thoughts

You can always tell an anger-triggering thought by how it frames reality. Here are the basic components of most trigger thoughts:

1. The perception that you've been harmed and victimized.

2. The belief that the provoking person harmed you deliberately.

3. The belief that the provoking person was wrong and bad to harm you, and should have behaved differently.

Let's examine some typical trigger thoughts and see how these three elements can be separated out:

1. "Why do I have to come home from work exhausted and shop and clean and cook and get zero help?"
   Harm: Overwork, exhaustion
   Done Deliberately: Implication that the provoking person chooses not to help, thus contributing to the exhaustion.
   And Wrong: Implication that giving zero help is unjust and unfair.

2. "It's a stupid way to operate a car, and I've said it a hundred times—you don't keep riding the brakes because it wears them out."
   Harm: Cost of a brake job; not being listened to.
   Done Deliberately: Implication that if the provoking person thought a little more, or made a reasonable effort, he or she could remember to use the brakes properly.
   And Wrong: Implies that riding the brakes is poor driving technique; and not heeding appropriate warnings is either lazy or careless.

3. "She's doing this to upset me (child jumping on the sofa following an angry exchange regarding staying at the table until breakfast is eaten)."
   Harm: Noise, dirt on sofa, not being listened to.
   Done Deliberately: Implies the child is choosing obnoxious behavior out of a need for revenge.
   And Wrong: Implies child is being manipulative and disobedient.

Now you try to identify the three elements of trigger thoughts for these next examples.

4. "How could he tell them about losing my job before I did? It's like he's trying to humiliate me."

   Harm:

   Done Deliberately:

   And Wrong:

5. "She doesn't care if the toilet flushes, just as long as I pay the rent. She's all about the money and doesn't give a damn about fixing anything."

   Harm:

   Done Deliberately:

   And Wrong:

Answer Key for Examples 4 and 5

4. *Harm:* Humiliated; *Done Deliberately:* The provoking person chose to reveal confidential information; *And Wrong:* Implies that it's wrong to embarrass someone.

5. *Harm:* Toilet doesn't work; *Done Deliberately:* Landlord chooses to save money and ignore problem; *And Wrong:* Unfair to renters not to maintain property.

Exercise: Dissecting Your Trigger Thoughts

Take four trigger thoughts from last week's Anger Log and identify the key elements.

Trigger Thought 1

_____

_____

Harm:

Done Deliberately:

And Wrong:

Trigger Thought 2

_____

_____

Harm:

Done Deliberately:

And Wrong:

Trigger Thought 3

_____

_____

Harm:

Done Deliberately:

And Wrong:

Trigger Thought 4

_____

_____

Harm:

Done Deliberately:

And Wrong:

Trigger Thoughts Make You Feel Helpless

All trigger thoughts assert that you've been harmed, deliberately and wrongly. But there's one more implication: Not only did the provoking person cause your pain, but they ought to change so the pain can stop. They are both responsible for the harm *and* required to fix it.

The problem with this thinking is that it leaves you feeling very helpless. The pain you experience is out of your control. Someone did it to you, and you won't feel better until they see the light and change their behavior. But, as you already know, *people rarely change*. They keep behaving in habitual ways. They do what's rewarding to them, what makes them feel good. Your anger may distress them briefly, but usually they quickly return to their old patterns. The whole time you're angry, waiting for them to change, you remain stuck. You keep hurting, and the problem feels beyond your control.

This feeling of angry helplessness starts a vicious cycle: You're hurt, the provoking person should fix it but doesn't, and you feel stuck and unable to escape the pain. The feeling of helplessness makes you feel even worse, even more angry, even more frustrated that the provoking person won't change.

Breaking the cycle requires that you take responsibility for changing what's painful, and not wait for the other person to do it. For example, imagine that you have a friend who's chronically late for lunch dates. Over and over you find yourself fuming in a restaurant. Of course, you can lambaste your friend each time you find yourself stuck waiting; you can complain about the thoughtlessness and disregard for your time. However, if you take responsibility for your own pain, you might:

■ always remember to bring a book and schedule extra time, or

■ never meet in a restaurant, or

- always include others so you'll have someone to talk to while you wait, or

- pick your friend up at home.

Instead of being helpless and angry, you take charge of the situation. Here's another example. Your partner never cleans up after himself. Clothes are on the floor, dishes and cups are left on the coffee table, the bathroom sink always has toothpaste residue. You can stay caught in the anger-helplessness-anger cycle, or you can:

- hire a weekly house cleaner at his expense;

- if there are two bathrooms, give him exclusive use of one;

- put the stuff he drops around the house on top of his desk or in a box;

- leave the dishes on his side of the bed;

- delay putting on the video till he's finished his cleanup tasks for the night;

- move out.

Think back for a moment to the situation described at the beginning of the chapter—feeling distracted by radio talk shows that coworkers listen to all day in the office. If the protagonist in the scene took responsibility for his or her own discomfort, here's how the situation might be reframed. "This is no big deal. They're having a good time. They don't know they're bugging me. I'll find a diplomatic way to get them to turn the radios down, or I'll get some headphones and listen to relaxing music." When you take responsibility, both anger and helplessness melt away. You're suddenly free to solve the problem. Instead of always asking the question, "Who's responsible for my pain?," you ask instead, "What can I do about it?"

Here are three coping mantras that can help you stay focused on taking responsibility:

1. I am responsible for what happens between us.

2. No point in blaming. I'll try a new strategy for taking care of myself.

3. What can I do about this?

Exercise: Taking Control

Review your Anger Log for the past week and complete this exercise for each provocative situation:

TAKING CONTROL—Worksheet

Provocative Situation	What I Expect from the Other Person	How I Can Take Responsibility and Control

Here's an example of how a thirty-year-old programmer responded to this exercise:

Provocative Situation	What I Expect from the Other Person	How I Can Take Responsibility and Control
1. My mother calls and asks for help paying my sister's nursing school tuition.	She ought to understand my financial situation and not embarrass me by asking for money. My sister should get a loan.	Tell her I can't help but don't reveal how truly screwed my finances are. Suggest sister get a loan that the government forgives when you work for the VA.
2. Boss gives me a new programming assignment before I finish the one I'm working on.	He should know I'm working as fast as I can, and not load me down so I have to work all night.	Tell him I'm unable to start a new assignment till I've met my current deadline.
3. My mother arranges a birthday party for me and invites a bunch of relatives I hate.	It's crazy to make a birthday party for someone that they'll hate. She should do something I enjoy—not what _she'd_ enjoy.	Tell her to have fun with her relatives, but that's not how I want to spend my birthday. Invite Bill and Carol and Roxanne out to dinner.
4. Roommate and her boyfriend lay all over the couch, leaving debris from a pizza, and then have a big, loud fight in the living room.	They should leave space for me to use my own living room, clean up their stuff, and fight where I can't hear it.	Tell her to clean up. Then turn up the radio in my room so I don't hear them fighting. Ask her to leave next month.

Trigger Thought Themes

It's time to once again review the trigger thoughts you've written in your Anger Log. Now the focus should be on identifying key themes and threads that run through your anger triggers. The following is a list of typical themes that occur in trigger thoughts. Put a check by the ones that underlie some of your angry thinking.

☐ 1. People ignore your needs.

☐ 2. People don't see or understand you.

☐ 3. People demand or expect too much.

☐ 4. People are inconsiderate or impolite.

☐ 5. People take advantage of or use you.

☐ 6. People control you.

☐ 7. People are selfish.

☐ 8. People are stupid and thoughtless.

☐ 9. People shame and/or criticize you.

☐ 10. People keep you waiting.

☐ 11. People are uncaring and/or ungenerous.

❑ 12. People are manipulative.

❑ 13. People are threatening and coercive.

❑ 14. People are mean or cruel.

❑ 15. People disrespect you.

❑ 16. People are unfair or unjust.

❑ 17. People are lazy or don't do their share.

❑ 18. You're helpless and stuck and have no choice.

❑ 19. People are incompetent.

❑ 20. People are irresponsible.

❑ 21. People don't help.

❑ 22. People don't do the right thing.

Add here any additional themes you discover:

_____

_____

_____

After reviewing your Anger Log, you'll probably find that there are between two and six themes that show up with some frequency. At the root of all of the themes is the notion that people are behaving in ways they shouldn't be, and that you have a right to be angry at them for it.

But what if that weren't true? What if provoking people are doing the only thing they know how to do to take care of themselves and survive? What if they are doing the best they can, given their own needs, fears, pain, and personal history? What if people are behaving based on what they know and don't know, their skills, their physical and emotional limitations, their values, what they find most rewarding, and their available resources? The next exercise explores how most annoying and provoking behavior actually represents the other person's best coping solution, given all of the above.

Exercise: People Are Doing the Best They Can

There's a simple way to prove that this is true. Think back to something you did that really angered another person. Now write down how the following influenced your behavior and choices:

1. Your needs at that moment:

_____

2. Your fears at that moment:

_____

3. Your pain or stress at that moment:

_____

4. Any personal history or experiences that influenced your behavior or choices:

_____

5. What you knew or didn't know at the time:

_____

6. Your skills or lack of skills that influenced your choice at the time:

_____

7. Any physical or emotional limitations that influenced you to act as you did:

_____

8. Personal values or beliefs that influenced your behavior:

_____

9. The prospects for rewards or pleasures that influenced your choice at that moment:

_____

10. Resources that you did or didn't have at that moment that could have influenced your choice:

_____

If you've really worked through this exercise, it should be clear that your behavior seemed the best available choice *at that moment.* You might, with hindsight, do something different. But it appeared to be the best response when you made it.

If you are still uncertain that you make the best choices available to you (even though they anger others), do the exercise with another situation or two. Or do it for a situation where *you* were angry, and try to identify the main influences on the other person's behavior.

A key understanding from this exercise can greatly reduce your anger response: *We are all doing the best we can to take care of ourselves.*

Homework

1. Record all anger experiences over 40 on the scale on Anger Log II. Pay careful attention to the distinction between sensory input (objective data) and the screen (your assumptions).

2. Implement at least one of the "How I can take responsibility and control" items from your Taking Control Worksheet.

3. Record practice dates for relaxation imagery, cue-controlled relaxation, and relaxation without tension on your Relaxation Log. Best results are achieved by practicing at least five out of seven days of the week.

Anger Log II

Provocative Situation Sensory Input (Objective data from what you hear, see, and touch)	The Screen (Your conclusions, assumptions, interpretations, beliefs, and trigger thoughts)	Anger Rating 0–100	Behavior	Outcomes -10 to +10 Self	Others

Relaxation Log II

Date	Relaxation Imagery	Cue-Controlled Relaxation	Relaxation without Tension

INSTRUCTIONS: Put a check mark under the relaxation exercises completed on each date.

CHAPTER 7

THE ANGER DISTORTIONS

We know that how you think about things determines to a large degree what you experience, and this is particularly true of anger. This chapter will help you to identify the six major categories of thought distortions that are most likely to increase your feelings of anger. For each one, we've included some alternatives: new, helpful coping thoughts. The concept of coping thoughts will be explored fully in the next chapter. For now, however, it's only necessary to understand that coping thoughts are different ways of conceptualizing or reframing a situation in order to help you to better manage your anger.

Blaming

This is the most self-destructive and damaging anger distortion. The mistaken belief that underlies blaming is that other people are doing bad things to you, usually on purpose—and they aren't going to get away with it. It's true that blaming other people can make you feel better sometimes, but it leaves you feeling helpless as well. By blaming others, you are giving up the power to change the situation that is causing you pain. You keep waiting for them to change their behavior. But, of course, they never do. This can cause you to be judgmental and vindictive, lashing out angrily. The other person then responds by pulling back or counterattacking. Now you've got two problems, the original situation and the mess you've made with your angry reaction.

Examples of Blaming

- I could really enjoy this vacation if it weren't for your constant complaining and always finding fault with things.

- If you really cared about me, you would have helped me with the résumé, and then I would have gotten that job.

- You always ask me to give you a ride and then take all day to get dressed, so I'll be late for my meeting.

It's useful to remember that people are mostly doing the best they can. Everyone (including you) tends to behave in ways that will meet their own needs. The people you're blaming are most likely just doing what they can to take care of themselves as best they know how.

When you use a blaming strategy, your entire focus is on trying to change the other person. What's easy to forget is that you're not stuck. You *can* make different choices. Remember that you have some options to change the situation—it doesn't all depend on the other person. The key to dealing with self-defeating blaming is to develop a new coping strategy. This requires you to take responsibility and make your own plan to change the situation, or to figure out a different way of responding to it. Forget the other person—they're not going to do anything different. Therefore, your plan shouldn't require any cooperation whatsoever from the person you blame.

Coping Thoughts to Replace Blaming

- I know that blaming makes me feel helpless, so what can I do to change the situation and make myself feel better?

- I can make a plan to take care of myself in this situation.

- I don't like what he's doing, but I know that he's just trying to take care of himself.

- I'm hurt and disappointed, but I believe that she's doing the best she can.

- I'm not helpless, and I can take care of myself in this situation.

- They're doing what they need to do, so I'll just have to do what I need to do.

Catastrophizing/Magnifying the Situation

This is more than just making a mountain out of a molehill or making things worse than they already are. It's the tendency to take something bad and really run with it, extrapolating a bad situation to the worst possible conclusion. By magnifying events and thinking of them as awful, terrible, or horrendous, you set yourself up to respond in an angry or hostile way. In effect, you behave as though your distorted and exaggerated view of the situation were actual fact.

Examples of Catastrophizing/Magnifying:

- Because of him, my presentation is totally screwed up, and I'm going to lose my job.

- Her behavior is so disgusting that our social life is becoming a complete nightmare.

- This is the worst thing imaginable. It's all over for me now. I'll never be able to show my face around here again.

- Complete disaster! Total betrayal! How could he do something like that?

Luckily, there are a few things that you can do to control the tendency to magnify a bad situation. First, make a realistic assessment of just how bad things are. Sure, things are bad, a hassle, messed up, and definitely not the way you would like them to be. Ask yourself, "How bad is it?" Then ask yourself, "How bad is it *really*?" Make every effort to answer the second question honestly and realistically. Second, be very accurate and precise in the language you use to describe the bad situation. The restaurant bill isn't "exorbitant and outrageous," it's just a lot more than you expected. And the service wasn't a total embarrassment, the waiter was just over worked and didn't bring your soup as quickly as you have would liked.

Third, look at the whole picture, not just the annoying piece. Every situation or relationship has its positive and negative aspects. Your girlfriend may never be ready on time when you pick her up for a date. On the other hand, she's really supportive and accepting. By focusing on the positive aspects, you can neutralize your anger.

Coping Thoughts to Replace Catastrophizing

- Yeah, this is frustrating, but it's not the end of the world.

- This is really no big deal. I don't like what's going on, but it will be history next week.

- I'll get through this okay if I just hang loose.

- Wow, this situation is really messed up, but I'll do the best I can and make the most of it.

- It's only a setback. It's not worth getting all bent out of shape about it.

Inflammatory Global Labeling

This anger distortion involves making sweeping, often inflammatory, negative judgments about people whose behavior you don't like. However, instead of focusing on the behavior, the label tends to paint the person as being totally wrong, bad, and worthless. This is accomplished by one-word epithets like "loser," "asshole," "jerk," "retard," "bitch," "bastard," or "schmuck." Global labels tend to fuel your anger by turning the person whose behavior you don't like into a worthless object. And, of course the labels are always false and misleading because they reduce the whole person to a single characteristic.

Examples of Inflammatory Global Labeling

- My girlfriend is a total bitch.

- That driver who just cut me off is a complete asshole.

- What a jerk. He doesn't know anything.

- That bastard deserves to be drawn and quartered for what he did to me.

- Look at that wimpy tennis serve—he's a real loser.

The best way to combat a tendency toward global labeling is to be specific. Focus on the annoying behavior and describe it with precision. What happened? When did it happen? How often? How did it affect you or others? Notice that this does not involve making judgments about the other person or making derogatory comments about his/her personality or parentage.

Coping Thoughts to Replace Inflammatory Global Labeling

- Why am I swearing? I feel frustrated, and things aren't going the way I would like. But I can cope with the situation.

- It's nothing more than a problem. I don't have to make her the wicked witch.

- What is really bothering me? Stick to the facts.

- He's not a jerk, just someone who wasn't properly trained to do his job.

Misattributions

This is all about jumping to conclusions and mindreading. When you find yourself feeling hurt or annoyed by other people's behavior, the simplest thing is to imagine that they did it on purpose. Rather than thinking about all the other reasons for why things might have happened as they did, you assume that you know the person's "real" motives. You focus on a single explanation. They were deliberately trying to be mean to you and cause you upset.

It's easy to guess at other people's motives. But if you've ever taken the trouble to check out your assumptions, you've no doubt discovered how often you were partly or completely mistaken. Sometimes misattributions can cause real problems, such as when you angrily act on your mistaken assumptions, only to find out later that the true situation was entirely different from what you imagined.

Examples of Misattributions

- He acted like he just wanted to correct my grammar, but he was really trying to make me look stupid.

- I know she was just doing that to embarrass me in front of everyone.

- What a dumb assignment. He's really out to get me.

- The only reason she's late is just to piss me off.

The best way to avoid misattributions is to pay attention and catch yourself making the assumptions. Then, if possible, check it out with the person directly or gather some relevant facts. If you're reluctant to directly check out your assumptions, at least keep an open mind to other possibilities. Consider asking someone you trust what they make of a certain situation, to get another point of view.

Sometimes your interpretations of other people's behavior might actually be correct. However, there are usually many other reasons or explanations for people's actions—things that might surprise you. Your anger may be way out of line or disproportionate to the situation. A good way to work on misattribution is to get into the habit of developing alternative explanations for other people's behavior. Really brainstorm: Try to think of as many different scenarios as you can, and think of your original assumption as just one of many possible explanations of how other people act.

Coping Thoughts to Replace Misattributions

- That's one possibility, but there are probably other reasons for her behavior.

- Stop trying to second-guess other people's motives.

- Getting angry won't help me figure out what's really going on. I need more facts.

- My assumption may not be accurate—I'd better check it out.

Overgeneralization

Any problem can be made to look bigger or more important by using words like "never," "always," "nobody," "everybody," etc. This is a way of making an occasional occurrence feel like an intolerable ongoing event. By exaggerating, you go way beyond the truth of the situation and set yourself up for an angry response.

Examples of Overgeneralizing

- She's always doing things like that to make me look bad.
- Nobody seems to know what they're doing around here.
- You're never ready on time, so we're always late for everything.
- Everybody is always asking me to do them a favor.

The best antidote for overgeneralization is to make a conscious effort to look for exceptions. Realizing that people act in a variety of ways makes their behavior less upsetting. Ideally, you want to avoid using generalizing terms as much as possible, so it helps to use accurate and specific descriptions of the situation. For example, "This is the second time you're late this week," instead of, "you're never on time."

Coping Thoughts to Replace Overgeneralization

- No need to get upset. Just focus on the facts and I'll get through this okay.
- I want to be accurate. How often has this really happened?
- Generalizing always makes things worse. Just relax and things will calm down.
- This doesn't *always* happen this way. There are lots of exceptions.

There is a special case of overgeneralization that is worth mentioning. It's when you think in terms of black and white only, with no grays in the middle. Everything falls into one of two polar opposites: things are 100 percent right or wrong, good or bad. People either love you or hate you, with no room for anything in between. This kind of dichotomous thinking often leads to anger when people behave in less than perfect ways. Since they're not entirely right, they must be all wrong. Or, since they're not acting friendly toward you, they must be your sworn enemy.

One way of dealing with polarized thinking is to get into the habit of using qualifying adjectives and adverbs such as "a little," "a lot," or "somewhat." This will serve to reintroduce shades of gray into a black-or-white world. Another strategy is to try to see people as the complex, confusing, and often contradictory beings that they really are. By looking closely at a person you despise you may be surprised to find aspects of their personality that you like, and other aspects about which you feel at least neutral.

Demanding/Commanding

This anger distortion is best exemplified by turning your personal preferences into the equivalent of the Ten Commandments. These thoughts often involve words like "should," "got to," "have to," or "ought to." Having a well-developed sense of values is a healthy thing. However, when these values are raised to the level of moral dictates, problems with anger can occur.

Specifically, anger can often be triggered when you judge others by a set of commandments about how people should or shouldn't behave. A typical theme involves entitlement, as in, "Bad things shouldn't happen to me." Another common theme involves perfectionism, as in, "That's not the correct way to do it. You should do it the right way." Fairness is another important theme, as in, "That's not fair. It isn't right when things aren't equal."

Examples of Demanding/Commanding

- They shouldn't have done that—it was absolutely wrong.

- He isn't being fair. He should listen to me once in a while.

- She ought to have known better. That was bound to hurt my feelings.

- This is the way it's got to be. Any other way is just plain stupid.

The biggest problem with a demanding/commanding strategy is that other people rarely do what you think they should. They're too busy taking care of themselves, attending to their own wants and needs. Just because you want something or believe in something doesn't mean that others have to agree with you. This may be hard to stomach, but in fact, there's absolutely no reason why things "should" be the way that you want.

The best way to cope with "shoulds" is to reframe them as things you want or would like. These are just personal preferences. When things don't go the way you would prefer, or you don't get what you want, it's reasonable to feel frustrated and disappointed. But putting it off on someone else's moral failings is a sure road to righteous anger. You're better off sticking with desire and disappointment over shoulds and moral weakness.

Coping Thoughts to Replace Demanding/Commanding

- This is disappointing. I'd rather things were different, but I'll be all right.

- So what if I don't get what I want. It's not the end of the world, and not a reason to blow up.

- This shouldn't be happening to me. I don't like what they're doing, but I live with it.

- There's no reason why she should do it my way, other than that's the way I want it. She's got her own needs to worry about.

Now it's time to practice recognizing and dealing with anger distortions as they occur in your everyday life.

Exercise: Identifying Distortions

Using the worksheet on the next page, fill in examples from your own life of situations where you responded with each anger distortion discussed above. Focus on your thoughts in these situations, because anger distortions grow from how you think about things—your assumptions and conclusions. For example, suppose your brother brings an uninvited guest to your Thanksgiving dinner. Your thoughts are, "He's destroying our evening, he's ruined the family feeling." This is an example of catastrophizing/magnifying and would be written into the appropriate place on the worksheet.

A complete, filled-out example follows the worksheet to help you with the exercise.

IDENTIFYING DISTORTIONS—Worksheet

Instructions: In the spaces provided below, fill in the details of anger-provoking situations in your everyday life, along with the thoughts that exemplify each anger distortion listed:

1. Blaming:

_____
_____
_____

2. Catastrophizing/magnifying:

_____
_____
_____

3. Inflammatory/global labeling:

_____
_____
_____

4. Misattributions:

_____
_____
_____

5. Overgeneralization:

_____
_____
_____

6. Demanding/commanding:

_____
_____
_____

IDENTIFYING DISTORTIONS—Example

Instructions: In the spaces provided below, fill in the details of anger-provoking situations in your everyday life, along with the thoughts that exemplify each anger distortion listed:

1. Blaming:

My visitation day at the park is being ruined by my kids, who keep fighting with each other and are demanding candy and popcorn. "They're always bothering me asking for stuff, so I can't enjoy the day." "If they would just stop all that bickering we could have fun."

2. Catastrophizing/magnifying:

My mother asks for help to pay a dental bill. "She's going to suck me dry." "She's going to end up totally helpless and I'll have to take care of everything."

3. Inflammatory/global labeling:

Tim is late picking me up for a date , again. "What a complete jerk. He doesn't even know how to be on time." "He's such a loser. What am I doing with him anyway?"

4. Misattributions:

Tim is still late for the date. "The only reason that he's late is because he doesn't care about me." "I'll bet he's doing this just to annoy me."

5. Overgeneralization:

Waiting for my friend Mary to get ready so I can drive her to our office party . "She's never ready on time, so we're always late." "She always has some stupid excuse. Everybody we know realizes what a flake she is."

6. Demanding/commanding:

Not happy with the way that Tim did the dishes. "That was absolutely wrong. He should have dried the wine glasses by hand." "Do it right or forget it; I'll do the damn dishes myself."

Exercise: Correcting Distortions

Using the worksheet on the next page, name the countermeasures that you would use to combat the anger distortions that you identified in the previous exercise. Refer back to the description of each distortion to see which countermeasure might work best for you. For example, countermeasures for overgeneralizing involve: (1) looking for exceptions, (2) avoiding generalizing terms, and (3) using accurate and specific descriptions. For the anger example where you had overgeneralized, you'd choose one of these countermeasures to correct the distorted thinking.

A complete, filled-out example follows the worksheet to help you with the exercise.

Doing the exercises to identify anger distortions and name appropriate countermeasures to correct them is the first step. Next, we want you to use this information as a guide to actually revise your distorted thinking in real-life situations.

Homework

1. Continue to record anger experiences over 40 on the scale on Anger Log II. As you write down trigger thoughts in the "Screen" column, also note any anger distortions that you recognize.

2. Implement at least one more of the "How can I take responsibility and control" items form the previous chapter.

3. Using the Relaxation Log, record practice dates for relaxation imagery, cue-controlled relaxation, and relaxation without tension.

CORRECTING DISTORTIONS—Worksheet

Instructions: In the spaces provided below, name the countermeasures that you would employ for the anger distortions that you listed on the previous worksheet, then rewrite each distortion.

1. Blaming:

_____

_____

_____

2. Catastrophizing/magnifying:

_____

_____

_____

3. Inflammatory/global labeling:

_____

_____

_____

4. Misattributions:

_____

_____

_____

5. Overgeneralization:

_____

_____

_____

6. Demanding/commanding:

_____

_____

_____

CORRECTING DISTORTIONS—Example

Instructions: In the spaces provided below, name the countermeasures that you would employ for the anger distortions that you listed on the previous worksheet, then rewrite each distortion.

1. Blaming:
My day at the park.... Countermeasures include: (1) understand that children are doing the best they can and (2) develop a new coping strategy. New thoughts: "They're just kids, probably wanting my attention. Let's all have popcorn and enjoy ourselves."

2. Catastrophizing/magnifying:
Mother needs help with dental bill.... Countermeasures include: (1) making a realistic assessment and (2) looking at the whole picture. New thoughts: "It's just one bill, and only because she doesn't have dental coverage." "The big picture is that she has Medicare and a pension—she has her own resources."

3. Inflammatory/global labeling:
Tim is late for date. ... Countermeasures include: (1) focus on the behavior and (2) avoid making derogatory judgments. New thoughts: " He's 45 minutes late. I don't like waiting, but I can handle it." "I'm not going to put him down when I don't know what happened."

4. Misattributions:
Tim is still late.... Countermeasures include: (1) avoid assumptions and (2) develop alternate explanations. New thoughts: "I'm not going to assume any-thing." "He may have had car trouble or got stuck at the office."

5. Overgeneralization:
Waiting for Mary.... Countermeasures include: (1) looking for exceptions and (2) accurate and specific descriptions. New thoughts: "She's punctual maybe half the time." "She drove me to that medical test I had at the hospital—on time."

6. Demanding/commanding:
Not happy with how Tim did dishes.... Countermeasure: (1) reframe as personal preference. New thoughts: "I wish that he had dried the wine glasses by hand, but it's not the end of the world—I can live with it."

Anger Log

Pain/Stress	Provocative Situation	Trigger Thoughts	Anger Rating 0–100	Behavior	Outcomes -10 to +10 Self	Others

Relaxation Log II

Date	Relaxation Imagery	Cue-Controlled Relaxation	Relaxation without Tension

INSTRUCTIONS: Put a check mark under the relaxation exercises completed on each date.

CHAPTER 8

CREATING COPING THOUGHTS

Congratulations, you've gotten this far in the workbook, so you've already achieved a lot. First of all, you've learned to monitor and pay attention to your anger. By itself, this is a major step in anger control. You've developed the ability to identify anger-triggering thoughts and connect them to important anger distortions. Another major achievement is learning and practicing your relaxation skills. You've rehearsed the relaxation techniques critical to anger control, and by now may be trying them out in real-life situations.

Learning to Cope with Arousal

Nearly thirty years ago, a psychologist named Donald Meichenbaum made an important observation while working with children. He noticed that while children are engaged in learning a new and challenging task, they coach themselves out loud through each step of the process. For example, a boy building an erector set structure might be heard whispering, "First I put the screw in . . . washer . . . hold the nut . . . keep it still . . . screw it tight," and so on. Meichenbaum called this kind of monologue *self-instruction*.

Self-instruction really works, but for some reason adults stop doing it. Kids learn new tasks more easily when they can talk themselves through it, and Meichenbaum wondered if adults might get the same benefit. In a series of experiments, he taught adults who suffered anxiety problems to "talk themselves through" periods of high stress. These techniques—called stress inoculation—have been very successful and are now widely used. Stress inoculation was primarily used for anxiety problems . Then a researcher named Raymond Novaco discovered that it works just as well with anger difficulties. We now call it anger inoculation, and later in this workbook you'll be using it yourself.

Just because children self-instruct out loud, you don't have to do that. You can use "coping thoughts" to remind yourself how to navigate provocative situations. When someone upsets you and you're starting to get steamed, you need to be able to remind yourself to calm down, relax, and manage your anger. What follows is a list of general coping thoughts that you can use as self-instructions whenever you find your anger escalating.

General Coping Thoughts List

- Take a deep breath and relax.
- Getting upset won't help.
- Just as long as I keep my cool, I'm in control.
- Easy does it—there's nothing to be gained in getting mad.
- I'm not going to let him/her get to me.
- I can't change him/her with anger; I'll just upset myself.
- I can find a way to say what I want to without anger.
- Stay calm—no sarcasm, no attacks.
- I can stay calm and relaxed.
- Relax and let go. There's no need to get my knickers in a twist.
- No one is right, no one is wrong. We just have different needs.
- Stay cool, make no judgments.
- No matter what is said, I know I'm a good person.
- I'll stay rational—anger won't solve anything.
- Let them look all foolish and upset. I can stay cool and calm.
- His/her opinion isn't important. I won't be pushed into losing my cool.
- Bottom line, I'm in control. I'm out of here rather than say or do something dumb.
- Take a time-out. Cool off, then come back and deal with it.
- Some situations don't have good solutions. Looks like this is one of them. No use getting all bent out of shape about it.
- It's just a hassle. Nothing more, nothing less. I can cope with hassles.
- Break it down. Anger often comes from lumping things together.
- Good. I'm getting better at this anger management stuff.
- I got angry, but kept the lid on saying dumb things. That's progress.
- It's just not worth it to get so angry.
- Anger means it's time to relax and cope.
- I can manage this; I'm in control.
- If they want me to get angry, I'm going to disappoint them.
- I can't expect people to act the way I want them to.
- I don't have to take this so seriously.

- I have a plan to relax and cope.
- This is funny if you look at it that way.

Most of the coping thoughts are focused on staying calm and relaxed. However, there's also a group of thoughts that center on keeping control and distancing yourself from the behavior of the provoking person. Right now, in the space provided, write down the three general coping thoughts that most appeal to you and seem likely to be helpful.

1. _____

2. _____

3. _____

Now take a moment to memorize the three coping thoughts you've selected. Stop. This is really important. Make a commitment that you'll use one or more of these thoughts whenever you begin to get angry during the next week. Research shows that this tool is extremely effective for maintaining control of anger and aggression.

Sometimes people find it difficult to remember to use their coping thoughts because provocations seem to erase all their good intentions. If this is likely to be a problem for you, there are some things you can do in advance to help you remember your coping thoughts. First, transfer your three coping thoughts to a piece of paper that you mount on your vanity or shaving mirror. Seeing them prominently displayed will keep them in your mind. Second, promise yourself a reward for using your coping thoughts. Especially for the first few times, you might reinforce using coping thoughts with a meal in your favorite restaurant, a new CD, a movie or video. Give yourself a treat when you succeed in remembering, regardless of whether you fully control your anger. Right now, remembering and making an effort are enough. Third, tell a friend about your effort to use coping thoughts, and ask him or her to check in with you to see if you're remembering them. Fourth, use a physical cue. It might help this week to wear a new or unusual piece of jewelry that's associated with your plan to use coping thoughts. Another option is to wear your watch on the wrong wrist or unusual shoes or a sweater you don't particularly like—anything that will remind you of your new effort to cope.

Perhaps the best strategy to help you remember your coping thoughts is to plan in advance for provoking situations. For example, if your kids dawdle most mornings getting ready for school, plan out exactly when and how you'll use your coping thoughts. First, you'll want to plan for a cue or reminder in the situation. In the case of slow-moving kids, you might want to place one or more of your coping thoughts on a sign near the kitchen table. Or you might put something strange and inappropriate on the table (your daughter's wire sculpture of a horsefly), so you're cued to cope. A second step in planning involves identifying a clear behavioral indicator that tells you to start managing your anger. It might be when you raise your voice, or start pushing the kids down in their chairs, or make particular attacking comments. A third stage in planning is to identify exactly *how* you will cope. For example, you might decide to take a deep breath and use your cue word, then tell yourself, "Easy does it—there's nothing to be gained in getting mad." The *how* of coping might also include walking out of the room for a minute so you can breathe and use your coping thoughts away from the children.

Exercise: Making a Coping Plan

This exercise will help you plan a coping response for one anger-provoking situation that's likely to occur in the next week. Start by identifying the situation, including enough details so you're clear about the exact set of circumstances that you're planning for. Then identify one or more cues to remind you of your coping thoughts and plan. Make sure that the cues will be present and prominent in the situation where your anger is likely to be triggered. Next, under When to Cope, write down the behavioral red flags that tell you it's time to deal with your anger. Whether it's criticizing or pointing your finger or laughing sarcastically, the red flag should be specific to the situation you're planning for. Finally, under How to Cope, note the specific coping thoughts you plan to use and any actions you want to take to keep your anger from escalating. Always include one of the relaxation strategies that's quick and easy to use as part of your How to Cope plan.

Coping Plan

1. Situation

_____

2. Cues to Cope

_____

3. When to Cope

_____

4. How to Cope

_____

Coping Thoughts for Prolonged Anger or Anger Distortions

Sometimes general coping thoughts aren't enough. You're too angry, or the situation is triggering anger distortions that inflame your feelings. Controlling anger in these cases requires more careful planning and the development of coping thoughts that are tailored to particular anger triggers and distortions.

You can use what you've learned about anger distortions in the previous chapter to dramatically change your thinking when provoked. The key is to identify which anger distortion a particular trigger thought derives from, then use the countermeasures appropriate for that distortion to generate more realistic thinking. Here's a quick refresher of the countermeasures you might use to rewrite trigger thoughts sparked by the following distortions.

Magnifying/Catastrophizing. (1) Be realistically negative (e.g., it's disappointing or frustrating, not terrible or awful). Ask, "How bad is it really?," then answer honestly. (2) Use very accurate language. (3) Look at the whole picture. Try to find evidence that the opposite is also true.

Overgeneralization. (1) Avoid general terms like "always," "all," and "every." (2) Use specific and accurate descriptions. (3) Look for exceptions to the rule. Recall how people sometimes act contrary to their tendencies.

Demanding/commanding. (1) People rarely do what they should do, only what they need or want to do. (2) Stay with your wants, desires, and preferences—not shoulds. Think, "I prefer," not "You ought to."

Inflammatory/global Labeling. (1) Be specific: focus on behavior, not the person as a whole.

Misattribution/Single Explanations. (1) Check out your assumptions about other people's motives. (2) Find alternative explanations for the problem behavior.

Blaming. (1) Make a coping plan to solve the problem yourself. (2) Recognize that people are mostly doing the best they can—what they think will best meet their needs.

Each of the above countermeasures is a guideline to help you revise trigger thoughts. Here are some examples of how to use the suggested countermeasures to develop less angry thinking:

1. **Situation**: Your mother-in-law invites you to dinner, but cooks a dish you're allergic to.

    Trigger thought: This is her typical crap—I'm total chopped liver to her, I never count. The only thing she cares about is her precious daughter.

    Anger distortion: Overgeneralization (total chopped liver, I never count). Misattribution/single explanations (she cooked this because she doesn't care about me).

    Counterresponse plan: For overgeneralization, look for exceptions. For misattributions, look for alternative explanations.

    Revised trigger thought: She cooked eggplant today, but it's also true she paid for my watercolor workshop and came over and made soup when I had the flu. She's seventy-five, so it may just be that she forgets.

2. **Situation**: Your husband is yelling at your daughter over not bringing an assignment home from school.

    Trigger thoughts: He's doing damage. This is going to ruin their relationship. He's crazy.

    Anger distortions: Magnifying/catastrophizing (he's doing damage, this will ruin their relationship). Inflammatory/global labeling (he's crazy).

    Counterresponse plan: For magnifying/catastrophizing, be accurate and look at the whole picture. For inflammatory/global labeling, focus on specific behavior, not the person as a whole.

    Revised trigger thought: He raises his voice maybe once a week, but most times they get through the homework okay. They even laugh a little. He doesn't hit her, he doesn't call her names. It's not crazy, it's just a bit loud and unsettling.

3. **Situation**: A male work colleague, who has sometimes been critical in the past, tells you that, "Women are not as committed to their careers as men."

    Trigger thoughts: Stupid jerk! He shouldn't open his mouth when he doesn't know what he's talking about. He says this kind of sh-- to annoy me.

    Anger distortions: Inflammatory/global labeling (stupid jerk). Demanding/commanding (shouldn't open his mouth if he doesn't know what he's talking about). Misattribution/single explanations (says this to annoy me).

    Counterresponse plan: For inflammatory/global labeling, focus on specific behavior, not the person as a whole. For demanding/commanding, remember that people do what they need to do, not what I want. For misattribution/single explanations, find an alternative explanation.

    Revised trigger thought: He makes ignorant remarks about women at times. I suspect he needs to do it because he feels very insecure and copes by putting women down. These comments may be a way to manage his poor self-esteem.

    The next two examples will require a little thought on your part. After you've read through the situation and trigger thoughts, try to identify the key anger distortions and a counterresponse plan for each of them. An answer key is provided at the end.

4. **Situation**: Your neighbor keeps blocking your driveway with his garbage can.

    Trigger thoughts: That f——ing idiot is making me late for work. He always does that.

Anger distortions: (hint—there are three anger distortions)

_____

Counterresponse plan:

_____

Revised trigger thoughts: Okay, the blind old coot got the can in my way. This is only the fourth time in six months, and it takes me exactly two minutes to pull it out of the way. I'll check the driveway before I get in the car. That'll make it easier.

5. **Situation**: Your roommate hasn't fed her dog or bird; the bird is screeching and the dog is constantly jumping on you when you come in from work.
    Trigger thoughts: I can't stand this ... this is too much, this is totally f—ed up. She's ruining my evening; she shouldn't have pets.
    Anger distortions: (hint—there are four anger distortions)

_____

Counterresponse Plan:

_____

Revised trigger thought: She forgets a few times a week. This is a brief, unpleasant moment till I feed them, but it's nothing horrible. She's scattered and forgetful. I'd prefer she remembered, but she's doing her best.

Answer Key

Example 4:
Anger distortions: inflammatory/global labeling (f—ing idiot), blaming (making me late for work), overgeneralization (he always does that)
Counterresponse plan: For inflammatory/global labeling, make a funny label. For blaming, make a problem-solving plan. For overgeneralization, be accurate.

Example 5:
Anger distortions: magnifying/catastrophizing (can't stand this; this is too much), inflammatory/global labeling (totally f—ed up), blaming (she's ruining my evening), demanding/commanding (she shouldn't have pets)
Counterresponse plan: For magnifying/catastrophizing, be realistically negative. For inflammatory/global labeling, focus on specific behavior. For blaming, recognize that she's doing the best she can. For demanding/commanding, stay with desires and preferences.

Creating Coping Thoughts

This is your chance to develop revised trigger thoughts for some of your own anger situations. Complete the Creating Coping Thoughts Worksheet for an anger situation recorded in your most recent Anger Log.

CREATING COPING THOUGHTS—Worksheet

Complete the following for each significant trigger thought in an anger situation from your most recent Anger Log:

1. Trigger thoughts that inflame my anger:

    a.

    b.

    c.

2. Anger distortions that underlie my trigger thoughts:

    a.

    b.

    c.

3. Counterresponse plan for each of my trigger thoughts (e.g., looking for exceptions, alternative explanations, preferences not shoulds, and so on). Revised trigger thought based on each counterresponse plan.

    a. Counterresponse plan:

       Revised trigger thought:

    b. Counterresponse plan:

       Revised trigger thought:

    c. Counterresponse plan:

       Revised trigger thought:

4. Helpful coping thoughts (see General Coping Thoughts List earlier in this chapter):

    a.

    b.

    c.

To give you an idea of how the worksheet can be used, an example follows from a forty-five-year-old customer service rep. She finds herself getting angry at customers who are themselves upset about delayed or mishandled orders.

1. Trigger thoughts that inflame my anger:

   a. I can't stand this.

   b. They use me as a punching bag because I can't fight back.

   c. Just an endless string of crazy people.

2. Anger distortions that underlie my trigger thoughts:

   a. Magnifying.

   b. Misattributions/single explanations.

   c. Overgeneralization and inflammatory/global labeling.

3. Counterresponse plan for each of my trigger thoughts:

   a. Counterresponse plan: Be accurate, look at the whole picture.
      Revised trigger thoughts: It's not that bad—usually only one customer in ten is really obnoxious.

   b. Counterresponse plan: Alternative explanations
      Revised trigger thoughts: They're frustrated and, I think, afraid they'll be screwed somehow.

   c. Counterresponse plan: Be specific and accurate.
      Revised trigger thought: It's 10 percent rude people and 90 percent nice ones.

4. Helpful coping thoughts:

   a. Just as long as I keep my cool, I'm in control.

   b. Take a deep breath and relax.

   c. Let them get all upset, I can stay calm.

Homework

There are four specific things you'll need to do over the next seven to ten days to strengthen the anger management skills you've learned so far:

1. Use one of your three general coping thoughts whenever you find yourself responding with anger.

2. Practice cue-controlled relaxation whenever you feel stressed or the beginnings of anger. Also continue to practice all three key relaxation skills and record the dates in your Relaxation Log.

3. Continue to note in your Anger Log all significant anger situations.

4. Use your Creating Coping Thoughts Worksheet to develop revised trigger thoughts for any significant anger situation recorded in your log. There are four extra worksheets at the end of this chapter.

Anger Log II

Provocative Situation Sensory Input (Objective data from what you hear, see, and touch)	The Screen (Your conclusions, assumptions, interpretations, beliefs, and trigger thoughts)	Anger Rating 0–100	Behavior	Outcomes -10 to +10 Self	Others

Relaxation Log II

Date	Relaxation Imagery	Cue-Controlled Relaxation	Relaxation without Tension

INSTRUCTIONS: Put a check mark under the relaxation exercises completed on each date.

CREATING COPING THOUGHTS—Worksheet

Complete the following for each significant trigger thought in an anger situation.

1. Trigger thoughts that inflame my anger:

   a.

   b.

   c.

2. Anger distortions that underlie my trigger thoughts:

   a.

   b.

   c.

3. Counterresponse plan for each of my trigger thoughts (e.g., looking for exceptions, alternative explanations, preferences instead of shoulds, etc.). Revised trigger thought based on each counterresponse plan.

   a. Counterresponse plan:

      Revised trigger thought:

   b. Counterresponse plan:

      Revised trigger thought:

   c. Counterresponse plan:

      Revised trigger thought:

4. Helpful coping thoughts (see General Coping Thoughts List earlier in this chapter):

   a.

   b.

   c.

CHAPTER 9

ANGER INOCULATION I

This chapter will begin to teach you a new set of coping skills and help you to keep track of which coping strategies work best for you during provocative situations. It's important to remember to use the relaxation skills that you've already mastered. Deep breathing, cue-controlled relaxation, and relaxation without tension (focused on one particularly tense area only) are all very helpful in provocative situations.

Second, remember to use the new coping thoughts you learned in the last chapter during provocative situations. Have a few key coping thoughts written down. Carry them with you and review them every day, to better keep them in mind. It's also good to keep in mind that behavioral coping strategies are available. During a provocative situation, you can reduce tension by lowering your voice, looking for a compromise, or agreeing to talk about it later. Finally, remember that you are not stuck. It's perfectly okay to simply leave a provocative situation if you see that you're on the slippery slope to an anger disaster.

How to Monitor Your Coping Efforts

We have developed a useful tool for you to keep track of all your coping strategies and their relative effectiveness. You will find a blank copy of Anger Log III on the next page. As you can see, there are several columns, providing spaces to list provocative situations and their associated anger ratings. There are also columns for listing coping strategies and outcomes.

Beginning with the provocative situation on the left side of the page, you can see that it's broken down into two parts. First, under Sensory Input, write down the actual objective data that you are aware of. This should include the things that you actually can hear, see, or touch. Next, under the heading, The Screen, we want you to write down your interpretations of the data. This would include assumptions, conclusions, beliefs, and trigger thoughts. To the right of that is a column for making an initial, baseline rating of your experience of anger associated with this situation. Use a rating scale of 0 to 100, with 0 being no anger at all, and 100 being absolute, total rage.

Now move your attention to the next column to the right. This is where we want you to write down the coping strategies (if any) that you tried in response to the provocative situation. Then rate the amount of anger experienced after your coping efforts. Use the same 0- to 100-point

Anger Log III

Provocative Situation Sensory Input (Objective data from what you hear, see, and touch)	The Screen (Your conclusions, assumptions, interpretations, beliefs, and trigger thoughts)	Anger Rating 0–100	Coping Strategies Breathing, relaxation, coping thoughts, coping behaviors.	Anger Rating 0–100	Outcomes Rating -10 to +10 Self Others

Anger Log III

Provocative Situation — Sensory Input (Objective data from what you hear, see, and touch)	Anger Rating 0–100	The Screen (Your conclusions, assumptions, interpretations, beliefs, and trigger thoughts)	Coping Strategies — Breathing, relaxation, coping thoughts, coping behaviors.	Anger Rating 0–100	Outcomes Rating −10 to +10 Self	Outcomes Rating −10 to +10 Others
A car swoops in front of me on the highway. I hit the brakes hard. Squealing sound. Hands clenched on wheel.	40	He did that on purpose because he wants to scare me. F--king a--hole?	Deep breathing, relax without tension, focus on hands. "It's not directed at me." "He's just out for a thrill"	5	+7	0
Teenager's room. A complete mess. Homework not done. Talking to friend on telephone.	50	She has absolutely no respect for me. I've told her a thousand times and she never listens.	Deep breathing, relaxation imagery. "She's just being a teenager." "I was the same way at her age."	20	+3	+2
Doctor's receptionist calls, canceling my appointment.	60	He doesn't give a damn about any of his patients.	No coping	60	−6	0

scale as before. By comparing these ratings to the baseline, you can assess how well your coping strategies have worked in this situation.

Finally, use the columns to the far right to evaluate the outcome of your anger in conjunction with any coping efforts. Negative numbers would indicate an unfavorable result, while positive numbers indicate a favorable outcome. By rating the outcomes for both yourself and others, you can see how your anger and your coping strategies have differential effects.

In order to help you with this process, we've included a completed sample log with three anger situations, following the blank log.

Anger Inoculation

Now it's time to learn more about a process known as *anger inoculation*. Don't worry—it has nothing to do with needles! Essentially, anger inoculation is similar to the more familiar technique called stress inoculation, but specifically designed to deal with anger. Anger inoculation is basically a structured rehearsal of your coping thoughts and relaxation coping skills. You simply practice your new coping skills in response to imagined anger scenes. Here's the basic sequence:

1. Create 2 mild to moderate (40–50 SUDS) anger scenes. Incidentally, SUDS stands for Subjective Units of Distress. You can create your own unique SUDS scale by assigning points to various situations, from 0 (none) to 100 (absolutely unbearable).

2. Next, identify the trigger thoughts and anger distortions in each scene.

3. Using the Creating Coping Thoughts Worksheet later in this chapter, develop two or three coping thoughts for each scene.

4. Then, relax using whichever brief method works best for you. Try relaxation imagery, cue-controlled relaxation, and perhaps relaxation without tension.

5. Once you feel relaxed, start to visualize the first mild to moderate anger scene. See all the detail, hear what's being said, and notice your feelings and any bodily sensations. Crank up your anger with a few juicy trigger thoughts. Stay with it. Allow the anger to intensify as much as possible. Maintain the scene for thirty seconds.

6. Then, mentally erase the scene and begin relaxation imagery, cue-controlled relaxation, and perhaps relaxation without tension (focused on a particular muscle area). Also rehearse two or three coping thoughts until you feel completely calm again.

7. Repeat the entire sequence again, using the second anger scene.

8. Keep alternating the two scenes for four to six repetitions of each.

Right now you should create the two mild to moderate (40–50 SUDS) anger scenes that you will use to practice anger inoculation. This technique works best when the images in the scene are clear and strong. That's why it's necessary to get as much detail into the scene as possible. The scene should be something that has really happened, and is fresh enough to easily recall. To develop a scene fully, start by closing your eyes. Mentally look around and notice the environment. What time of day is it? Be aware of the temperature. Listen to the sounds around you. What are people saying? Notice feelings inside your body. Is there a tingling or tense sensation somewhere in your body? Are there any smells? Use the following Creating Anger Scenes Worksheets to write down your notes.

We've also provided a sample worksheet with two examples, filled out by Suzy, a young woman with an overly protective uncle and a less-than-perfect boyfriend.

CREATING ANGER SCENES—Worksheet
Mild-to-Moderate (40–50 SUDS) Anger Scenes

Instructions: In the spaces provided below, fill in the details of two situations in which you would experience mild-to-moderate anger. Include details about the physical environment and what other people are saying and doing. Also describe your own trigger thoughts, feelings, and physiological reactions.

Mild-to-Moderate Anger Situation 1:

Mild-to-Moderate Anger Situation 2:

CREATING ANGER SCENES—Examples
Mild-to-Moderate (40–50 SUDS) Anger Scenes

Instructions: In the spaces provided below, fill in the details of two situations in which you would experience mild-to-moderate anger. Include details about the physical environment and what other people are saying and doing. Also describe your own trigger thoughts, feelings, and physiological reactions.

Mild-to-Moderate Anger Situation 1:

I'm on my way to meet Uncle Willy for lunch. And I'm already feeling a knot in my stomach. I know that he's going to say something judgmental. Warm day, outside café. Uncle Willy waves me over to the table, but his face looks serious. Even before the waiter comes to take our order, Uncle Willy says, "I want to talk to you about your boyfriend. I don't know why you put up with him. He's not good enough for you. He has that stupid pizza job and I think that he's taking advantage of you." I think, "There you go again. Always putting me down and trying to run my life." I sit there and seethe for the rest of the lunch. I can't get what he said out of my mind.

Mild-to-Moderate Anger Situation 2:

Here's Randy, on time for dinner but never on time for anything else. "You know, Randy, I like having dinner with you, and I don't mind cooking for you. But I wish that you would contribute in some way. Maybe bring flowers or a bottle of wine." My neck starts to tense up, but I continue anyway. "And you never even offer to help with the cleanup or the dishes. I'm sick and tired of feeling unappreciated." Then Randy goes, "Take a chill pill, you're always kicking my ass about something. Your problem is you don't know how to enjoy yourself." Then I think to myself that maybe Uncle Willy was right.

The next step is to identify some trigger thoughts and anger distortions associated with the scene. Visualize each scene you've created and notice what you're thinking. Once the trigger thoughts become clear, try to link them to the appropriate anger distortion. With this in mind, we want you to fill out a Creating Coping Thoughts Worksheet for each anger scene that you created. There are two blank worksheets on the following pages.

To give you an example of how the worksheet looks, we've enclosed a sample filled out by Tom, a fifty-three-year-old middle manager working in a large printing firm. He keeps finding himself getting angry at some younger employees whom he considers unmotivated.

Now, let's follow along as Tom goes through the anger inoculation sequence:

First, he begins the relaxation process by doing some deep breathing. Then he closes his eyes and calls up his relaxation image, which for him is a deserted beach on the island of Molokai. He can feel the gentle breeze and warm sun, and he can hear waves lapping up on shore. He does some cue-controlled relaxation, feeling himself let go completely.

Then, he switches to the mild-to-moderate anger scene. He comes to work and the first thing he notices is a couple of the younger employees hanging around the coffee room. They should be working. When they see him, they stop talking and Tom thinks he sees one of them hide a smirk. Tom feels a knot in his stomach as they saunter off without saying a word. Tom's trigger thoughts: "Lazy . . . self-centered . . . deadwood like that is running the company." [Thirty seconds go by quickly.]

Now, he mentally erases the anger scene. He pictures a slow fade-out like in a movie he once saw. He tries to get back to the beach on Molokai, but it won't come. A few deep breaths and he switches to cue-controlled relaxation. Then relaxation without tension focused on the knot in his stomach. That's it. He's feeling more relaxed. Now he rehearses two of his favorite coping thoughts. "Just take a deep breath and relax"; "I'm in control, just keep cool." After several minutes, he feels completely calm again.

Switching to his second scene, Tom imagines that it's lunchtime at the plant. As he's leaving for lunch, he sees the two young employees leaving the boss's office. They see him, whisper something to each other, and walk off in the other direction. He's sure that they've just been bad-mouthing him to his boss. Trigger thoughts: "They're in there sucking up. Probably covering their asses by blaming others for not getting the work done." Tom holds a mental picture of the scene for thirty seconds.

Scene does slow fade-out. And Tom focuses on his stomach, relaxation without tension. That's it, just let go. Now some deep breathing with his cue word, and here comes the beach on Molokai. All right. Now some coping thoughts: "I can stay calm, I'm in control." "Their work habits don't affect me." Within a short while Tom feels completely calm again, and thinks to himself, "Yes. This is really working."

Tom keeps alternating the two scenes for a repetition of five times each.

Homework

1. Develop two anger scenes and practice four to six repetitions of each scene, on two separate occasions, before moving on to the next chapter.

2. Keep practicing relaxation and keep up the notations in the Relaxation Log.

3. Keep your record of anger events using Anger Log III.

We know that this chapter makes a lot of demands on your time and energy. But it's worth it to minimize the devastating effects anger can have on you and your loved ones. The stronger your commitment to this healing process, the better your life will feel.

CREATING COPING THOUGHTS—Worksheet

Complete the following for each significant trigger thought in an anger situation.

1. Trigger thoughts that inflame my anger:

   a.

   b.

   c.

2. Anger distortions that underlie my trigger thoughts:

   a.

   b.

   c.

3. Counterresponse plan for each of my trigger thoughts (e.g., looking for exceptions, alternative explanations, preferences instead of shoulds, etc.). Revised trigger thought based on each counterresponse plan.

   a. Counterresponse plan:

      Revised trigger thought:

   b. Counterresponse plan:

      Revised trigger thought:

   c. Counterresponse plan:

      Revised trigger thought:

4. Helpful coping thoughts (see General Coping Thoughts List earlier in this chapter):

   a.

   b.

   c.

CREATING COPING THOUGHTS—Worksheet

Complete the following for each significant trigger thought in an anger situation.

1. Trigger thoughts that inflame my anger:

    a.

    b.

    c.

2. Anger distortions that underlie my trigger thoughts:

    a.

    b.

    c.

3. Counterresponse plan for each of my trigger thoughts (e.g., looking for exceptions, alternative explanations, preferences instead of shoulds, etc.). Revised trigger thought based on each counterresponse plan.

    a. Counterresponse plan:

       Revised trigger thought:

    b. Counterresponse plan:

       Revised trigger thought:

    c. Counterresponse plan:

       Revised trigger thought:

4. Helpful coping thoughts (see General Coping Thoughts List earlier in this chapter):

    a.

    b.

    c.

CREATING COPING THOUGHTS—Example

Complete the following for each significant trigger thought in an anger situation.

1. Trigger thoughts that inflame my anger:

    a. *Lazy ... self-centered ... deadwood*

    b. They're ruining this company.

    c.

2. Anger distortions that underlie my trigger thoughts:

    a. *Global labeling*

    b. *Magnifying*

    c.

3. Counterresponse plan for each of my trigger thoughts (e.g., looking for exceptions, alternative explanations, preferences instead of shoulds, etc.). Revised trigger thought based on each counterresponse plan.

    a. Counterresponse plan: *Accurate statements, no put-down labels*

    Revised trigger thought: *They're taking more frequent breaks than they should, but their work habits don't affect me.*

    b. Counterresponse plan: *Be accurate and specific.*

    Revised trigger thought: *They're wasting 5 to 10 minutes, that's all. That will have zero impact on a big company like this.*

    c. Counterresponse plan:

    Revised trigger thought:

4. Helpful coping thoughts (see General Coping Thoughts List earlier in this chapter):

    a. *Just take a deep breath and relax.*

    b. *I'm in control, just keep cool.*

    c.

Anger Log III

Provocative Situation Sensory Input (Objective data from what you hear, see, and touch)	The Screen (Your conclusions, assumptions, interpretations, beliefs, and trigger thoughts)	Anger Rating 0–100	Coping Strategies Breathing, relaxation, coping thoughts, coping behaviors.	Anger Rating 0–100	Outcomes Rating -10 to +10 Self Others	

Relaxation Log II

Date	Relaxation Imagery	Cue-Controlled Relaxation	Relaxation without Tension

INSTRUCTIONS: Put a check mark under the relaxation exercises completed on each date.

CHAPTER 10

ANGER INOCULATION II

Before moving on to this next level, take a moment to look at and evaluate the results from your most recent entries in Anger Log III. Have you begun to cope with provocative situations as they arise? If so, what coping strategies are working best for you? In the space provided below, write in anything that's worked well for each category:

1. Relaxation Coping:

   _____

   _____

2. Coping Thoughts:

   _____

   _____

3. Coping Behaviors:

   _____

   _____

Anger Inoculation—Moderate Anger Scenes

Now it's time to start practicing anger inoculation with two moderate (50–60 SUDS) anger scenes. Just like last time, we want you to imagine an anger-producing scene and then manage the anger by using relaxation and coping thoughts.

It's really important to try hard to make these anger scenes as vivid as possible. That means including lots of specifics: what you see and hear, even smells associated with the scene, and also kinesthetic aspects like temperature and texture. It's also good to include details about emotional and physical reactions that are occurring during each scene. If you've been practicing all along, this will get easier and easier to accomplish over time.

Next, identify the trigger thoughts and anger distortions in each scene. These are important to include in your visualization because they crank up your anger.

Now, using the Creating Anger Scenes Worksheet on the next page, write out two moderate anger scenes. In order to give you an idea of what this should look like, we've provided a sample worksheet with two examples.

When you feel completely prepared, you can go to a quiet, comfortable place and start the relaxation process. It usually works best to begin with relaxation imagery, then make a segue into cue-controlled relaxation, and perhaps relaxation without tension.

Once you feel relaxed, you can start the moderate anger scene, like pushing the PLAY button on your VCR remote control. Allow the anger to intensify by focusing on the images and trigger thoughts that really outrage you. Stay in the scene for thirty seconds.

Now erase the scene, like pushing the STOP button on the VCR remote, and then go back to the relaxation process again. Be sure, at the very least, to use cue-controlled relaxation. As you feel yourself begin to relax physically, repeat some of your coping thoughts. Continue until you feel completely calm.

Repeat the entire sequence again using the second anger scene. Keep alternating the two scenes for four to six repetitions of each. In a day or two, do the entire series (four to six alternating repetitions of each scene) once more.

By way of example, let's follow Jenny, a fifty-two-year-old divorced accountant, as she goes through the process with a moderate anger scene.

She begins relaxing by picturing herself in a childhood summer cabin in the Catskill Mountains. A gentle breeze is coming off the lake, and some birds are chirping. She can smell her mother's apple pie cooling in the kitchen.

Now the scene shifts dramatically. It's a retirement "home," where the harsh odor of antiseptics doesn't quite mask the sweet, sickly, "old people" smell in the air. Jenny is coming to visit her mother, her heels clicking on the nearly empty hallway. "Why is it always me who has to take care of Mom? My brothers and sisters never help at all." Her stomach starts to tighten as she nears the room. Open door, "Hi Mom." "Oh, it's you, finally. Nobody ever comes to see me. I guess it's 'cause I'm not cooking. After everything I did for you I think you could at least show up here once in a while." Jenny thinks, "I can't stand this for even one second more."

After thirty seconds, CLICK, mercifully the scene ends and Jenny is back in the Catskills. Cue-controlled relaxation, and Jenny thinks, "My brothers and sisters are doing the best they can, they have kids of their own to take care of." "I'll only stay for fifteen minutes—my mother deserves that much." After a few minutes, she feels calm again.

Now a new scene begins to take shape. Jenny is at the supermarket. It's crowded at this time of day. Feeling good about getting the last shopping cart, she starts to smile. This quickly turns into a grimace as she realizes that it has a bad wheel, veering to the left with a constant squeaking noise. Her hands tighten on the cart's handle. Finally, finished shopping, she gets on line at the checkout counter. The line moves along fairly quickly until the last person ahead of her starts having an argument with the clerk. "This was on sale, three for a dollar." The clerk calls for an assistant to go check out the price.

All the other lines are moving nicely except this one. "This always happens to me. At this rate I'll miss the evening news on TV." Assistant returns, the customer was mistaken. Now she's fumbling through her purse looking for discount coupons. Finally, giving up, she says, "Okay, I'll write you a check." When the clerk asks for ID she doesn't have any. The clerk calls for a manager. Jenny's stomach is tightening up. Minutes go by. Nothing happens. The clerk calls again for a manager. "Oh, come on! What a goddamned idiot!"

CREATING ANGER SCENES—Worksheet
Moderate (50–60 SUDS) Anger Scenes

Instructions: In the spaces provided below, fill in the details of two situations in which you would experience moderate anger. Include details about the physical environment and what other people are saying and doing. Also describe your own trigger thoughts, feelings, and physiological reactions.

Moderate Anger Situation 1:

Moderate Anger Situation 2:

CREATING ANGER SCENES—Examples
Moderate (50–60 SUDS) Anger Scenes

Instructions: In the spaces provided below, fill in the details of two situations in which you would experience moderate anger. Include details about the physical environment and what other people are saying and doing. Also describe your own trigger thoughts, feelings, and physiological reactions.

Moderate Anger Situation 1:

Last weekend I decided it's time to do my laundry. Finally got all the dirty, smelly clothes into a large garbage bag. I'm walking to the Laundromat when it starts to pour. I'm hurrying, but have to stop at a red light. A car speeds around the corner, nearly hitting me, and splashing my shoes. I feel my body go tense. I get to the Laundromat. There's only one empty washing machine and I run to get it, putting my coins in the slot, and jamming them home. Then I notice a small sign saying it's out of order. I push the coin return button and nothing happens. I kick the side of the washer and say, "Damn machine." I feel a surge of anger.

Moderate Anger Situation 2:

It's Friday evening. I finally get home after an hour and a half on the road. I feel tired and uptight, just wanting to relax and be taken care of. My wannabe writer husband comes out of his "den," unshaven and looking sheepish. "I haven't had time to go shopping. I've been too busy with this new poem." My neck gets tense. I snap out, "Thanks a lot," and go into the living room. The morning newspaper is still strewn all over the place. "Do I have to do everything myself?" I mumble under my breath through clenched teeth. I feel my anger start to rise. I go into the kitchen and find the dirty dishes still in the sink. "You're useless, Bob," I shout as my husband enters the room.

CREATING COPING THOUGHTS—Worksheet

Complete the following for each significant trigger thought in an anger situation.

1. Trigger thoughts that inflame my anger:

    a.

    b.

    c.

2. Anger distortions that underlie my trigger thoughts:

    a.

    b.

    c.

3. Counterresponse plan for each of my trigger thoughts (e.g., looking for exceptions, alternative explanations, preferences instead of shoulds, etc.). Revised trigger thought based on each counterresponse plan.

    a. Counterresponse plan:

       Revised trigger thought:

    b. Counterresponse plan:

       Revised trigger thought:

    c. Counterresponse plan:

       Revised trigger thought:

4. Helpful coping thoughts (see General Coping Thoughts List earlier in this chapter):

    a.

    b.

    c.

CREATING COPING THOUGHTS—Worksheet

Complete the following for each significant trigger thought in an anger situation.

1. Trigger thoughts that inflame my anger:

   a.

   b.

   c.

2. Anger distortions that underlie my trigger thoughts:

   a.

   b.

   c.

3. Counterresponse plan for each of my trigger thoughts (e.g., looking for exceptions, alternative explanations, preferences instead of shoulds, etc.). Revised trigger thought based on each counterresponse plan.

   a. Counterresponse plan:

      Revised trigger thought:

   b. Counterresponse plan:

      Revised trigger thought:

   c. Counterresponse plan:

      Revised trigger thought:

4. Helpful coping thoughts (see General Coping Thoughts List earlier in this chapter):

   a.

   b.

   c.

CLICK, back in the Catskills, a sunny afternoon. "It's okay, they're doing the best they can." "So what if I miss the news. It'll be in the paper tomorrow anyway." Cue-controlled relaxation, relaxation without tension focusing on her stomach, more coping thoughts, more relaxation, and eventually calm.

Jenny alternates the two scenes—anger at her mother, and then anger at the supermarket lady—for four to six repetitions each.

Anger Inoculation—New Format

When you feel comfortable managing moderate anger scenes, it's time to move up a notch to moderate-to-high (60–75 SUDS) anger. This time, however, you will not be erasing the scene as before. We want you to continue visualizing the provocative scene while *simultaneously* using a variety of coping strategies to reduce the anger. In other words, you'll cope with your anger *in* the scene, not after it.

Begin by creating two moderate-to-high anger scenes, using lots of detail, and write them out on the Creating Anger Scenes Worksheet provided on the next page. Next, identify the trigger thoughts and anger distortions in each scene. Then, develop coping thoughts for each scene, recording all of the information on the Creating Coping Thoughts Worksheets provided. Once you've finished all the preparatory work, relax and start to visualize the first scene. *Note:* Don't start any coping strategies until the scene is fully developed

Now, here's the important part: We want you to maintain the image of the provocation, while at the same time practicing your coping skills. Hold on to the image while using cue-controlled relaxation, and perhaps releasing tension in a tight area of your body. Continue to stay locked on to the image, and use one or two coping thoughts. Then go back to cue-controlled relaxation, more coping thoughts, etc. It's not easy to do several things at the same time. But, with practice, you will be able to balance the visualization with the coping strategies. Only when you feel completely calm in the anger scene should you erase it and take a break using relaxation imagery.

As an example, we can follow along as Jim, a forty-two-year-old, married, freelance building contractor with two kids, works his way through the moderate-to-high anger scene that he's created. He's already prepared himself by identifying trigger thoughts, anger distortions, and the appropriate countermeasures. Now he goes to his den, closes his eyes, and begins to relax by visualizing a meadow in Yosemite National Park. Deep breath. Filtered sunlight, shadows float across the meadow, a doe and a fawn shyly step out of the forest. Cue-controlled relaxation.

CLICK. Now to work. Jim is riding in his old pickup truck, bouncing along as his worn-out shocks make a creaking noise. His hands tense on the steering wheel as he hits a pothole. "Damn, I need a new truck, but I can't afford it." Cell phone rings. It's Carstairs, complaining that the crew that was supposed to be putting in the new roof hasn't shown up yet, and it's nearly noon. "Shit, I can't afford to mess up on this job too. Everybody is complaining about something, and I'm not getting any new referrals." He thinks to himself, "That's what I get for using cheap labor—those guys are just plain lazy and don't want to work. They're all worthless pieces of crap."

With this scene firmly established, and feeling quite angry as he relives it, Jim is ready to start coping. Cue-controlled relaxation, that's better. Coping thoughts: "My job is solving problems. That's what I do. No big deal. Breathe and relax. I can handle it." Jim focuses on relaxing his stomach, which is tight, letting each deep breath loosen the knot. More coping thoughts, more cue-controlled relaxation until his whole body seems to have let go and he feels calm again.

CREATING ANGER SCENES—Worksheet
Moderate-to-High (60–75 SUDS) Anger Scenes

Instructions: In the spaces provided below, fill in the details of two situations in which you would experience moderate-to-high anger. Include details about the physical environment and what other people are saying and doing. Also describe your own trigger thoughts, feelings, and physiological reactions.

Moderate-to-High Anger Situation 1:

Moderate-to-High Anger Situation 2:

CREATING COPING THOUGHTS—Worksheet

Complete the following for each significant trigger thought in an anger situation.

1. Trigger thoughts that inflame my anger:

   a.

   b.

   c.

2. Anger distortions that underlie my trigger thoughts:

   a.

   b.

   c.

3. Counterresponse plan for each of my trigger thoughts (e.g., looking for exceptions, alternative explanations, preferences instead of shoulds, etc.). Revised trigger thought based on each counterresponse plan.

   a. Counterresponse plan:

      Revised trigger thought:

   b. Counterresponse plan:

      Revised trigger thought:

   c. Counterresponse plan:

      Revised trigger thought:

4. Helpful coping thoughts (see General Coping Thoughts List earlier in this chapter):

   a.

   b.

   c.

CREATING COPING THOUGHTS—Worksheet

Complete the following for each significant trigger thought in an anger situation.

1. Trigger thoughts that inflame my anger:

    a.

    b.

    c.

2. Anger distortions that underlie my trigger thoughts:

    a.

    b.

    c.

3. Counterresponse plan for each of my trigger thoughts (e.g., looking for exceptions, alternative explanations, preferences instead of shoulds, etc.). Revised trigger thought based on each counterresponse plan.

    a. Counterresponse plan:

       Revised trigger thought:

    b. Counterresponse plan:

       Revised trigger thought:

    c. Counterresponse plan:

       Revised trigger thought:

4. Helpful coping thoughts (see General Coping Thoughts List earlier in this chapter):

    a.

    b.

    c.

Only when the anger is completely gone does he click off the scene. Now he returns to the relaxation imagery of the Yosemite meadow.

Now Jim switches to his second moderate-to-high anger scene.

Jim comes home at seven P.M., exhausted. His wife Shirley meets him at the door and says, "I've had it with your son. He won't clean his room. You deal with him." Jim stomps to Chad's room, which looks like a cyclone hit it. He can smell the remains of half-eaten pizza, and sees pizza cartons and empty soda cans strewn all over. His son is lying on an unmade bed chatting on the telephone, while MTV blares on the TV. "Hang up that phone son, we need to talk." Chad replies, "Oh man, can't you see I'm busy?" Jim feels himself get cold all over. His right arm tenses as his hand forms a fist. "Get off that damn phone and clean up this room right now." Chad, not really paying attention, says, "All right, Dad, I'll do it later." With a snarl, Jim grabs the receiver and hangs up the phone. "Do it now, or get out of my house," he yells.

Still quivering with anger, and attention locked on the scene, Jim begins to use his coping strategies. First, cue-controlled relaxation, then coping thoughts. "I'm still in control. Keep cool now." Relaxation without tension focused on his forearm, biceps, and fist. "He's just a kid, go easy on him." Deep breathing. Slowly, a sense of calm returns.

Only after the anger is completely gone does he click back to the relaxation image in Yosemite.

Jim switches back and forth between each scene four to six times. Within a day or two, he does the entire series (four to six alternating repetitions of each scene) once more.

Homework

1. Continue to track your anger experiences and coping efforts using Anger Log III.

2. Continue to practice cue-controlled relaxation whenever stressed, and notice how much easier it's getting to relax whenever you put your mind to it. Practice all three key relaxation skills and note the details in the Relaxation Log.

3. Use the Creating Coping Thoughts Worksheet for any provocative situation where you couldn't manage your trigger thoughts or control your anger.

4. Make sure you've completed two entire series (four to six alternating repetitions of each scene) for both the moderate and moderate-to-high anger level scenes.

Anger Log III

Provocative Situation Sensory Input (Objective data from what you hear, see, and touch)	The Screen (Your conclusions, assumptions, interpretations, beliefs, and trigger thoughts)	Anger Rating 0–100	Coping Strategies Breathing, relaxation, coping thoughts, coping behaviors.	Anger Rating 0–100	Outcomes Rating -10 to +10 Self Others	

Relaxation Log II

Date	Relaxation Imagery	Cue-Controlled Relaxation	Relaxation without Tension

INSTRUCTIONS: Put a check mark under the relaxation exercises completed on each date.

CHAPTER 11

ANGER
INOCULATION III

Before we move on to the highest levels of anger inoculation, it's useful to spend some time reviewing the information that has accumulated in your Anger Log III records. In particular, we want you to look back on times when you felt upset but somehow weren't able to mobilize and use your new skills.

On the checklist below, mark the categories of anger situations where you either forget to use your new skills, or they don't seem to work.

❑ Anger with people you supervise.

❑ Anger with authority figures.

❑ Anger with spouse/partner/lover.

❑ Anger with children.

❑ Anger with close friends.

❑ Anger with strangers (i.e., road rage, anger at store clerks, receptionists, etc.)

❑ Anger with parents.

❑ Anger when you feel criticized.

❑ Anger when you feel disrespected.

❑ Anger when you feel hurt.

❑ Anger when you feel pressured to do something.

❑ Anger when you feel humiliated/shamed.

❑ Anger when you feel disappointed.

❑ Anger when you feel frustrated.

❑ Anger when you feel threatened.

❑ Anger when you feel guilty or wrong.

❑ Anger when you're scared something bad will happen.

❑ Anger when you're tired/overwhelmed/pushed to the limit/running on empty.

❑ Anger when people don't live up to your expectations.

❑ Anger when people don't listen to you.

The categories you marked represent ongoing problems. Now, go back over the list and put a star next to the top three in terms of their impact on you. Then, for each of the starred categories, we want you to identify the following:

1. One strategy to remind you to use your coping skills.

2. An intervention point, i.e., the "red flag" behavior or step in the escalation process when you're going to do something different.

3. One (foolproof) coping response you're sure to use. This can be either a relaxation skill, a coping thought, or something you'd say or do differently.

Here are some examples:

One of the starred items on Maggie's list was "Anger with children"—specifically, her teenage daughter Ashley, who was an expert at pushing her buttons. Since many angry situations began in the kitchen, Maggie decided to use the refrigerator as a reminder site. She found a picture of an atomic bomb explosion and attached it to the door with magnets, as a subtle hint about going ballistic. Her red-flag behavior was when she started to sound like her own mother, hearing her voice get high and sharp. For a surefire coping response, Maggie chose cue-controlled relaxation, using the cue word "floating."

One of Bob's starred items was "Anger with people you supervise." He put a wood carving of an African warrior on his desk at work to remind him this *wasn't* a battle. For his intervention point, he chose to be aware of tapping his right foot and talking in a harsh, lecturing tone. Bob had noticed that when he felt annoyed at Lester, whom he supervised, he would start to tap his foot and talk as if Lester were stupid. He then chose the coping thought, "He's doing his best and I'm not going to mess with him," as his foolproof coping response.

There are three blank Target Problem Worksheets available at the end of this chapter. Fill out one for each of your identified target problems.

Anger Inoculation—High Anger Situations

Now it's time to move on to anger inoculation with high (75–85 SUDS) anger situations. Use the Creating Anger Scenes Worksheet on the next page to develop two scenes that are rich in detail. An example of a completed worksheet is also provided. Next, identify the trigger thoughts and anger distortions in the scene. Then, develop some appropriate coping thoughts and record them on the Creating Coping Thoughts Worksheets on the following pages.

CREATING ANGER SCENES—Worksheet
High (75–85 SUDS) Anger Scenes

Instructions: In the spaces provided below, fill in the details of two situations in which you would experience high levels of anger. Include details about the physical environment and what other people are saying and doing. Also describe your own trigger thoughts, feelings, and physiological reactions.

High Anger Situation 1:

High Anger Situation 2:

CREATING ANGER SCENES—Examples
High (75–85 SUDS) Anger Scenes

Instructions: In the spaces provided below, fill in the details of two situations in which you would experience high levels of anger. Include details about the physical environment and what other people are saying and doing. Also describe your own trigger thoughts, feelings, and physiological reactions.

High Anger Situation 1:

I"m sitting in my cold super's office thinking, "I'm a glorified janitor." People call me at all times of the day and night, expecting me to drop everything and fix this, fix that. Canfield, that looney tune in #15, calls to complain that I didn't clean up enough when I fixed his sink. He's an a—hole, like a lot of them in this building. Then Canfield says I should get a move on and clean under his sink right now or he's going to complain to the landlord. Stomach tense. I tell him to clean his own damn sink, and he says f—k you. Hands balled into fists. I've had it with his crazy shit. I'm only getting a lousy couple of hundred bucks for this. Treating me like dirt.

High Anger Situation 2:

Being a little league baseball coach. I'm sitting in the car sopping wet, driving half the players home from our rained-out ballgame. Most of the parents don't even show up for the games, and when they do, they're all over my ass about why their kid isn't batting cleanup. Stomach knots up. First, the damn kids don't want to practice, and then they throw a fit if I don't give them enough playing time. This kid Sal tells me to drop him off way the hell over at the Hillsdale mall. I tell him to forget it. He says maybe he'll quit the team then. I can feel how wet my clothes are, sticking to the seat. Flushed feeling in my face. I want to kick him out of the goddamned car right there in the rain. "Who needs you?" I tell him. Who the hell needs a kid like you on his team?" Feel the rage going up and down my body.

CREATING COPING THOUGHTS—Worksheet

Complete the following for each significant trigger thought in an anger situation.

1. Trigger thoughts that inflame my anger:

    a.

    b.

    c.

2. Anger distortions that underlie my trigger thoughts:

    a.

    b.

    c.

3. Counterresponse plan for each of my trigger thoughts (e.g., looking for exceptions, alternative explanations, preferences instead of shoulds, etc.). Revised trigger thought based on each counterresponse plan.

    a. Counterresponse plan:

       Revised trigger thought:

    b. Counterresponse plan:

       Revised trigger thought:

    c. Counterresponse plan:

       Revised trigger thought:

4. Helpful coping thoughts (see General Coping Thoughts List earlier in this chapter):

    a.

    b.

    c.

CREATING COPING THOUGHTS—Worksheet

Complete the following for each significant trigger thought in an anger situation.

1. Trigger thoughts that inflame my anger:

   a.

   b.

   c.

2. Anger distortions that underlie my trigger thoughts:

   a.

   b.

   c.

3. Counterresponse plan for each of my trigger thoughts (e.g., looking for exceptions, alternative explanations, preferences instead of shoulds, etc.). Revised trigger thought based on each counterresponse plan.

   a. Counterresponse plan:

      Revised trigger thought:

   b. Counterresponse plan:

      Revised trigger thought:

   c. Counterresponse plan:

      Revised trigger thought:

4. Helpful coping thoughts (see General Coping Thoughts List earlier in this chapter):

   a.

   b.

   c.

The sequence for this anger inoculation set is the same as the one used in the last chapter with moderate-to-high anger scenes. Begin by relaxing, then visualize the scene and let the anger build. Once you've achieved a level of anger, remember to *stay in the scene* and use your coping strategies. Do the entire series (four to six alternating repetitions of each scene) on two separate occasions.

Here's an example from Cheryl, a thirty-eight-year-old waitress who lives with her younger sister, Patti. She's already done the preparation by identifying trigger thoughts and distortions, and figuring out coping countermeasures.

She begins by visualizing a scene at the beach. Warm sun, slight breeze coming in from the ocean, the salty air, and sounds of seagulls complete the picture. When she finds herself feeling quite relaxed, she's ready to move on.

CLICK. It's Saturday night, close to the end of my shift at the restaurant. My feet are killing me from waiting tables all day. Every time I go into the kitchen for an order, I smell the grease on the grill going rancid. I hate this lousy job, and all the cheapskate customers with their measly tips. Beginning to get angry, I feel my stomach start to churn.

Then there's this disgusting family of four. The kids have a water fight and I have to clean up the spilled glasses. Goddamn kids running all over the place, driving me crazy. I'm gritting my teeth. Parents letting their kids run amok. They shouldn't be allowed to have kids. Then they tell me the kids are wild because the food is so late. They tell me to hurry it up. Why the hell are they eating in a restaurant in the first place with these little monsters? Whole body like a coiled spring.

Staying with the imagery of the scene, and trembling slightly with rage, Cheryl starts her coping strategies. First, some deep breathing. Then, "They were just kids having a good time." Cue-controlled relaxation. Starting to feel calmer. "I'm under control. This won't affect me." More deep breathing. Only when she feels completely relaxed does Cheryl let go of the restaurant scene. Immediately she returns to the beach, relaxing in the warm air, taking a few deep breaths.

CLICK. Sunday afternoon and I'm home alone, listening to jazz on the radio. Patti is out having a picnic with her boyfriend. I go into the kitchen and find that she left the breakfast dishes in the sink for me to clean up. My jaw tightens. "Who does she think I am? The goddamn maid?"

Looking through my closet, I discover that Patti borrowed my new sweater without even asking me. I think, "She's always taking advantage of me." Boy, that makes me mad. I don't know why I put up with that selfish bitch. I slam the closet door, picturing her face on the other side.

Holding on to the image of the scene, and still seething inside, Cheryl begins to breathe deeply. She practices relaxation without tension, focusing on her jaw. Now some coping thoughts: "I can handle this. Just breathe and relax." Cue-controlled relaxation. Cheryl decides to set some limits with Patti. "I don't have to be a victim." More deep breathing, and finally relaxed again.

Anger Inoculation—Extreme Anger Situations

This is the last, and perhaps the most important, phase of the anger inoculation process—the one that may save your life. Develop two scenes where provocation can lead to anger scores in the 85–100 SUDS range. Use the Creating Anger Scenes Worksheet to fully flesh out the details. As before, identify potential trigger thoughts and anger distortions. Next, use the Creating Coping Thoughts Worksheets to prepare your coping strategy.

CREATING ANGER SCENES—Worksheet
Extreme (85–100 SUDS) Anger Scenes

Instructions: In the spaces provided below, fill in the details of two situations in which you would experience extreme levels of anger. Include details about the physical environment and what other people are saying and doing. Also describe your own trigger thoughts, feelings, and physiological reactions.

Extreme Anger Situation 1:

Extreme Anger Situation 2:

CREATING COPING THOUGHTS—Worksheet

Complete the following for each significant trigger thought in an anger situation.

1. Trigger thoughts that inflame my anger:

   a.

   b.

   c.

2. Anger distortions that underlie my trigger thoughts:

   a.

   b.

   c.

3. Counterresponse plan for each of my trigger thoughts (e.g., looking for exceptions, alternative explanations, preferences instead of shoulds, etc.). Revised trigger thought based on each counterresponse plan.

   a. Counterresponse plan:

      Revised trigger thought:

   b. Counterresponse plan:

      Revised trigger thought:

   c. Counterresponse plan:

      Revised trigger thought:

4. Helpful coping thoughts (see General Coping Thoughts List earlier in this chapter):

   a.

   b.

   c.

CREATING COPING THOUGHTS—Worksheet

Complete the following for each significant trigger thought in an anger situation.

1. Trigger thoughts that inflame my anger:

    a.

    b.

    c.

2. Anger distortions that underlie my trigger thoughts:

    a.

    b.

    c.

3. Counterresponse plan for each of my trigger thoughts (e.g., looking for exceptions, alternative explanations, preferences instead of shoulds, etc.). Revised trigger thought based on each counterresponse plan.

    a. Counterresponse plan:

       Revised trigger thought:

    b. Counterresponse plan:

       Revised trigger thought:

    c. Counterresponse plan:

       Revised trigger thought:

4. Helpful coping thoughts (see General Coping Thoughts List earlier in this chapter):

    a.

    b.

    c.

When you feel fully prepared, follow the same sequence that you used in the last set. Begin by relaxing completely. Visualize the scene, and let the anger build up as much as possible. Hold on to the scene and start to implement your coping strategies. Maintain the scene until you've managed to relax, and only then click off the first scene. Return briefly to your relaxation imagery, take a few deep breaths, and move on to the second scene.

Do the entire series (four to six alternating repetitions of each scene) on two occasions.

Homework

1. Continue to track your anger experiences and coping efforts using Anger Log III.

2. Continue to practice cue-controlled relaxation whenever stressed. By this time, it should feel as easy as a hot knife cutting through butter. Also practice the three relaxation skills and note the dates in the Relaxation Log.

3. Continue to use the Creating Coping Thoughts Worksheets for any provocative situations that are still giving you some difficulty.

4. Make sure you've completed two entire series (four to six alternating repetitions of each scene) for both high and extreme anger level scenes.

5. Implement plans on Target Problems Worksheet.

Anger Log III

Provocative Situation Sensory Input (Objective data from what you hear, see, and touch)	Anger Rating 0–100	The Screen (Your conclusions, assumptions, interpretations, beliefs, and trigger thoughts)	Coping Strategies Breathing, relaxation, coping thoughts, coping behaviors.	Anger Rating 0–100	Outcomes Rating -10 to +10 Self Others

Relaxation Log II

Date	Relaxation Imagery	Cue-Controlled Relaxation	Relaxation without Tension

INSTRUCTIONS: Put a check mark under the relaxation exercises completed on each date.

TARGET PROBLEMS—Worksheet

Instructions: In the spaces provided below, fill in the identified target problem and the steps that you'll take to deal with it differently in the future.

Target Problem:

1. Strategy for using coping skills:

2. Intervention point (red flag event):

3. Foolproof coping response:

TARGET PROBLEMS—Worksheet

Instructions: In the spaces provided below, fill in the identified target problem and the steps that you'll take to deal with it differently in the future.

Target Problem:

1. Strategy for using coping skills:

2. Intervention point (red flag event):

3. Foolproof coping response:

TARGET PROBLEMS—Worksheet

Instructions: In the spaces provided below, fill in the identified target problem and the steps that you'll take to deal with it differently in the future.

Target Problem:

1. Strategy for using coping skills:

2. Intervention point (red flag event):

3. Foolproof coping response:

CHAPTER 12

PROBLEM-SOLVING COMMUNICATION

This chapter will help you to reduce anger experiences by focusing on improving two vital skills: problem solving and communication. A useful place to begin is by examining three different coping styles: passive, aggressive, and assertive.

Coping Styles

The *passive* coping style is characterized by a desire to avoid offending people at all costs. It simply feels too scary to push for what you want if it conflicts in any way with the needs of others. Often this means saying nothing—certainly nothing about your own wants and needs. At best, you express your wants indirectly. When you need to set limits, you tend to do it by avoiding the situation or just by dragging your feet. The advantage of this coping strategy is that people will rarely be angry at you, since on the surface you appear good, sweet, and compliant. The downside, of course, is that people don't see you for who you really are. You're like the invisible man. You never get what *you* want, and often feel overwhelmed by the demands of others. What you *do* get is the opportunity to carry a load of resentment because no one seems to see or acknowledge what's important to you.

The *aggressive* coping style is characterized by pushing people around, loudly demanding that you get things your way, and punishing people who don't give you what you want. The advantage of this coping strategy is that aggressive people often *do* get what they want. This might mean having things go their way regarding chores at home, or getting the last fresh rye bread at the bakery.

There is, however, a downside as well to the aggressive coping style. The people you try to intimidate and push around will find some way to retaliate, either directly through confrontation or indirectly through avoidance. Confrontation leads to escalation and the dangers of a knock-down-drag-out fight (either physically or psychologically). Avoidance leads to a feeling of isolation and loneliness. And, the aggressive person can never be quite sure if even those close to him/her are cooperating out of love or fear.

A note about the "passive-aggressive" style: Inside every "long-suffering," passive-coping-style person is a lot of anger. When you're afraid to ask directly for what you want, resentment and pain build up inside. A "nice-guy," passive coping style leaves you feeling stuck and helpless, until the pressure builds to the breaking point. Then, any convenient trigger will serve to precipitate a vicious outburst—often indirect, yet lethal nonetheless.

The *assertive* coping style, which we recommend, is characterized by the belief that everyone has the right to express their own legitimate needs. You *are* allowed to say what you want, express feelings, stand up for your rights, and set appropriate limits. All this can be accomplished without violating the rights of others, who, by the way, also have a right to express their needs.

The assertive style allows you to work toward a settlement without anger. It makes it possible to seek a solution where both parties get something they want. The assertive style allows you to protect yourself without blaming others, and lets you set limits without turning other people off. Being assertive (rather than passive or aggressive) works well in every aspect of interpersonal interaction, whether it be struggles about money, conflicts at work, or intimate issues like sexuality. Clear, direct, and nonattacking communication will usually bring the best results.

In order to clarify these different coping styles, here are several examples of real-life situations.

Mark goes to a convenience store, picks up a six-pack of soda, and pays for it at the counter. As he's leaving the store, mentally reviewing the change he got from his ten-dollar bill, and with one foot out the door, he suddenly realizes that he's a dollar short. What does he do?

If Mark habitually used a passive coping style, he would probably say something to himself like, "Oh well, it's only a dollar. Maybe I made the mistake, and the line at the counter is awfully long." He would leave the store having avoided a potentially unpleasant confrontation. But Mark would carry a residual amount of resentment, wondering if the clerk was really trying to rip him off.

If Mark were the kind of person who used an aggressive coping style, he would respond in a different way. He'd probably whirl around, push his way back to the front of the line, and in a loud voice demand his money. "You don't even know how to make correct change. I'm a dollar short and you better give it to me." Mark would probably get his dollar, but he would also be met with hostility and resentment on future visits to the store.

But Mark is a person who uses an assertive coping style. He returns to the counter and waits until the clerk has finished with the next customer. Then, speaking up briskly, he says to the clerk, "I think that you've made a mistake. The change that you gave me is a dollar short. (Showing the change in his hand) I gave you a ten-dollar bill." If the clerk refuses to make the correction, then Mark would say, "Please let me speak with your manager."

Another example comes from Joan, who has a friend (Sally) in need of a ride. Joan has a car, but her friend does not, and since they're both going to the same meeting, she agrees to give Sally a lift. When Joan arrives, her friend is not ready—she's just getting out of the shower. It's clear that, unless Sally really gets herself in gear, they won't get to the meeting on time.

If Joan were using a passive coping style, she would just stand around encouraging Sally to "hurry up," or try to help her find her shoes. As the time drags on, Joan would feel her stomach tighten, knowing that they would be late for the meeting, and building up resentment that would resurface later.

If Joan habitually used an aggressive coping style, she would probably say to Sally, "I'm getting goddamn sick of waiting. I'm going to the meeting and you can call a cab," slamming the door and leaving her friend in the lurch.

If Joan used an assertive coping style, she'd say, "Look, Sally, I really want to get to the meeting on time. I can wait for five minutes, but if you're not ready by then I'll have to leave. If you want, I'll call a cab for you before I go." Joan gets to the meeting on time, while giving her friend as much support and help as possible.

Assertive Statements

An assertive message is characterized by the use of the three "F's": facts, feelings, and fair requests.

"Just the *facts*, ma'am," is a familiar phrase from a popular detective drama of the sixties. Joe Friday was right. The first component of an assertive statement is an objective description of what you observe—things you see, hear, or notice. It presents the facts, as you perceive them, without making judgments, trying to place blame, or guessing at the intentions of the other person.

Here are some examples of factual observations that are not tainted by judgments or blame.

- "I notice that the sink is full of the dirty dishes from last night's dinner."

- "I see that the videos that we rented are still on the table near the door, waiting to be returned."

- "It looks like the grass on the front lawn is getting pretty high."

Sometimes it's hard to separate the facts from the feelings, but it's the first step in reducing the anger spiral. When you state the facts, it opens up the topic for discussion, and you'll be more likely to get cooperation from the other person. By contrast, beginning a discussion with an insulting comment like, "Are you too lazy to do the dishes now?" or "Lame brain, you forgot to return the videos and our lawn looks like a jungle," only serves to fuel your own anger. And comments like these are also likely to make the other person defensive and angry as well.

The second component of an assertive statement acknowledges your honest reaction, your personal *feelings*. It lets the other person become aware of how his/her behavior has affected you. It's important to state this in a way that avoids making the other person feel defensive. So you need to steer away from statements that are blaming or guilt slinging.

Here are some examples of statements that acknowledge personal feelings without judging or blaming others.

- "When I come home from work and find dirty dishes in the kitchen sink, I feel angry."

- "When you spend much of your free time either watching TV or on the Internet, I feel lonely and resentful. I miss you."

- "When we go to a party and you ignore me, paying attention to other men, I feel jealous and abandoned."

The last—and most important—part of the assertive statement is making a *fair request*. This is basically just saying what you want. There are, however, some guidelines that will make this part of the assertive statement more effective. First, make a *specific* request, and see to it that it's reasonably "doable." "I want you to be a millionaire," although specific, and an understandable desire, does not meet the criterion. "I want us to take three weeks off this summer and spend it in the mountains," is more like it.

Another important thing to remember is to make just *one* request at a time. It may be true that you want your wife to cook more French meals, spend less money on antiques, be more supportive of your career aspirations, make the azaleas bloom, and model Victoria's Secret intimate apparel. But if you bring these issues up all at once, she's bound to feel overwhelmed, criticized, and attacked.

Finally, a fair request is characterized by the fact that it seeks a *behavioral change*. It's useless to ask people to change their attitudes, values, or feelings. For example, it's reasonable for you to ask your husband to attend the office Christmas party, and he may agree to go for your sake. But asking him to *want* to go is an exercise in futility.

Now, putting it all together, here are some examples of complete assertive statements.

■ "When I drove the car to work this morning I noticed that the gas tank read almost empty. (Facts) I felt annoyed and angry. (Feelings) When you use the car on the weekend, I would like you to make sure that you refill the tank, so I won't be inconvenienced." (Fair request)

■ "You spend a lot of time at work, and even bring more work home with you to do on the weekends. (Facts) I feel lonely and miss our intimate times together. (Feelings) I would like to make a date with you for a quiet, romantic dinner this weekend." (Fair request)

Consequences

When you don't get results by using all the elements of assertive communication—facts, feelings, and fair request—it may be time to add a more forceful component. In the absence of willing cooperation, it might be necessary to add *consequences* to the equation.

Some people will be naturally motivated to go along with your assertive statements. They might value your friendship, or seek to maintain your continued goodwill. They might see the fairness in your request, or just want to make you happy. But when people aren't motivated to meet your needs, you'll have to up the ante by providing some form of reinforcement. Using positive reinforcement (rewards) is best, simply because it usually works better than punishment, which tends to create resistance and resentment.

Unfortunately, there are times when positive rewards just won't do the job. No amount of praise or promised goodies will get the results you want. One solution is to institute consequences in the form of sanctions. Simply put, this means the other person will have to pay a price for not going along with what you want. The purpose of applying sanctions is to motivate the other person to cooperate with you or to respect your boundaries. Used judiciously, appropriate sanctions can help you get your needs met without anger.

Here are four rules for using consequences most effectively.

1. **Consequences should be specific**. Be precise about exactly what behavior will trigger the consequence. And be precise about what will happen next. Vague threats like, "If you don't stop bugging me, you'll be sorry," don't give the other person enough information and are unlikely to get results. A better formulation is, "If you don't stop calling me several times a day, I'll use my answering machine to screen calls, and won't talk to you for twenty-four hours after your last call."

2. **Consequences should be reasonable**. Setting reasonable consequences helps you feel in control, and it allows other people to make sensible decisions. Avoid setting consequences that involve threats of violence or public humiliation. For example, from a mother to her teenage son: "If you don't watch your mouth I'm going to slap you silly." These types of unreasonable sanctions will tend to make people angry, and they'll be less likely to want to cooperate with you. A better reformulation of the mother-son example is, "If you speak to me again in a disrespectful manner, there'll be no allowance this week."

3. **Consequences should be consistent**. If you've said that you're going to do something, like not respond to pestering phone calls, then you have to do it. And do it *every time* the situation comes

up. If you don't follow through, the other person will learn not to take you seriously. Being consistent will teach the other person to respect you and your limits, both now and in the future.

4. **Be sure that you can live with the results yourself.** That means, don't bite off your nose to spite your face. It doesn't make sense to try to get rid of the ant problem by dynamiting your house. The consequences you set should be problematic for the other person, not for you. Bob's divorced mother, Marion, told him that she would not fly out for his college graduation unless he shaved off what she called "that silly beard that makes you look like a bum." He decided that it was time for him to take a stand for independence. Besides, his girlfriend really thought the beard was cute. True to her word, Marion boycotted the graduation, leaving her ex-husband as the sole family representative. Dad had a great time with his son—it turned out to be a real bonding experience. To this day, Marion still regrets missing an important milestone in her son's life, and the rift it created in their relationship.

A cautionary word about making dramatic ultimatums: Be careful about using consequences like threatening to file for a divorce or kill yourself. Although these statements may seem appropriate in the heat of battle, they usually end up hurting you more, and they rarely get you what you want anyway.

Exercise: Practicing Assertiveness

On the Assertive Scripts Worksheets provided, write out an assertive script for two problematic situations in your life. Be sure to include all the elements of facts, feelings, and fair request, and a consequence that meets all the criteria mentioned above. Finally, we want you to make a commitment to change by setting a date and time for implementation.

Negotiation

Another way to minimize angry interactions is to learn how to *negotiate* when there is a conflict of interest or needs. This isn't easy, because it requires that you listen and try to understand the other person's point of view. It's much easier to simply picture the other person as wrong or stupid. Then, all you have to do is convince them, by any means possible, that you're right and they should do it your way.

Negotiation requires that you start with the premise that the other person's needs are as important to him/her as yours are to you. Trying to angrily bully your way into getting what you want will usually not get others to change their point of view. When you have a conflict of needs, negotiation allows you to find a middle ground where both of you can get some of what you want.

There are six steps to a successful negotiation:

1. **Know what it is that you want.** This isn't as easy as it sounds. Sure, you "want to be happy," but what exactly does that mean? You need to be as specific as possible.

"I want us to go to Maine for two weeks this summer."

2. **State what you want in behavioral terms.** This means saying what, specifically, you want the other person to do or not do.

"I want you to wash the dishes before watching any TV."

"I don't want you to work late at the office."

3. **Listen to the other person's point of view.** The purpose of this step is to gather information so that you can understand his position, not to argue. Use active listening skills such as asking

ASSERTIVE SCRIPTS—Worksheet 1

In the spaces provided below, begin by sketching out a problematic situation in your life that needs to change. Then, write out in detail an assertive script to make that happen. Be sure to fill in all the elements of facts, feelings, and fair request. Next, add a consequence that is specific, reasonable, and one that you can consistently apply without hurting yourself. Finally, write in a date and time when you plan to implement this plan.

Problematic Situation 1:

Assertive Script

FACTS:

FEELINGS:

FAIR REQUEST:

CONSEQUENCES:

DATE & TIME OF IMPLEMENTATION:

ASSERTIVE SCRIPTS—Worksheet 2

In the spaces provided below, begin by sketching out a problematic situation in your life that needs to change. Then, write out in detail an assertive script to make that happen. Be sure to fill in all the elements of facts, feelings, and fair request. Next, add a consequence that is specific, reasonable, and one that you can consistently apply without hurting yourself. Finally, write in a date and time when you plan to implement this plan.

Problematic Situation 2:

Assertive Script

FACTS:

FEELINGS:

FAIR REQUEST:

CONSEQUENCES:

DATE & TIME OF IMPLEMENTATION:

questions, clarifying, and paraphrasing what you think the other person is trying to say. Understanding a point of view doesn't mean that you have to agree with it. Having gotten this far, you can now take the next step, which is . . .

4. Make a proposal. Your proposal should take into account what the other person needs or wants in this situation. What's in it for him or her to do what you want? This may take some creative thinking and a flexible attitude.

5. Ask for a counterproposal. If the other person doesn't like your proposal, encourage him or her to come up with an alternative. Remember, you're trying to come up with something that you both can live with.

6. Achieve a compromise. This is the heart of the negotiation process. In some situations, you might say something like, "It's really important to me that we do it this way now. What would it take for you to go along this time?" Here are some sample compromise solutions:

- "When the kids are in my house, I'll make the rules for watching TV. When they're at your house, you make the rules."

- "Let's try it my way for week and see if it works. If you don't like it, we'll go back to doing it the old way."

- "When you're driving we'll do it your way, and when I'm driving we'll do it my way."

- "Let's split the difference."

- "If we do it my way this time, I'll agree to do it your way next time."

Setting Limits

Every day, you are bombarded with requests. Some of them, like going to lunch with a friend, are requests that you are glad to agree to do. Then there are all the others. Incessant calls from telemarketers trying to sell you something. Subtle requests from your boss to volunteer for a new project or put in some unpaid overtime. A call from your sister trying to guilt-trip you into taking care of your invalid father on the East Coast.

The ability to say no is a critical skill. Saying no sends a message to the world that you have your own needs, wishes, and priorities. That you are able to defend yourself against other people's demands. A statement of your own boundaries lets other people know that you're not a pushover. That you're worthy of respect, and that you value your own needs alongside the needs of others.

It is the people who can't set limits who are at risk for experiencing chronic anger. They feel taken advantage of, helpless in the face of the demands others make on their time, space, or money. They can feel like a prisoner in an intimate relationship, giving, giving, giving, all the time. They expend all their energy on people or activities that give them little pleasure or satisfaction, and they end up having little time for those things that could provide some real happiness.

There are three basic steps for setting limits:

1. Acknowledging the other person's needs. First, you may need to get more information about what the other person wants. Feel free to ask specific questions. What exactly is entailed in a request to "help out with the party," "be more intimate," or "advertise the new product"? Once you understand what is being requested, you can rephrase and repeat it back. This assures the other person that you have heard correctly.

2. Stating your own position. This is your reason for setting the limit. It may include your feelings, preferences, or perception of the circumstances. State your position without apologizing, as confidently and assertively as possible. Just describe what is true or right for you, without putting yourself down. "I need to rest this weekend." "I don't like playing golf."

3. Saying no. This is the essence of setting a limit. "No thanks." "I don't want to do that." "I've decided not to go." "It just doesn't feel right for me." "I'm not willing to drive."

Here are some examples of setting limits:

- "I understand that you need help with the party, and you want me to do all the shopping. (Acknowledging) I don't have the time next weekend. I'm working on a voter registration drive. (Your position) So, I won't be able to help you." (Saying no)

- "I'm aware that you feel attracted to me. (Acknowledging) I feel flattered, and enjoy spending time with you—but just as a friend. (Your position) I don't want to have a sexual relationship with you." (Saying no)

- "When you said that you wanted help to advertise the new product, you meant for me to create a full-blown ad campaign, including a color brochure. (Acknowledging) My other deadlines and commitments don't allow me the necessary time to do this project. (Your position) I have to ask you to give this project to someone else." (Saying no)

Exercise: Setting Limits

On the Setting Limits Worksheet provided, we want you to write out two limit-setting scripts, following the model provided above. Focus on *current* problem situations where you need to set a boundary, and commit yourself to implementing these ideas at the next available opportunity.

Saying no and setting limits can be difficult to accomplish at first—especially if you're not used to standing up for yourself. Here are some suggestions that will make it easier to get started:

Don't apologize. When you apologize for setting a limit, it communicates to the other person that you don't feel that you have the right to take care of yourself. Excessive apologies will invite the other person to put more pressure on you or ask for a different favor to "make it up" to them.

Don't put yourself down. Saying things like "I can't help you because . . . I'm too weak . . . clumsy . . . afraid . . ." is not a good way to set a limit. The other person will try to convince you that you *can* do it, leaving you stuck with having to prove that you can't. Saying "I won't" or "I don't want to" is a much better strategy because it leaves the other person less room to argue with you.

Be aware of voice and body language. When you set a limit, look the other person in the eye. If you're on the telephone, speak with a clear, confident voice. You want your tone of voice and body posture to match your assertive statement.

Delay your response. If you're someone who tends to automatically say yes to things, stall for time. You'll probably think more clearly without the pressure of an immediate response. Tell them, "I'll let you know this afternoon," or "I'll have to get back to you on that."

Be specific. If you don't want to say no outright, be clear about exactly what you are and are not willing to do. "I'm willing to review your design for the brochure, but I won't get involved in the production end." "I'm willing to bring a bottle of wine to the party, but I can't make the salad."

SETTING LIMITS—Worksheet

In the spaces provided below, write out two scripts for saying no in a current problematic situation.

Situation 1

Acknowledge:

State your position:

Set limit:

Next implementation opportunity:

Situation 2

Acknowledge:

State your position:

Set limit:

Next implementation opportunity:

Dealing with Criticism

Criticism can be very painful. It can evoke memories from childhood when your behavior was minutely scrutinized for mistakes. Then you were judged and made to feel wrong, bad, guilty, and worthless. Each of these feelings has the potential for triggering anger, which is used to avoid and cover up the painful emotions.

There is a way of hearing criticism that can be beneficial to you. Accept the comment as feedback, separate out what is appropriate and useful, and disregard what is not. Here are the steps you need to take.

First, *stop the attack*. Don't allow yourself to be verbally battered by angry, abusive attacks from others. Even if you are wrong, or feel guilty about the situation, you don't deserve to be kicked around. If the other person continues to attack you, despite your request to stop, you can call for a time-out and walk away.

Whenever Sharon called her mother, Etta, she was inevitably subjected to a scathing critique of her child-rearing skills. Nothing Sharon did seemed to be right, from the way she fed her children to the clothes they wore. Etta not only gave advice freely, she also yelled at her daughter, calling her an incompetent mother. Sharon would leave each telephone call feeling devastated. Eventually, with the help of a therapist, she learned how to handle the situation. Whenever Etta started to yell or call her names, Sharon would say, "Mother, please stop shouting or I'll hang up." If her mother continued, Sharon was instructed to say, "Oh, well. Gotta go now. Bye," and hang up. She would then leave the house so that she couldn't hear the phone ring every ten minutes.

Next, remind yourself that what you're hearing is only *one person's opinion* about a specific aspect of your behavior. The criticism is about something you've done, not about who you are. The report that you submitted may be deemed "worthless" by your supervisor, but that doesn't mean that you are a worthless person, or that all your work in the past has been worthless. Accept the fact that you don't always do your best job, often because of being rushed or not having all the information you need.

Some criticism can be constructive and helpful. Before you fly into a rage or slink away in embarrassment, make sure you know exactly what the critic is trying to tell you. In order to get the most value out of the situation, you will have to *ask for more information*. Although it's uncomfortable to encourage the critic, probing for more information may provide you with the useful feedback you need to improve future performance—or your relationship.

When Jim wrote the report for his company, he included lots of historical analysis and comparisons to other industries. His supervisor, Bob, returned the report to him, saying it was "useless." Jim felt hurt and devastated, but he was also curious. He asked Bob what exactly he would have liked to see in the report. It turns out that what was wanted was a current market analysis, comparison with other companies in the same industry, and projections for the next five years. The report Jim submitted, although good background material, was indeed useless. What Jim learned is that Bob doesn't always communicate his needs well. Next time he will ask more questions and get all the information he needs before writing a report.

Trevor thought that his relationship with MaryLou was going pretty well, despite fights now and then. So he was really surprised and hurt when MaryLou became critical and attacked him, apparently out of the blue. "You're just never there for me. All you care about is yourself and your own needs." Gathering courage, Trevor asked her what she meant. "Remember last year, when you broke your ankle and it was in a cast for six weeks? I was at your house every other day, cleaning up, cooking your food, and waiting on you hand and foot. I've been sick with the flu for more than a week and you just go on with your life, and don't even come by to see how I am." Trevor was indeed "clueless," but now he has some more information. MaryLou would feel cared for if he paid more attention to her and did some things to help her out when she was down.

There are three techniques that you can use to deflect criticism, prevent escalation, and disarm the critic.

1. **Clouding** is a strategy in which you partially agree with the criticism without accepting it completely. This requires that you listen carefully to the critic and agree with the part of the criticism that you feel is accurate. Other options are to agree in principle, or agree in probability.

For example, the *criticism* might be, "You spend money like it grows on trees. At this rate we'll be penniless in no time." You can *agree in part* by saying, "Yeah, we have been spending more money since we bought those horses." Or you could *agree in principle*, by saying, "I think you're right, it's not a good idea to spend too much money." Lastly, you could choose to *agree in probability* by saying something like, "It's probably true that we're spending quite a bit right now."

2. Making an **assertive preference** is a way of shutting off the critic completely. You use this technique by acknowledging the criticism, but disagreeing with it. There's no need to give a lengthy explanation or rationale for your behavior—you simply state that that's the way you want to do things. This technique assumes an equal power situation and is a very effective way of stopping further discussion without attacking the other person. And you can do it without getting angry.

For example, if the criticism is, "That's a dumb way to deal with your kids coming home after curfew," you can respond with an assertive preference statement by saying, "I hear that you don't agree with how I'm handling this situation, but I prefer to do it this way." If the critic tries to continue by pointing out the dangers of doing it your way, you can respond by saying, "Thanks for your concern, but I'm willing to take that risk."

3. You can make a **content-to-process shift** to prevent a discussion from heating up into a full-blown conflagration, or when you think that underlying feelings are fueling the fire. When you make a content-to-process shift, the focus of the discussion changes from the issue (content) to what's going on inside you or the quality of the interaction (process). It allows you to get to the real or more important issue that lies at the bottom of the conflict.

For example, "I know that you like me to look good in public, but we're always arguing about how much money I spend on clothes. I end up feeling accused and attacked by you. What's going on between us that we're feeling angry all the time?"

Exercise: Dealing with Criticism

Use the worksheet on the next page to prepare some more effective ways to deal with criticism. Begin by writing a description of a recent provocative scene in which you felt criticized and attacked. Then, write out what words or actions you would have employed to stop the attack. Next, write what specific questions you would have asked to learn more about the other person's needs, feelings, or problems. Finally, write down some ways in which you could have used clouding, assertive preference, or content-to-process shift to deflect the attack.

Homework

1. Monitor anger and coping responses on Anger Log III.

2. Use the Creating Coping Thoughts Worksheet to develop better anger management responses following situations where you lapsed into anger.

DEALING WITH CRITICISM—Worksheet

In the space below, write a description of a recent provocative scene in which you felt criticized and attacked. Then, *in retrospect*, fill out the rest of the worksheet with strategies that you could have used to change the outcome.

Provocative scene involving criticism:

If you decided to stop the attack, how could you accomplish it?

Words:

Actions:

If you wanted to learn more about the other person's position, what specific questions would you ask to ascertain the following:

Feelings:

Problems:

What they want:

If you wanted to deflect the attack, how would you use:

Clouding:

Assertive preference:

Content-to-process shift:

Anger Log III

Provocative Situation Sensory Input (Objective data from what you hear, see, and touch)	The Screen (Your conclusions, assumptions, interpretations, beliefs, and trigger thoughts)	Anger Rating 0–100	Coping Strategies Breathing, relaxation, coping thoughts, coping behaviors.	Anger Rating 0–100	Outcomes Rating -10 to +10 Self Others

CREATING COPING THOUGHTS—Worksheet

Complete the following for each significant trigger thought in an anger situation.

1. Trigger thoughts that inflame my anger:

    a.

    b.

    c.

2. Anger distortions that underlie my trigger thoughts:

    a.

    b.

    c.

3. Counterresponse plan for each of my trigger thoughts (e.g., looking for exceptions, alternative explanations, preferences instead of shoulds, etc.). Revised trigger thought based on each counterresponse plan.

    a. Counterresponse plan:

       Revised trigger thought:

    b. Counterresponse plan:

       Revised trigger thought:

    c. Counterresponse plan:

       Revised trigger thought:

4. Helpful coping thoughts (see General Coping Thoughts List earlier in this chapter):

    a.

    b.

    c.

CREATING COPING THOUGHTS—Worksheet

Complete the following for each significant trigger thought in an anger situation.

1. Trigger thoughts that inflame my anger:

   a.

   b.

   c.

2. Anger distortions that underlie my trigger thoughts:

   a.

   b.

   c.

3. Counterresponse plan for each of my trigger thoughts (e.g., looking for exceptions, alternative explanations, preferences instead of shoulds, etc.). Revised trigger thought based on each counterresponse plan.

   a. Counterresponse plan:

      Revised trigger thought:

   b. Counterresponse plan:

      Revised trigger thought:

   c. Counterresponse plan:

      Revised trigger thought:

4. Helpful coping thoughts (see General Coping Thoughts List earlier in this chapter):

   a.

   b.

   c.

CHAPTER 13

YOUR PLAN FOR REAL-LIFE COPING

This chapter will be an opportunity to synthesize much of what you've learned so far about anger management. The first step will be an exercise to help you recognize and remember the coping thoughts that have worked best for you.

Best Coping Thoughts

Look back over the three chapters where you used anger inoculation to cope with anger in visualized scenes. Review each Creating Coping Thoughts Worksheet that you filled out and write down on a separate piece of paper the coping thoughts that seemed most effective. Now go back and review the "coping efforts" column from each Anger Log III that you've completed. Add any good coping thoughts that you find in your logs to the list you're compiling.

Now it's time to turn the list you just made into something that can really help you. The Best Coping Thoughts Exercise you're about to complete will organize the random coping thoughts from your list into nine specific coping categories. The categories for best coping thoughts are:

1. **Cool thoughts.** These are simple reminders to use your relaxation skills.

2. **Problem-solving thoughts.** This type of coping thought identifies alternative solutions to a problem. Anger is just a signal to start looking for new answers.

3. **Escape routes.** These thoughts remind you to walk away from something upsetting, to remove yourself from the situation before things escalate.

4. **Self-confidence thoughts.** These remind you that you have the ability to manage your anger in provocative situations. No matter what happens, you recognize that you have the skills to cope.

5. New explanations. These thoughts help you identify alternative ways of thinking about people's problematic behavior. Why else might they be acting as they do? Instead of assuming that you're a target, these coping thoughts look for more benign interpretations.

6. See the whole picture. This type of coping thought looks for exceptions to overgeneralizations. You try to remember balancing facts or events that help you see the other person in a less negative light.

7. Getting accurate. These are self-reminders that encourage you to stay with the facts of a situation while avoiding any kind of magnifying or exaggerating. Getting accurate can also mean recognizing how a situation is *realistically negative*, but not awful or unbearable.

8. Preferences, not shoulds. This category of coping thoughts changes absolute "should" statements into simple preferences. Instead of focusing on unbendable rules for living, you soften angry expectations into personal wants and desires.

9. People doing their best. These coping thoughts remind you that people are trying to survive their own pain and struggles. They're trying to manage their life circumstances as best they can.

Exercise: Best Coping Thoughts*

This exercise includes the nine categories of coping thoughts just discussed. Under each category, you'll find some examples. Then there's a space for you to fill in coping thoughts of your own (from the list you just compiled) that seem to fit that category.

When you've worked your way through all nine coping thought categories, go back and do another pass. Read each of the example coping thoughts that are included in the exercise. Put a star by any of the example coping thoughts that you think might be helpful for you.

As a final step, focus on the coping thoughts categories where you've written nothing down. Take some time to think about each of these categories and see if you can create some coping thought of your own for them. If you have difficulty, go back and look at the General Coping Thoughts list in chapter 8.

Cool Thoughts

"Just stay cool, getting all pissed off won't help."

"It's just not worth it. Take a few deep breaths and chill out."

"This too shall pass. Others have to deal with this kind of stuff without going crazy mad."

Your coping thoughts:

Problem-Solving Thoughts

"It's not the end of the world, just a problem to be solved."

"It's okay to feel annoyed, but it's just a hassle to be dealt with."

"Develop a plan. So, the first thing I would want to do is . . ."

"Break the frustration down. I can deal better with it that way."

---

*   Adapted from *Overcoming Situational and General Anger* by Jerry Deffenbacher and Matthew McKay.

Your coping thoughts:

Escape Routes

"I can always walk away rather than lose it totally."

"It's okay to take time out. Move away, get your act together, then come back and deal with it."

"Better to walk away than to be a screaming idiot."

"Bottom line, I walk before I hit or do something dumb."

Your coping thoughts:

Self-Confidence Thoughts

"I can handle this—I've done it before."

"I'm hanging in and coping."

"I have what it takes to get through this hassle."

"I'm getting better at this anger management stuff."

Your coping thoughts:

New Explanations

"They're probably just (scared, overwhelmed, not understanding, confused, out of the loop, hurting, etc.)"

"Cut them some slack. I'd hope they'd do the same for me if I were having a bad time."

Your coping thoughts:

See the Whole Picture

"Look at the other side."

"There are exceptions. For example . . ."

"Time to look for some of the good for a change."

Your coping thoughts:

Getting Accurate

"Cut the angry crap. Tell it like it is."

"Just the facts."

"Tell it simple and straight."

"I'm frustrated and disappointed. Better stay there and quit while I'm only somewhat behind."

Your coping thoughts:

Preferences, Not Shoulds

"It doesn't have to be my way, I just prefer it."

"What I want and what has to be are two different things."

"This is what I *need*, not a *should*."

"Nobody appointed me God. So give it up. Be human and focus on your wants."

Your coping thoughts:

People Doing Their Best

"They're doing what they know how to do."

"They're coping the best they can, all things considered."

"I don't like how they do it, but they're just trying to survive."

Your coping thoughts:

Best Coping Behaviors

Now it's time to look back again at the "coping efforts" column of Anger Log III. This time, pay attention to how you behave in response to anger provocations. What are you doing or not doing that is different from your old anger response? Do you try to speak in a quieter voice? Do you choose words that are less inflammatory? Do you withdraw at times from a provocative situation rather than explode? Do you find a way to express your needs assertively rather than use blaming attacks? Have you on occasion suggested a solution or a compromise instead of going on the warpath?

While you may find some examples of good coping behaviors in the Anger Log, many of your best coping efforts may be in situations where you never got angry enough to write anything down. Your very success made your coping efforts easy to forget. The exercise that follows is an opportunity to record your best and most successful coping behaviors. In the space provided in the exercise, write examples from your own recent experience of each category of coping behavior. Don't be surprised if you have no examples that fit some of the categories. No one person is going to use all of these coping strategies.

Exercise: Best Coping Behaviors

1. Expressed needs in nonattacking ways. Examples:

2. Softened inflammatory language. Examples:

3. Lowered my voice. Examples:

4. Suggested an alternative solution or compromise. Examples:

5. Tried to express understanding of the other person's views. Examples:

6. Withdrew from a situation rather than let it escalate. Took time to think things through. Examples:

7. Agreed to disagree and let it go. Examples:

8. Described a problem without blaming the other person. Examples:

9. Tried to listen to the other person to get a better awareness of what they want. Examples:

10. Tried to change the subject so things wouldn't escalate. Examples:

11. Other coping behaviors:

Once filled in, this exercise provides you a good list of coping behaviors that work for you. You can use it as a resource and return to it again and again for ideas about how to manage your anger in difficult situations.

Advance Planning: The Key to Real-Life Anger Management

Learning to cope with visualized anger scenes is one thing. Managing your anger in the face of real-life provocations is quite another. All the practicing you've done with anger inoculation has served to give you more effective coping skills. Now it's time to make a strong commitment to use these skills where it counts—with your friends, family, and coworkers.

Exercise: Anger Planning**

This anger planning exercise has six sections: anger precipitants, trigger thoughts, coping thoughts, relaxation, coping behavior, and problem solving. Right now, fill in the Anger Planning Exercise using a recent provocation as an example situation. Start off by writing down all the anger precipitants in the situation. Mostly these would be the actual events, although precipitants might include memories or even feelings that preceded your anger. For trigger thoughts, write down every inflammatory thought that fueled your anger. For the coping thoughts section, we suggest that you review the Best Coping Thoughts Exercise that you completed earlier in the chapter. Try to find several that would be useful to manage your anger in this particular situation. In the relaxation section, write in the specific relaxation skill that you feel would be most effective while facing this particular provocation. Under coping behavior, try to develop at least one strategy that might keep this situation from escalating in the future. Use the list you created in the Best Coping Behaviors Exercise for ideas. Finally, in the problem-solving section, note any alternative solution or problem solving scenario you can think of. Do you have any idea of how you could structure things to avoid this problem in the future? Is there something you could say or do when you aren't upset that would alter the provocative situation in some way?

Anger Precipitants:
      What events, memories, associations, or feelings preceded my anger?

Trigger Thoughts:
      What inflammatory thoughts set off my anger?

Coping Thoughts:
      Look at Best Coping Thoughts Worksheet for help.

Relaxation:
      How can I use my relaxation skills in this situation (e.g., take a deep breath before I say anything, etc.)?

Coping Behavior:
      What can I say or do that will calm things down?

Problem Solving:
      Is there a way to solve this problem and avoid conflict?

** Adapted from *Overcoming Situational and General Anger* by Jerry Deffenbacher and Matthew McKay.

Here's an example of how Roger, a short-order cook, completed the Anger Planning Exercise.

Anger Precipitants:
Thelma (waitress) takes a long time picking up her orders. The server shelf fills up and I have nowhere to put new orders.

Trigger Thoughts:
Where's Mrs. Molasses? She's slower than a damn double amputee. She's lazy. She's screwing me up.

Coping Thoughts:
Cool down, you can handle this. You can solve the problem and chill. She's probably doing the best she can.

Relaxation:
Deep breath; use phrase, Let it be. Relax my tight shoulders.

Coping Behavior:
Stop constantly ringing the bell and trying to get her attention; put the order under the warmer and wait till she asks for it.

Problem Solving:
Ask restaurant owner about a second server shelf.

At the end of this chapter, you'll find multiple copies of this exercise, labeled Anger Planning Worksheet. You are encouraged to fill out the worksheet for chronic provocations and anger situations you can anticipate during the coming week. Anger planning is an excellent tool to make sure you have effective responses to any upset or provocation that you can anticipate.

Homework

1. Continue to track your anger experiences and coping efforts using Anger Log III.

2. For any anger situation where you didn't respond adequately, fill out an Anger Planning Worksheet. Draw on your Best Coping Thoughts and Best Coping Behaviors Exercises to complete the worksheet. If you have difficulty developing appropriate coping thoughts for a specific provocation, use a Creating Coping Thoughts Worksheet.

Anger Log III

Provocative Situation	Anger Rating 0–100	Coping Strategies	Anger Rating 0–100	Outcomes Rating −10 to +10	
Sensory Input (Objective data from what you hear, see, and touch)		Breathing, relaxation, coping thoughts, coping behaviors.		Self	Others
The Screen (Your conclusions, assumptions, interpretations, beliefs, and trigger thoughts)					

CREATING COPING THOUGHTS—Worksheet

Complete the following for each significant trigger thought in an anger situation.

1. Trigger thoughts that inflame my anger:

    a.

    b.

    c.

2. Anger distortions that underlie my trigger thoughts:

    a.

    b.

    c.

3. Counterresponse plan for each of my trigger thoughts (e.g., looking for exceptions, alternative explanations, preferences instead of shoulds, etc.). Revised trigger thought based on each counterresponse plan.

    a. Counterresponse plan:

       Revised trigger thought:

    b. Counterresponse plan:

       Revised trigger thought:

    c. Counterresponse plan:

       Revised trigger thought:

4. Helpful coping thoughts (see General Coping Thoughts List earlier in this chapter):

    a.

    b.

    c.

CREATING COPING THOUGHTS—Worksheet

Complete the following for each significant trigger thought in an anger situation.

1. Trigger thoughts that inflame my anger:

    a.

    b.

    c.

2. Anger distortions that underlie my trigger thoughts:

    a.

    b.

    c.

3. Counterresponse plan for each of my trigger thoughts (e.g., looking for exceptions, alternative explanations, preferences instead of shoulds, etc.). Revised trigger thought based on each counterresponse plan.

    a. Counterresponse plan:

       Revised trigger thought:

    b. Counterresponse plan:

       Revised trigger thought:

    c. Counterresponse plan:

       Revised trigger thought:

4. Helpful coping thoughts (see General Coping Thoughts List earlier in this chapter):

    a.

    b.

    c.

ANGER PLANNING—Worksheet

Anger Precipitants:
    What events, memories, associations, or feelings preceded my anger?

Trigger Thoughts:
    What inflammatory thoughts set off my anger?

Coping Thoughts:
    Look at Best Coping Thoughts Worksheet for help.

Relaxation:
    How can I use my relaxation skills in this situation (e.g., take a deep breath before I say anything, etc.)?

Coping Behavior:
    What can I say or do that will calm things down?

Problem Solving:
    Is there a way to solve this problem and avoid conflict?

ANGER PLANNING—Worksheet

Anger Precipitants:
    What events, memories, associations, or feelings preceded my anger?

Trigger Thoughts:
    What inflammatory thoughts set off my anger?

Coping Thoughts:
    Look at Best Coping Thoughts Worksheet for help.

Relaxation:
    How can I use my relaxation skills in this situation (e.g., take a deep breath before I say anything, etc.)?

Coping Behavior:
    What can I say or do that will calm things down?

Problem Solving:
    Is there a way to solve this problem and avoid conflict?

ANGER PLANNING—Worksheet

Anger Precipitants:
    What events, memories, associations, or feelings preceded my anger?

Trigger Thoughts:
    What inflammatory thoughts set off my anger?

Coping Thoughts:
    Look at Best Coping Thoughts Worksheet for help.

Relaxation:
    How can I use my relaxation skills in this situation (e.g., take a deep breath before I say anything, etc.)?

Coping Behavior:
    What can I say or do that will calm things down?

Problem Solving:
    Is there a way to solve this problem and avoid conflict?

ANGER PLANNING—Worksheet

Anger Precipitants:
        What events, memories, associations, or feelings preceded my anger?

Trigger Thoughts:
        What inflammatory thoughts set off my anger?

Coping Thoughts:
        Look at Best Coping Thoughts Worksheet for help.

Relaxation:
        How can I use my relaxation skills in this situation (e.g., take a deep breath before I say anything, etc.)?

Coping Behavior:
        What can I say or do that will calm things down?

Problem Solving:
        Is there a way to solve this problem and avoid conflict?

CHAPTER 14

BLOCKS TO REAL-LIFE COPING

Anyone who's been on this earth more than ten minutes knows that things aren't perfect. This is never more true than when you're trying to change a habit. There are plenty of times when you'll forget or get caught up in some of the powerful reinforcers that created the habit to begin with. Your new anger management program is bound to have some spectacular failures scattered among the times you successfully cope.

Number one, don't condemn yourself. Old ways die hard. Number two, learn from your mistakes. Fill out an Anger Planning Worksheet after any occasion where your coping efforts didn't work. But perhaps most important, take a realistic look at the factors that may be blocking use of your new anger management skills. This chapter will help you do that. The exercise that follows will allow you to examine the six most common obstacles to effective anger control.

Exercise: Blocks to Real Life Coping

1. You expect to be embarrassed if people notice you practicing your relaxation skills.

You're not alone if you worry about this. But how obvious is it when you take a deep breath? To find out, try this experiment: Stand in front of a mirror and take several slow breaths using cue-controlled relaxation. Be objective. Does it look like anything more than a sigh or the deep breath that people often take in the middle of a tense situation? Most people, watching themselves take a breath in the mirror, report that it doesn't look odd. Right now, commit yourself to taking one or two deep breaths and using your cue word every time you're in an angry encounter. It will look as normal as a sigh.

2. When angry you can't remember to use your coping skills.

Most people struggle with this because anger tends to erase everything else from your mind. It's a storm that seems to blow away your best intentions and plans. Nonetheless, the problem can be overcome. What you need is a reminder to use your coping skills. When someone gets in your face, or does something that seems totally irresponsible, you can cue yourself to relax and use your coping thoughts. A simple strategy is to wear something that's unusual and acts as a reminder that you have to stop and cope. A new ring or piece of jewelry could work, or an unusual color of nail polish. Something as simple as putting your watch on the other wrist might act as a cue to use your new skills. When you do any of these things deliberately, as part of a plan to jog your memory, you improve your chances of noticing them when a situation gets hot. Additional strategies might involve using signs—on your vanity or shaving mirror. You could tape up a file card that says, "Breathe when you're pissed." Or you could put a reminder in your wallet, in your desk drawer, or by a light switch.

Right now, take a moment to look over your Anger Logs for the past few weeks. Focus on the Coping Strategies column. First off, give yourself some credit for the times you successfully coped. Every time you've replaced your old anger pattern with a new coping strategy, it represents a lot of hard work.

Second, each occasion when you've successfully coped could be a gold mine of information that would help right now. Think back. How did you *remember* to use your new coping skills? Was it spontaneous? Did someone remind you? Did you use a cue or a sign? Did you try to fix in your mind beforehand a criterion behavior—some response on your or the other person's part—that would be a signal to cope? Typical criterion behaviors could be raising your voice, a belittling or attacking tone, pointing gestures, foul language or name calling, and so on. Some criterion behaviors might even be internal events, like muscle tension or a particular negative thought.

Looking back, did you use any other strategies to remember your skills? For example, did you ever promise someone whose opinion matters that you'd try to cope more effectively in a particular target situation? Or did you ever try reminding yourself throughout the day of your commitment to cope with anger? One man actually programmed a watch to beep every hour as a way to keep his coping plans in mind.

The following chart may help you get clearer about some of the strategies you already use to remember your skills. In the left hand column of the Remembering to Cope Worksheet, write down each of your anger coping efforts from the past two weeks. Don't write a lot, just a sentence or even a couple of words to identify the incident. Then, in the right hand column, write the word or phrase that describes how you remembered to cope. Examples of memory strategies are written across the top of the worksheet, but it's okay to develop your own labels for ways *you* remember to cope.

Examine your memory strategies listed on the worksheet. Do you find that you rely on only one or two strategies? If so, you might consider testing additional strategies that seem potentially helpful. Select three anger situations that you run into with some consistency, and where you often forget to use your coping skills. Write them in the left-hand column:

Anger Provocation

1.

2.

3.

Memory Strategy

1.

2.

3.

Now that you have the provocations listed, look back at the example memory strategies at the top of the Remembering to Cope Worksheet. Select one that you haven't tried before for each of the above provocations and write it in the space under Memory Strategy. Right now make a commitment to yourself to implement the selected memory strategy for each of the provocations.

3. You can't recall any coping thoughts during a provocation.

No one thinks clearly when they're upset. As you learned in the last chapter, any provocation that shows up with regularity will have a better outcome when you do some advanced planning. You can deal with such provocations using the Anger Planning Worksheet.

REMEMBERING TO COPE—Worksheet*

Spontaneously remembered; reminded by someone; memory cue; signs; criterion behavior; promise to someone; self-reminding throughout day

Coping Efforts	Memory Strategies
1.	1.
2.	2.
3.	3.
4.	4.
5.	5.
6.	6.
7.	7.
8.	8.
9.	9.
10.	10.
11.	11.
12.	12.

*   From *Overcoming Situational and General Anger* by Jerry Deffenbacher and Matthew McKay.

There are, of course, provocations you can't plan for. They come at you from out of the blue. For these you need a generic coping thought that feels strong and "right." Refer to the General Coping Thoughts list in chapter 8 to find something that might be effective as an all-purpose coping response. Write it in the space below.

Generic Coping Thought:

_____

Now strongly commit yourself to using this coping thought whenever you start getting upset. Memorize it. Practice recalling it throughout the day.

4. You won't be listened to if you cope successfully and stop being angry.

Many people are afraid to lose their anger. They expect no one will listen if they aren't aggressive and attacking. They're so used to getting loud that talking in a normal voice feels like they've been silenced. Paradoxically, the exact opposite is true. When you're always loud and angry, people *stop* listening. They get defensive and resistant, and they look for reasons to ignore you. Right now, do a quick mental inventory of some of your recent anger experiences. Did you feel heard? Did the target of your anger express conern about your needs and feelings? Was your viewpoint appreciated? Chances are, if you look at it objectively, most of these anger experiences didn't have a positive outcome. People were too busy protecting themselves from your ire to really hear what you had to say.

5. When you're upset, you want to punish people for their mistakes.

If you control your anger, no one pays for their transgressions. This feeling is not uncommon. It's hard to cope with and modulate your anger when at the same time you want to use it as a weapon. But this desire, understandable as it is, has had a negative impact on your relationships and your life. That's why you've been working so hard on this program. The exercise you did in chapter 2 helped you identify the effects of your anger on both your personal and work life. Right now, in the space below, write down one reason you are ready to let go of anger as a tool for punishing wrongdoers.

_____

_____

If you can't think of a single reason that feels true and motivating, this could be a serious impediment to your anger control efforts. You are strongly encouraged, in this case, to seek the help of a psychotherapist or pastoral counselor who can open this issue to deeper exploration.

6. Anger feels like the only way you can protect yourself.

Anger functions to protect you from two kinds of threats. First, anger can help you repel pressures, demands, and attacks from others. It can mobilize you to fight back. Anger also can help to block internal threats—emotions such as shame, hurt, fear, and guilt that feel as though they might overwhelm you.

When someone is really pushing you around or threatening you, anger can be an appropriate, healthy response. It's a signal for others to back off. Most of the time, however, anger is overkill. You don't need it. A clear, assertive statement is usually enough to get people to listen. Right now, make a list of the last six anger situations noted in your logs. Write a phrase to remind you of each in the left-hand column below.

Anger Situations	Assertive Alternative	Outcome + or -
1.	1.	1.
2.	2.	2.
3.	3.	3.
4.	4.	4.
5.	5.	5.
6.	6.	6.

When you've finished filling in the six anger situations, go back over each one and write down in the column labeled Assertive Alternative an assertive statement you could have used to replace your angry ones. In the column marked Outcome, write + or -, depending on whether the assertive statement would likely have had a better or worse result than your anger response.

The purpose of this exercise is to get a sense of how often anger is necessary and healthy as a response to threats. People tend to find, when looking at outcomes, that few if any of the anger situations actually require anger. Most would have better results using assertive statements.

As previously noted, anger can protect you internally as well as externally. It can be an effective defense against painful emotions. In the space below, write down the feeling or feelings from which anger has historically protected you. Be honest. When you get really steamed, is there another emotion that often comes first, that seems sometimes to actually trigger your anger?

If you often employ anger as a defense against the feeling or feelings listed above, if your reflex is to blow up rather than experience painful emotions, this is more than understandable. But it's also dangerous. While the anger is protecting you from overwhelming feelings, it is simultaneously damaging. You may need help from a trained therapist to cope more effectively with the feelings your anger has traditionally blocked.

Homework

1. Continue recording any significant anger incidents in Anger Log III, along with your coping efforts.

2. Fill out Anger Planning Worksheets (provided at the end of the chapter) for each anger situation where your coping efforts are not successful.

Anger Log III

Provocative Situation Sensory Input (Objective data from what you hear, see, and touch)	The Screen (Your conclusions, assumptions, interpretations, beliefs, and trigger thoughts)	Anger Rating 0–100	Coping Strategies Breathing, relaxation, coping thoughts, coping behaviors.	Anger Rating 0–100	Outcomes Rating -10 to +10 Self　　Others	

CREATING COPING THOUGHTS—Worksheet

Complete the following for each significant trigger thought in an anger situation.

1. Trigger thoughts that inflame my anger:

    a.

    b.

    c.

2. Anger distortions that underlie my trigger thoughts:

    a.

    b.

    c.

3. Counterresponse plan for each of my trigger thoughts (e.g., looking for exceptions, alternative explanations, preferences instead of shoulds, etc.). Revised trigger thought based on each counterresponse plan.

    a. Counterresponse plan:

       Revised trigger thought:

    b. Counterresponse plan:

       Revised trigger thought:

    c. Counterresponse plan:

       Revised trigger thought:

4. Helpful coping thoughts (see General Coping Thoughts List earlier in this chapter):

    a.

    b.

    c.

CREATING COPING THOUGHTS—Worksheet

Complete the following for each significant trigger thought in an anger situation.

1. Trigger thoughts that inflame my anger:

   a.

   b.

   c.

2. Anger distortions that underlie my trigger thoughts:

   a.

   b.

   c.

3. Counterresponse plan for each of my trigger thoughts (e.g., looking for exceptions, alternative explanations, preferences instead of shoulds, etc.). Revised trigger thought based on each counterresponse plan.

   a. Counterresponse plan:

      Revised trigger thought:

   b. Counterresponse plan:

      Revised trigger thought:

   c. Counterresponse plan:

      Revised trigger thought:

4. Helpful coping thoughts (see General Coping Thoughts List earlier in this chapter):

   a.

   b.

   c.

ANGER PLANNING—Worksheet

Anger Precipitants:
    What events, memories, associations, or feelings preceded my anger?

Trigger Thoughts:
    What inflammatory thoughts set off my anger?

Coping Thoughts:
    Look at Best Coping Thoughts Worksheet for help.

Relaxation:
    How can I use my relaxation skills in this situation (e.g., take a deep breath before I say anything, etc.)?

Coping Behavior:
    What can I say or do that will calm things down?

Problem Solving:
    Is there a way to solve this problem and avoid conflict?

ANGER PLANNING—Worksheet

Anger Precipitants:
      What events, memories, associations, or feelings preceded my anger?

Trigger Thoughts:
      What inflammatory thoughts set off my anger?

Coping Thoughts:
      Look at Best Coping Thoughts Worksheet for help.

Relaxation:
      How can I use my relaxation skills in this situation (e.g., take a deep breath before I say anything, etc.)?

Coping Behavior:
      What can I say or do that will calm things down?

Problem Solving:
      Is there a way to solve this problem and avoid conflict?

CHAPTER 15

BEING GOOD TO YOURSELF

We've discussed at other times in this book how anger is most often a response to pain. Something feels very wrong, and anger seems like a way of coping with it. Whether the distress is emotional or physical, for a moment the anger masks it.

This chapter is about dealing with distress in proactive ways so anger will be less and less needed in your life. It's about nourishing and being good to yourself. It's about creating a life where your physical and emotional well-being are high priorities.

The first step in taking better care of yourself is learning to be more aware of what we call TLC issues:

Tired/stressed

Lonely

Craving (food, peace, stimulation, meaning, etc.)

Our experience shows that at least half of all anger episodes are in some way associated with TLC problems. It's far more effective to work on TLC issues directly, as a problem to solve, than to cover the distress with angry words. You'll end up feeling a lot better, and so will those around you.

The Big Question

A simple but important discipline in anger control is to ask, every time you're starting to get hot, "What's my TLC level?"

- Am I tired or physically distressed in any way? Do I need to sit, take a break, sleep, relax my muscles?

- Am I feeling a need for contact? Would it help if I talked to someone right now? Or just spent time doing something fun with someone?

- Am I hungry for something? Do I need food or quiet or something interesting to do?

Once you identify a TLC problem, shift the focus to what you can do about it. The royal road to anger is feeling stuck and helpless, so solving TLC distress is a high priority. Don't put it off if you can help it. Make a plan right away for how and when you'll get rest, contact a friend, or do something fun. If at all possible, plan to address a TLC issue on the same day you notice it. That way relief is in sight. You can look forward to feeling better rather than feeling helpless and angry.

Put a Cork in the Self-Hating Voice

People who struggle with anger often have strong judgments about others. But that gun points both ways. They frequently reserve the most negative, hateful judgments for themselves. This self-attacking voice has been called the "pathological critic." It's usually a whole load of judgments you've internalized from things your parents said over and over. The critic calls you stupid, lazy, or selfish; it says you're ugly, crazy, incompetent, or boring.

Sometimes the pathological critic attacks you for a lot more than your parents actually said. It condemns you for what their actions *suggest* they felt toward you. For example, if they paid you little attention and rarely helped when you needed it, the critic might call you "worthless" or a "burden to everyone."

The main function of the critic is to keep you feeling as rotten as you did as a child, to keep that old negative identity intact. The critic's main weapon is a stream of vicious, negative labels. And the result of all the critic's work is a hidden world of shame and self-contempt. In the end, you're in so much pain that the slightest hurt or criticism from others feels intolerable, and you fly into a rage.

So you see how the attacks of your pathological critic feed into your anger problem. The worse you feel about yourself, and the more shame and vulnerability you carry, the more likely you are to cope using anger. Doing something about your anger requires that you also do something about the critic and all its judgments. There are three key steps you can take to overcome the influence of your critic:

1. Find core qualities in yourself that you value.

2. Practice acceptance.

3. Reinforce healthy thinking.

Finding Core Qualities You Can Value

Deep down, you know there are good things inside you. You can draw on that for ammunition to fight the critic. So it's time to find out more about some of your positive core qualities. The following exercise will help you explore what's good about yourself.

Exercise: Core Qualities Inventory

Answer the following questions in the space provided, using one word or very brief descriptions of each quality.

1. Qualities in you that others have praised and appreciated:

_____

_____

2. Qualities the person who loved you most appreciated in you:

_____

_____

3. Qualities that helped you survive life's struggles, pain, and dangers:

_____

_____

4. Qualities that helped you reach certain life goals:

_____

_____

5. Qualities that allowed you to help or bring happiness to others:

_____

_____

6. Qualities that helped you at times feel happy, proud, or good about yourself:

_____

_____

7. Things you're good at . . .
   with your romantic partner:

_____

_____

with your children:

_____

_____

with your family/friends:

_____

_____

at work/school:

_____

_____

sports, hobbies, recreation:

_____

_____

creativity, crafts, etc.:

_____

_____

taking care of your home and home environments:

_____

_____

taking care of yourself:

_____

_____

Now carefully review the list of personal qualities you developed in this exercise. Write the top three, the ones you believe most and feel best about, in the space below:

_____

_____

_____

Exercise: Active Integration

It isn't enough to recognize positive qualities in yourself. You must actively work to keep them in mind. One strategy for increasing awareness of core qualities is called active integration. This involves each day finding an example from your past for up to three of your positive qualities. Here's how Emily, an out-of-work accountant, used active integration for three of her core qualities.

Date: 6/13

Quality 1: __caring__. I visited my grandmother daily when she was in the hospital last spring.

Quality 2: __take risks__. The time I asked Rick out, even though I'd just met him in a supermarket.

Quality 3: __lighthearted__. I kind of make people feel more up, like getting everybody laughing at Lisa's birthday party.

Date: 6/14

Quality 1: __caring__. When I went right over to Jason's house to comfort him after his mother announced she was divorcing his dad.

Quality 2: __take risks__. I told my boss about some problems with his leadership style.

Quality 3: __lighthearted__. Even after that skiing accident, I was still joking with everyone and not getting all down about it.

We suggest you make photocopies of the following worksheet so you can begin finding examples of your own positive core qualities. Try to remember examples of three qualities each day. Start with your top three from the Core Qualities Inventory. Keep working on them for several days to a week, and then move on to three other core qualities from the inventory.

ACTIVE INTEGRATION—Worksheet

Date: _____

Quality 1:

_____

_____

_____

Quality 2:

_____

_____

_____

Quality 3:

_____

_____

_____

Date: _____

Quality 1:

_____

_____

_____

Quality 2:

_____

_____

_____

Quality 3:

_____

_____

_____

Exercise: Affirm Your Worth

Go back over the Core Qualities Inventory, and in the space below write a summary of the main positive qualities you uncovered. Also include some of the situations or relationships where that quality is manifested:

_____

_____

_____

_____

_____

_____

Emily's core qualities summary looked like this:

"I'm a sunny, lighthearted person who cheers people around me. I'm supportive and caring, particularly when people are sick or hurting. I give people courage when they're scared, and I show them how to face situations through my own example. I take risks to achieve goals. I'm a good athlete, an honest and loyal friend, and a terrific (as yet unpublished) writer of children's stories. I have a good aesthetic sense and know how to make myself attractive."

Read your core qualities summary over each morning. Make it part of your daily rituals so that the words become incredibly familiar, even memorized. The idea is to use the summary as an affirmation of qualities that you need to remember and cherish in yourself.

Practice Acceptance

The key to self-acceptance is to recognize that you're doing the best you can. This is hard to remember sometimes because the pathological critic would rather have you believe that you are willfully screwing up, making one deliberate mistake after another. The facts are quite different. If you went back, with an open mind, to explore the actual process by which you made a regrettable decision, you'd find that you made the choice that seemed best at the time.

Exercise: People Doing the Best They Can

This exercise can be found in chapter 6, p. 53. The idea is to explore all the influences on your behavior and choices, including your needs, fears, stresses, personal history, and a host of other factors. Go through this exercise for several unfortunate acts or choices and take an honest look at everything that influenced you. After you do, we believe that you may revise some of your judgments. You may, in fact, discover that mistakes are something you can only see in hindsight. At the moment the choice is made, it feels right. It feels like the thing you have to do. There may be doubts, but you go ahead, hoping and expecting that things will turn out okay.

Exercise: Ending Negative Self-Labels

In the left-hand column below, write all the negative labels your critic slings at you—ugly, dumb, loser, etc. Think back over the past few months to times when you felt particularly down on yourself. What was the critic telling you? What pejorative word or phrase did the critic use to describe your behavior?

ENDING NEGATIVE LABELS—Worksheet

Negative Labels

Alternative Thinking
(Accurate and specific, balancing realities)

1.

1.

2.

2.

3.

3.

4.

4.

5.

5.

6.

6.

Now, in the column headed Alternative Thinking, it's time to revise some of these hurtful labels. First of all, the label is far too global. Make it accurate and specific. How often do you behave this way? Once a week? Once a month? Once in a lifetime? What exactly *is* the problem or undesirable behavior? Describe it specifically. If, for example, the label is "stupid," how often do you act this way? What exactly, behaviorally, does stupid mean? That the checkbook is seven dollars out of balance? That you forgot the PTA meeting twice in the last year? That you told a friend about a problem that you wish you hadn't? The point is to define carefully what these negative words are supposed to be describing.

Also, under Alternative Thinking, note any balancing realities—positive things you do that counterweight the negative. For example, you're often awkward in conversation with strangers, but are warm and engaging talking to friends. Or you have several nasty fights a year with your mother, but are faithful about calls and visits.

The first items on Emily's Ending Negative Labels Worksheet looked like this:

ENDING NEGATIVE LABELS—Example

Negative Labels	Alternative Thinking (Accurate and specific, balancing realities)
1. *foolish and impulsive*	1. *Basically this means I bought several outfits I shouldn't have for about $350 total. On the other hand, I'm paying the card down and looked great at the reunion.*
2. *airhead*	2. *I got in trouble three times at last job for math mistakes, but they also said I had a good knowledge of tax law.*
3. *self-centered bitch*	3. *My brother's line. I think a lot about my appearance and my own needs; I am also generous with my time and support to friends, and family.*

From now on, any time you catch yourself using a negative label, challenge it. Turn it into a statement that's specific and accurate, and find other, positive qualities that balance it.

Reinforce Healthy Thinking

Softening and changing negative judgments takes committed effort. One way to maintain that commitment is to make a contract with a friend or family member. Write down on a piece of paper what you're planning to do (i.e., active integration, affirming your worth, or ending negative labels). Commit yourself to one or more of these efforts for a specific period of time. Sign the contract and give it to your friend or family member. Ask them to check in with you regularly about your progress dealing with the critic.

A second strategy for reinforcing healthy thinking is to use a system of rewards. Each time you revise a negative label, give yourself a treat. It might be reading the next chapter in an exciting book, renting a video, or calling a good friend. After affirming your worth each morning, make sure you have a really delicious breakfast or have time to read the paper and enjoy your coffee. Think of these pleasant activities as a reward for remembering your core positive qualities.

Nourish Yourself

There are three main components to self-nourishment: physical comfort, connectedness, and emotional balance. The Self-Nourishment Checklist that follows is an opportunity to review a variety of activities that might be beneficial to include in your daily life. Put a check mark by each item that might improve the quality of your life.

Self-Nourishment Checklist

Physical Comfort

- ☐ Temperature/Warmth
  Keeping optimal room temperature; hot showers or tubs

- ☐ Clothes
  Pleasing texture and color; loose rather than constricting

- ☐ Bed
  Good support; warm and comforting

- ☐ Furniture
  At least one good, comfortable chair; a work space with room to spread out

- ☐ Food
  Healthy, good-tasting foods to look forward to

- ☐ Drink
  Warm or cool, good-tasting beverages; avoid caffeine

- ☐ Massage/Sensuality
  Relaxing physical touch

- ☐ Tension Level
  Relaxation exercises; meditation

- ☐ Energy
  Rest; sleep; quiet time

- ☐ Movement
  Aerobic exercises; stretching; athletics

- ☐ Pain Level
  If pain can be remedied, get immediate treatment or something to soothe it

- ☐ Smell
  Avoid unpleasant odors; consider using scents

- ☐ Grooming
  Manicure, haircuts, etc.

- ☐ Pace of life
  Avoid rushing—plan space between appointments and events; generous deadlines

Connectedness

- ☐ Friends
  Regular contact through phone and visits; plan shared activities

- ☐ Groups
  Sense of belonging to a regularly scheduled group activity: sports, hobbies, political or community action, educational or creative groups, etc.

- ☐ Family
  Regular contact with supportive and interested family members

- ☐ Generosity
  Giving and doing things for others

❑ Partner
Creating time alone with each other; scheduling fun; planning sensual or sexual experiences; small gifts (objects or time and energy)

❑ Community
Church activities; PTA; town hall; neighborhood association

Emotional Balance

❑ Meaning
Setting and pursuing a goal; service to others; creating something

❑ Pleasure
Scheduling time for things you enjoy

❑ Limits
Saying no to things you don't want to do or experience

❑ Gratitude
Daily meditation on what you appreciate and value in your life

❑ Mindfulness
Disciplining your mind to focus on the moment—what it feels like to wash the dishes, drive with the window open, take long strides as you walk home; mindfulness meditation

❑ Creativity
Making things—whether poetry and art or hemming new curtains

❑ Aesthetics
Arranging your environment so there are more things you like to look at

❑ Nature
Planning regular periods (however brief) in your favorite natural environments

❑ Learning
Enjoying new knowledge; developing a new skill

❑ Affirmation
Reminding yourself regularly of your positive core qualities (see Affirming Your Worth in this chapter)

❑ Time alone
Scheduling private time to think, reflect, and plan

❑ Stress breaks
Scheduling brief recovery periods (from a few minutes to a few days) to help manage stressful situations

❑ After-work cool-out
Time to decompress immediately after getting home

❑ Passive relaxation
Books, videos, plays, etc.

❑ Active relaxation
Hobbies, interests, projects

Having completed the checklist, it's time to go back and circle the three self-nourishment activities you want to try first. With this accomplished, you can move on to the next section—making a self-nourishment plan. It's not enough to want to do something. You have to plan for it and integrate it's into your life.

Exercise: Self-Nourishment Plan

Item 1 _____

When (day/time) _____

Where _____

Frequency (if applicable) _____

Rescheduling (what do you have to change or arrange or stop doing to make room for this self-nourishment experience?) _____

_____

_____

Item 2 _____

When (day/time) _____

Where _____

Frequency (if applicable) _____

Rescheduling (what do you have to change or arrange or stop doing to make room for this self-nourishment experience?) _____

_____

_____

Item 3 _____

When (day/time) _____

Where _____

Frequency (if applicable) _____

Rescheduling (what do you have to change or arrange or stop doing to make room for this self-nourishment experience?) _____

_____

_____

CHAPTER 16

GETTING UNSTUCK

Sometimes, no matter how hard you've worked on anger management skills, a provocative situation will get the best of you. It can be discouraging—and costly, particularly if your temper pushes you into some seriously aggressive or destructive behavior.

Don't give up. If you look back over your Anger Logs, you'll see a lot of ups and downs over the weeks. There are flare-ups; then there are periods when you are coping more effectively. There are also particular provocations that are clearly harder than others. So if you've been charting your progress, you would see a "sawtooth" profile. On *average*, though, despite the setbacks, you are probably angry less often and less intensely than you were at the start of this program.

That said, what can you do now if some provocation really gets to you? Or if a problem or conflict has become chronically upsetting? There are four things you can do.

Use your Anger Plans Worksheet

Go back to chapter 13, "Your Plan for Real-life Coping," and complete the Anger Plans Worksheet for any provocation that gets the better of you. This is important. Planning is 50 percent of anger management; the other 50 percent is practice. Find out what trigger thoughts are seducing you into a blowup. Look for or develop coping thoughts (see Best Coping Thoughts Worksheet) that are specific antidotes for your anger triggers. And while you're at it, plan one or two coping behaviors that help you disengage from the upset.

Identify and Cope with the Feelings Underneath Your Anger

One function of anger, as you learned in chapter 3, is to cover or cope with emotional pain. Anger tends to block awareness of feelings such as shame, fear, or hurt. It's like a great big boulder that obscures a lot of your emotional landscape.

If anger usually gets the upper hand with certain provocations, it often means that the anger is highly reinforced because it protects you from some other feeling—a feeling you'd prefer not to face. Overcoming anger in this situation may necessitate identifying that underlying feeling and finding an alternative way to cope with it.

Exercise: What's Underneath the Anger

Visualize a recent provocation where your anger got the upper hand. Close your eyes and form an image of the setting—colors, shapes, sounds, smells, and physical sensations such as heat or texture. Notice who's there and listen to what's being said. Also notice any trigger thoughts you may have. Take some time to really anchor yourself in the scene.

Now hit the rewind button and go back to the beginning, just as your anger was getting started. And then keep going a little further back—before the trigger thoughts and the anger—to what you first felt. Notice your inner climate at that moment. Stay with it. Take a few deep breaths and try to capture the emotion.

Now look at the following list to see if any of these feelings were present *before* the anger hit:

- Guilt—a sense of having done something wrong.

- Shame—a deep feeling of being unacceptable, flawed, or contemptible.

- Hurt—a feeling of being devalued or denigrated by others.

- Loss—a feeling that something you needed or counted on is lost or missing.

- Hunger/Frustrated Drive—an aching for something; a strong sense of incompleteness.

- Helplessness—the feeling that there's nothing you can do about your pain; crucial elements of your life are beyond your control.

- Anxiety/Fear—a dread of something that could happen; a sense of danger; a fear of certain things or situations.

- Feeling Unworthy—a sense that you aren't good enough, that you are bad or wrong or without intrinsic value.

- Emptiness—a sense either of numbness or a hollowness that requires constant attention and activity.

Three Strategies to Cope with Painful Feelings

If you've identified one of the above emotions as present just before your anger surged, chances are the anger was functioning as a breakwater to keep the feeling from overwhelming you. Now there is an important task ahead: You need to find an alternative way to cope with this feeling *besides anger*. There are three basic strategies to manage painful emotions.

One is to simply accept and "hold" the feeling for a while. It won't last forever. A common delusion when we're in pain is that there will never be an end to it. If you think back to struggles with similar emotions, you know that even the hardest ones to bear are time limited—eventually they pass. So notice the wave hit, crest, and gradually recede. Take some deep breaths. Imagine the pain is next to you, not *in you*, or see it from a distance. Give it a color and shape. Watch while it slowly, slowly shrinks in size.

The second strategy is to use coping thoughts, just like you've learned to do with anger. Begin by noticing the thoughts that trigger your feeling. What are you saying to yourself that intensifies the pain? Write these thoughts down. Now *rewrite* the negative thoughts following these key rules:

- Make the thoughts *accurate* rather than exaggerated.

- Make the thoughts *specific* rather than general.

- Use nonpejorative language.

- Include balancing realities and alternative explanations. Ask yourself what's the positive part of the picture that you're leaving out?

The following three self-help books are recommended for developing coping thoughts in response to a wide variety of painful feelings:

- *Thoughts and Feelings: Getting Control of Your Moods and Your Life* by Matthew McKay, Martha Davis, and Patrick Fanning

- *Mind Over Mood* by Dennis Greenburger and Christine Pedesky

- *Feeling Good: The New Mood Therapy* by David Burns

The third strategy for coping with difficult feelings is to develop a problem-solving plan. What can you change in your life, in your relationships, or in your behavior to diminish this painful feeling? If you stop the angry blaming, maybe there is something *you* can do to make things different. Begin by writing out a clearly stated goal. Now brainstorm some alternative solutions. List as many as you can think of. Quantity is better than quality. Don't evaluate your ideas, just generate a lot of them.

After you've listed between ten and twenty alternative solutions, try to rule out the obviously unworkable ones. For the solutions that remain, list the positive and negative consequences for each one. Try to identify both the short- and long-term outcomes. Finally, select one or more alternative solution that you would like to try. Be sure to decide on a first step toward implementation—including when and where you'll take it.

So whether you're afraid of something, or feeling helpless and stuck, or yearning for something you don't have, problem solving may help you to create real changes in the situation.

Example: Ricardo's Vacation

To illustrate the value of problem solving for anger control, consider Ricardo's struggle to take needed time off from his interior design business. He's irritable, exhausted, plus he wants to spend time with his mother in New Mexico. Problem is, he has a one-man office. He's afraid of alienating his clients and dropping the ball on some important projects if he takes time off.

Ricardo started with the clear goal: "I want two weeks both to relax and spend time with my mother." While brainstorming solutions, he came up with fourteen ideas ranging from "carry blueprints with me and conduct business by e-mail" to "send clients some French Chardonnay and tell them to chill for two weeks."

Ricardo listed positive and negative consequences for his top three solutions. For example, "get a cell phone hook-up in Gallup to talk to clients" had some clear advantages and disadvantages:

Advantages	*Disadvantages*
Can "put out fires" at work	Expense
Stay in touch with key clients	Vacation can be interrupted any time
	Never really relax
	Feel cheated

Ricardo finally settled on the following idea: "Take two week-long vacations separated by a brief catch-up period." He planned to make no calls while he was gone, except emergencies. Decision made, Ricardo immediately called his travel agent.

Identify the Anger Payoffs

Something others do in response to your anger may be reinforcing it. Anger can be an effective coercive strategy. People back off or give in when you get angry. You end up getting your way, and anger gives you a temporary feeling of control. In the long run, of course, people get inured to your anger and resistant to coercion. They stop giving in and just go away. But in a particular relationship or situation, anger may still be quite rewarding, and it may be hard for you to give up such a reliable tool for getting things to go the way you want.

Exercise: What's Reinforcing the Anger?

On the worksheet below, identify three recent anger situations where you got upset and would like to change your behavior in the future. In the middle column of the worksheet, identify the positive outcomes from your anger response in each situation. In other words, what did people do that you wanted them to do? How did people react to your anger that was beneficial or rewarding for you? What short-term positive changes came about as a result of your blowup? In the right-hand column of the worksheet, identify an alternative coping strategy that might have yielded the same result—for example, an assertive statement about your needs and feelings. Or a clear, but non-hostile, statement about your limits in the situation. Or efforts toward negotiation. Or making your own coping plan (independent of others) to change the situation. We've included a sample worksheet filled out by Ronnie, a thirty-six-year-old single woman living with a roommate.

This worksheet can be an important resource for identifying anger reinforcers and finding an alternative way to get your needs met. Whenever you're puzzled by an anger response that seems hard to change, do this simple three-step analysis to see how your anger is being rewarded, and how you can get the same reward using strategies that don't damage your relationships.

Make a Contract

In chapter 1, you started your anger management program by making a twenty-four-hour promise to behave calmly. That was a helpful exercise because it taught you that you could control your anger—one day at a time. This is an opportunity to make a different kind of contract. Instead of agreeing to stay calm for twenty-four hours, you are going to promise a particular individual that you will never engage in a specific target behavior with them again. For example, if you have an ongoing problem of name-calling with a particular person, and you believe this behavior is damaging and needs to change, you can sign a contract to do so.

The contract (a sample can be found at the end of the chapter) has five provisions. First, it is a promise made to a particular individual. Second, it should contain a clear description of the target anger behavior. It's best if the contract focuses on *one behavior only*. Promising too much, and trying to remember too much, will sabotage your effort. Third, the contract should identify a signal that the other person can use to warn you when your target behavior is starting. The signal should be clearly described and defined. Fourth, there should be a provision to stop everything and take a time-out as soon as you see the signal. This means that you don't say another word. You shut up and the issue is dropped until you can talk about it more calmly later on. Fifth, the contract should identify at least two other support people who know and care about your

WHAT'S REINFORCING THE ANGER—Worksheet

Anger Situation	Positive Outcomes	Alternative Coping
1		
2		
3		

WHAT'S REINFORCING THE ANGER—
Ronnie's Worksheet

Anger Situation	Positive Outcomes	Alternative Coping
1 Boss dumps huge pile of work on my desk at 4:30 and says he needs it by tomorrow. I get angry and sarcastic.	He gives half of it to someone else.	Assertively explain that I can only work till 6:30. So if he wants it done, someone else will have to help
2 Melinda (close friend) asks if it's okay if she goes out with my ex. I explode, call her "someone with an instinct for betrayal."	Melinda apologizes. Calls Jeff (my ex) and tells him he should never have asked.	Share my feelings without blaming her. Explain that it hurts too much to see him happily dating my best friend, and that it could distance us.
3 Roommate wakes me up when she comes in, loud and rowdy with her boy-friend. Scream, "Shut up, you F---heads."	They cool it, she stops bringing him home.	Come in the living room and ask calmly. Negotiate an evening quiet time—say after 11 P.M.

promise. They may sign the contract as witnesses, but at the very least, they should agree to check in with you periodically about your promise.

You're a Whole Lot Stronger Than You Used to Be

It takes two things to change. First, you need determination—you need a big reason and a strong resolve. The fact that you've read this far means that you've got the determination to make a real change in your life.

Second, you need skills. This book has given you the skills. Every time you successfully control your anger, you get stronger. It's like a muscle that develops each time you exercise it. You've been doing anger management "push-ups" for weeks or months now. In the beginning, it took everything you had, every fiber of your resolve, to remember to breathe and relax and use your coping thoughts. More and more, this has become second nature, and it isn't so hard now because the anger management muscle is strong and buffed. Keep at it. Don't neglect your skills. Don't forget to breathe and cope. The quality of your life, and the lives of those you love, are so much better because you've done this work.

ANGER CONTRACT

Date _____

I, _____, on this date commit myself to _____ that I will never engage in the following anger behavior with him/her:

Description of behavior: (one behavior only)

_____

_____

_____

I will watch for the following signal, to be given at the first sign of the anger behavior:

_____

_____

Whenever the signal is given, I will stop talking and end the discussion until I'm calm enough to deal with it. I will absolutely, positively cease the target behavior.

There are at least two other people who know about my promise and will check in with me to help me keep it. Their names are:

_____

_____

_____
Your Signature

_____
Witness

_____
Witness

APPENDIX

RESEARCH ON THE EFFECTS OF ANGER

Physiological Costs of Anger

Anger and Hypertension

The following studies have shown the connection between unexpressed anger (anger-in) and hypertension:

Alexander, F. 1939. Emotional factors in hypertension. *Psychosomatic Medicine* 1:175–179.

Diamond, E.L. 1982. The role of anger and hostility in essential hypertension and coronary heart disease. *Psychological Bulletin* 92:410–433.

Dimsdale, J.E., C. Pierce, D. Schoenfeld, A. Brown. 1986. Suppressed anger and blood pressure: The effects of race, sex, social class, obesity, and age. *Psychosomatic Medicine* 48:430–436.

Esler, M.S., S. Julius, A. Zweifler, O. Randall, E. Harburg, H. Gardiner, and E. De Quattro. 1977. Mild high-rennin essential hypertension: Neurogenic human hypertension? *New England Journal of Medicine* 296:405–411.

Gentry, W.D. 1982. Habitual anger-coping styles: Effect on mean blood pressure and risk for essential hypertension. *Psychosomatic Medicine* 44:195–202.

Hamilton, J.A. 1942. Psychophysiology of blood pressure. *Psychosomatic Medicine* 4:125–133

Harburg, E., J.C. Erfurt, L.S. Hauenstein, C. Chape, W.J. Schull, and M.A. Schork. 1973. Socio-ecological stress, suppressed hostility, skin color, and black-white male blood pressure: Detroit. *Psychosomatic Medicine* 35:2726–296.

Kahn, H.A., J.H. Medalie, H.N. Newfield, E. Riss, and U. Goldbourt. 1972. The incidence of hypertension and associated factors: The Israel ischemic heart disease study. *American Heart Journal* 84:171–182.

Miller, C., and C. Grim. 1979. Personality and emotional stress measurement on hypertensive patients with essential and secondary hypertension. *International Journal of Nursing Studies* 16:85–93.

Thomas, S.P. 1997. Women's anger: relationship of suppression to blood pressure. *Nursing Research* 46:324–30.

Additional Annotated Studies

Harburg, E., S. Julius, N.F. McGinn, J. McLeod, and S.W. Hoobler. 1964. Personality traits and behavior patterns associated with systolic blood pressure levels in college males. *Journal of Chronic Diseases* 17:405–414. Harburg and associates demonstrated the correlation between high blood pressure and hypertension in a college population.

Van der Ploeg, H.M., E.T. Van Buuren, and P. Van Brummelen. 1985. The role of anger in hypertension. *Psychotherapy & Psychosomatics* 43:186–193. Van der Ploeg and associates studied 208 subjects in the Netherlands. Their results supported a psychosomatic theory of hypertension, and found that hypertensives tend to avoid showing anger.

The following studies have shown the connection between expressed anger (anger-out) and hypertension:

Baer, P.E., F.H. Collins, G.C. Bourianoff, and M.F. Ketchel. 1983. Assessing personality factors in essential hypertension with a brief self-report instrument. *Psychosomatic Medicine* 45:59–63.

Harburg, E., E.H. Blakelock, and P.J. Roeper. 1979. Resentful and reflective coping with arbitrary authority and blood pressure: Detroit. *Psychosomatic Medicine* 41:189–202.

Kaplan, S., L.A. Gottschalk, E. Magliocco, D. Rohovit, and W. Ross. 1961. Hostility in verbal productions and hypnotic dreams in hypertensive patients. *Psychosomatic Medicine* 23:311–322.

Mann, A.H. 1977. Psychiatric morbidity and hostility in hypertension. *Psychological Medicine* 7:653–659.

Schachter, J. 1957. Pain, fear, and anger in hypertensives and normotensives. *Psychosomatic Medicine* 19:17–29.

Anger, Hostility and Cardiovascular Disease

The following studies have shown the connection between anger, hostility and various forms of cardiovascular disease:

Barefoot, J.C., W.G. Dahlstrom, and R.B. Williams, Jr. 1983. Hostility, CHD incidence, and total morbidity: a 25-year follow-up study of 255 physicians. *Psychosomatic Medicine* 45:59–63.

Barefoot, J.C., T.L. Haney, R.R. Harper, T.M. Dembroski, and R.B. Williams, Jr. 1990. Interview assessed hostility and the severity of coronary artery disease. Paper presented at the 98th Annual Convention of the APA. Boston MA.

Friedman, M. and R.H. Rosenman. 1974. *Type A Behavior and Your Heart.* New York: Alfred A. Knopf.

Grunnbaum, J.A., S.W. Vernon, and C.M. Clasen. 1997. The association between anger and hostility and risk factors for coronary heart disease in children and adolescents: a review. *Annals of Behavioral Medicine* 19:179–189.

Kawachi, I., D. Sparrow, A. Spiro, P. Vokonas, and S.T. Weiss. 1996. A prospective study of anger and coronary heart disease. The Normative Aging Study. *Circulation* 94:2090–2095.

Rosenman, R.H. 1985. Health consequences of anger and implications for treatment. In *Anger and Hostility in Cardiovascular and Behavioral Disorders,* edited by M.A. Chesny and R.H. Rosenman. Washington DC: Hemisphere Publishing Co.

Shekelle, R.B., M. Gale, A.M. Ostfeld, and O. Paul. 1983. Hostility, risk of coronary heart disease, and mortality. *Psychosomatic Medicine* 45:109–114.

Siegman, A.W., T.M. Dembroski, and N. Ringel. 1987. Components of hostility and severity of coronary artery disease. *Psychosomatic Medicine* 49:127–135.

Additional Annotated Studies

Joesoef, M.R., S.F. Wetterhall, F. DeStefano, N.E. Stroup, and A. Fronek. 1989. The association of peripheral arterial disease with hostility in a young, healthy population. *Psychosomatic Medicine* 51:285–289. In a cross-sectional study of U.S. army veterans, Joesoef and associates found that those with higher hostility scores were more likely to have peripheral artery disease.

Ricci, B., E. Pio, P. Gremgni, G. Bertolotti, and A.M. Zotti. 1995. Dimensions of anger and hostility in cardiac patients, hypertensive patients, and controls. 64:162–172. Ricci and associates studied 240 patients in Italy. They found that the frequency and extent to which people experienced anger arousal had pathogenic effects. Specifically, their results indicate that the more aggressively people tend to respond, the more likely they are to experience coronary heart disease.

Williams, R.B., T.L. Haney, K.I. Lee, J. Kong, J.A. Blumenthal, and R.E. Walen. 1980. Type A behavior, hostility, and coronary atherosclerosis. *Psychosomatic Medicine* 42:539–549. Williams and associates, testing 424 patients referred for coronary angiography (X-rays of the heart's blood supply), found that 70 percent of those with higher hostility scores had significant atherosclerosis.

Anger, Hostility, and Death from All Causes

The following studies have shown the connection between anger, hostility and total mortality:

Chesney, M.A., M. Hecker, and G.W. Black. 1989. Coronary-prone components of Type A behavior in the WGSC: A new methodology. In *Type A Behavior Pattern: Research, Theory, and Intervention*, edited by B.K. Houston and C.R. Snyder. New York: Wiley.

Koskenvuo, M. J. Kaprio, R.J. Rose, A. Kasaniemi, K. Heikkila, and H. Langinvainio. 1988. Hostility as a risk factor for mortality and ischemic heart disease in men. *Psychosomatic Medicine* 50:330–340.

Schekelle, R.B., M. Gale, A.M. Ostfeld, and O. Paul. 1983. Hostility, risk of coronary heart disease, and mortality. *Psychosomatic Medicine* 45:109–114.

Additional Annotated Studies

Carmelli, D., G.E. Swan, R.H. Rosenman, M.H. Hecker, and D.R. Ragland. 1989. Behavioral components and total mortality in the WGSC. Paper presented at the meeting of the Society of Behavioral Medicine. San Francisco, CA. Carmelli and associates found that anger scores predicted total mortality over a 22-year follow-up period.

Carmody, T.P., J.R. Crossen, and A.N. Wiens. 1989. Hostility as a risk factor: Relationships with neuroticism, Type A behavior, attentional focus, and interpersonal style. *Journal of Clinical Psychology* 45:754–762. Carmody and associates studied 2204 psychologically normal and physically healthy males, aged 20–43. Their findings support the idea that hostility is one dimension of the disease-prone personality.

Deshields, T., J.O. Jenkins, and R.C. Tait. 1989. The experience of anger in chronic illness: A preliminary investigation. *International Journal of Psychiatry in Medicine* 19:299–309. Deshields and associates reported that the chronic patient groups they studied differed significantly from the nonpatient control group. The chronic patient group reported more anger in general and a greater frequency of anger experiences. They also reported greater severity of health problems.

Emotional and Interpersonal Costs of Anger and Hostility

The following studies have shown the connection between anger, hostility and less satisfactory social supports. This section also includes studies relating to damaged friendships, increased fights with family members, and difficulties at school or in the workplace.

Blumenthal, J.A., J.C. Barefoot, M.M. Burg, and R.B. Williams, Jr. 1987. Psychological correlates of hostility among patients undergoing coronary angiography. *British Journal of Medical Psychology* 60:349–355.

Deffenbacher, J.L. 1992. Trait anger: Theory, findings, and implications. In Spielberger, C.D. and Butcher, J.N. (Eds.) *Advances in Personality Assessment*. 177-201. Lawrence Erlbaum Associates, Inc. Hillsdale, NJ.

Greenglass, E.R. 1996. Anger suppression, cynical distrust, and hostility: Implications for coronary heart disease. In Spielberger, C.D. and Sarason, I.G. (Eds.) *Stress and emotion: Anxiety, anger and curiosity.* 205-225.

Hansson, R.D., W.H. Jones, and B. Carpenter. 1984. Relational competence and social support. *Review of Personality and Social Psychology* 5:265–284.

Hardy, J.D. and T.W. Smith. 1988. Cynical hostility and vulnerability to disease: Social support, life stress, and physiological response to conflict. *Health Psychology* 7:447–459.

Hazaleus, S., and J. Deffenbacher. 1986. Relaxation and cognitive treatments of anger. *Journal of Consulting and Clinical Psychology* 54:222–226.

Houston, B.K., and K.E. Kelley. 1989. Hostility in employed women: Relation to work and marital experiences, social support, stress, and anger expression. *Personality and Social Psychology Bulletin* 15:175–182.

Jones, W.H., J.E. Freeman, and R.A. Gasewick. 1981. The persistence of loneliness: Self and other determinants. *Journal of Personality* 49:27–48.

Liebsohn, M.T., E.R. Oetting, and J.L. Deffenbacher. 1994. The effects of trait anger on alcohol consumption and consequences. *Journal of Adolescent Substance Abuse* 3:17–32.

Smith, T.W., and K.D. Frohm. 1985. What's so healthy about hostility? Construct validity and psychosocial correlates of the Cook & Medley Ho scale. *Health Psychology* 4:503–520.

Smith, T.W., M.K. Pope, J.D. Sanders, J.D. Allred, and J.L. O'Keeffe. Cynical hostility at home and work: Psychosocial vulnerability across domains. *Journal of Research in Personality* 22:525–548.

Additional Annotated Studies

In this series of articles, Deffenbacher and associates, using primarily college students and adolescents as subjects, studied people who identified anger as a personal problem. They selected those subjects who scored in the upper quartile on Spielberger's Trait Anger Scale. This sample was found to express their anger in outward, negative, and poorly controlled ways. The research suggests that these individuals were more likely to suffer damaged friendships, as well as having more fights with family members.

Deffenbacher, J.L., R. Lynch, E.R. Oetting, and C.C. Kemper. Anger reduction in early adolescents. *Journal of Counseling Psychology* 43:149–157.

Deffenbacher, J.L., E.R. Oetting, M.E. Huff, and G.R. Cornell. Evaluation of two cognitive-behavioral approaches to general anger reduction. *Cognitive Therapy and Research* 20:551–573.

Deffenbacher, J.L., E.R. Oetting, R.S. Lynch, and C.D. Morris. 1996. The expression of anger and its consequences. *Behavior research and Therapy* 34:575–590.

Deffenbacher, J.L., E.R. Oetting, G.A. Thwaites, R.S. Lynch, D.A. Baker, R.S. Stark, S. Thacker, and L. Eiswerth-Cox. 1996. State-Trait anger theory and the utility of the Trait Anger Scale. *Journal of Counseling Psychology* 43:131–148.

Deffenbacher, J.L., and P.M. Sabadell. 1990. A combination of cognitive, relaxation, and behavioral coping skills in the reduction of general anger. *Journal of College Student Development* 31:351–358.

SUGGESTED READINGS

Beck, A. 1999. *Prisoners of Hate: The Cognitive Basis of Anger, Hostility & Violence.* New York: HarperCollins.

Burns, D. 1980. *Feeling Good: The New Mood Therapy.* New York: William Morrow.

Davis, M., E.R. Eshelman, and M. McKay. 1998. *Relaxation and Stress Reduction Workbook* (Fourth Edition). Oakland, CA: New Harbinger Publications.

Deschner, J.P. 1984. *The Hitting Habit.* New York: The Free Press, Macmillan Publishers.

Ellis, A. 1998. *How to Control Your Anger Before It Controls You.* Secaucus, NJ: Carol Publishing Group.

Greenberger, D. and C.A. Pedesky. 1995. *Mind Over Mood.* New York: Guilford Press.

Lerner, H.G. 1985. *The Dance of Anger.* New York: Harper & Row.

McKay, M., M. Davis, and P. Fanning. 1998. *Thoughts and Feelings* Second Edition. Oakland, CA.: New Harbinger Publications.

McKay, M., K. Paleg, P. Fanning, and D. Landis. 1996. *When Anger Hurts Your Kids.* Oakland, CA New Harbinger Publications.

McKay, M., P.D. Rogers, and J. McKay. 1987. *When Anger Hurts.* Oakland, CA.:New Harbinger Publications.

McKay, M., P.D. Rogers, J.D. Blades, and R. Gosse. 1999. *The Divorce Book.* Oakland, CA: New Harbinger Publications.

Neidig, P.H. and D.H. Friedman. 1984. *Spouse Abuse: A treatment Program for Couples.* Champaign, IL:Research Press.

Potter-Efron, R. 1994. *Angry All the Time.* Oakland, CA.: New Harbinger Publications.

Tavris, C. 1989. *Anger: The Misunderstood Emotion.* New York: Simon & Schuster.

For Therapists:

Deffenbacher, J.L. and M. McKay. 2000. *Overcoming Situational and General Anger (Therapist Protocol).* Oakland, CA: New Harbinger Publications.

Matthew McKay, Ph.D., is the Clinical Director of Haight-Ashbury Psychological Services in San Francisco. Dr. McKay is the coauthor of thirteen popular books, including *The Relaxation & Stress Reduction Workbook, When Anger Hurts, Couple Skills, Thoughts & Feelings, When Anger Hurts Your Kids, Self-Esteem,* and several professional titles.

Peter Rogers, Ph.D. is the Administrative Director of Haight-Ashbury Psychological Services in San Francisco, and the past Director of the Alcohol and Drug Treatment Program at Kaiser Permanente in Redwood City, California. Dr. Rogers is coauthor of *The Divorce Book* and *When Anger Hurts,* and author of book chapters and articles on alcohol and drug abuse.

More New Harbinger Titles

WHY ARE WE STILL FIGHTING?

Explains how our mental models about the world can short-circuit our relationships and offers strategies for effective long-term change.

Item FIGH $15.95

TOXIC COWORKERS

This is the first guide to explain how to deal with a dysfunctional coworker who has a full-fledged personality disorder.

Item TOXC $13.95

WORKING ANGER

This step-by-step program is designed to help anyone who has had trouble dealing with their own anger or other people's anger at work.

Item WA $12.95

ANGRY ALL THE TIME

This emergency guide helps you change anger-provoking thoughts, deal with old resentments, ask for what you want without anger, and stay calm one day at a time.

Item ALL Paperback, $12.95

LETTING GO OF ANGER

Helps you recognize the ten destructive ways that people deal with anger and identify which anger styles may be undermining your personal and work relationships.

Item LET Paperback, $12.95

BETTER BOUNDARIES

If you feel like you have trouble saying no to others, at work or at home, this book can help you establish more effective boundaries.

Item BB Paperback, $14.95

Call **toll-free 1-800-748-6273** to order. Have your Visa or Mastercard number ready. Or send a check for the titles you want to New Harbinger Publications, 5674 Shattuck Avenue, Oakland, CA 94609. Include $3.80 for the first book and 75¢ for each additional book to cover shipping and handling. (California residents please include appropriate sales tax.) Allow four to six weeks for delivery.

Prices subject to change without notice.

Some Other New Harbinger Self-Help Titles

Multiple Chemical Sensitivity: A Survival Guide, $16.95
Dancing Naked, $14.95
Why Are We Still Fighting, $15.95
From Sabotage to Success, $14.95
Parkinson's Disease and the Art of Moving, $15.95
A Survivor's Guide to Breast Cancer, $13.95
Men, Women, and Prostate Cancer, $15.95
Make Every Session Count: Getting the Most Out of Your Brief Therapy, $10.95
Virtual Addiction, $12.95
After the Breakup, $13.95
Why Can't I Be the Parent I Want to Be?, $12.95
The Secret Message of Shame, $13.95
The OCD Workbook, $18.95
Tapping Your Inner Strength, $13.95
Binge No More, $14.95
When to Forgive, $12.95
Practical Dreaming, $12.95
Healthy Baby, Toxic World, $15.95
Making Hope Happen, $14.95
I'll Take Care of You, $12.95
Survivor Guilt, $14.95
Children Changed by Trauma, $13.95
Understanding Your Child's Sexual Behavior, $12.95
The Self-Esteem Companion, $10.95
The Gay and Lesbian Self-Esteem Book, $13.95
Making the Big Move, $13.95
How to Survive and Thrive in an Empty Nest, $13.95
Living Well with a Hidden Disability, $15.95
Overcoming Repetitive Motion Injuries the Rossiter Way, $15.95
What to Tell the Kids About Your Divorce, $13.95
The Divorce Book, Second Edition, $15.95
Claiming Your Creative Self: True Stories from the Everyday Lives of Women, $15.95
Six Keys to Creating the Life You Desire, $19.95
Taking Control of TMJ, $13.95
What You Need to Know About Alzheimer's, $15.95
Winning Against Relapse: A Workbook of Action Plans for Recurring Health and Emotional Problems, $14.95
Facing 30: Women Talk About Constructing a Real Life and Other Scary Rites of Passage, $12.95
The Worry Control Workbook, $15.95
Wanting What You Have: A Self-Discovery Workbook, $18.95
When Perfect Isn't Good Enough: Strategies for Coping with Perfectionism, $13.95
Earning Your Own Respect: A Handbook of Personal Responsibility, $12.95
High on Stress: A Woman's Guide to Optimizing the Stress in Her Life, $13.95
Infidelity: A Survival Guide, $13.95
Stop Walking on Eggshells, $14.95
Consumer's Guide to Psychiatric Drugs, $16.95
The Fibromyalgia Advocate: Getting the Support You Need to Cope with Fibromyalgia and Myofascial Pain, $18.95
Healing Fear: New Approaches to Overcoming Anxiety, $16.95
Working Anger: Preventing and Resolving Conflict on the Job, $12.95
Sex Smart: How Your Childhood Shaped Your Sexual Life and What to Do About It, $14.95
You Can Free Yourself From Alcohol & Drugs, $13.95
Amongst Ourselves: A Self-Help Guide to Living with Dissociative Identity Disorder, $14.95
Healthy Living with Diabetes, $13.95
Dr. Carl Robinson's Basic Baby Care, $10.95
Better Boundries: Owning and Treasuring Your Life, $13.95
Goodbye Good Girl, $12.95
Fibromyalgia & Chronic Myofascial Pain Syndrome, $19.95
The Depression Workbook: Living With Depression and Manic Depression, $17.95
Self-Esteem, Second Edition, $13.95
Angry All the Time: An Emergency Guide to Anger Control, $12.95
When Anger Hurts, $13.95
Perimenopause, $16.95
The Relaxation & Stress Reduction Workbook, Fourth Edition, $17.95
The Anxiety & Phobia Workbook, Second Edition, $18.95
I Can't Get Over It, A Handbook for Trauma Survivors, Second Edition, $16.95
Messages: The Communication Skills Workbook, Second Edition, $15.95
Thoughts & Feelings, Second Edition, $18.95
Depression: How It Happens, How It's Healed, $14.95
The Deadly Diet, Second Edition, $14.95
The Power of Two, $15.95
Living Without Depression & Manic Depression: A Workbook for Maintaining Mood Stability, $18.95
Couple Skills: Making Your Relationship Work, $14.95
Hypnosis for Change: A Manual of Proven Techniques, Third Edition, $15.95

Call **toll free, 1-800-748-6273,** or log on to our online bookstore at **www.newharbinger.com** to order. Have your Visa or Mastercard number ready. Or send a check for the titles you want to New Harbinger Publications, Inc., 5674 Shattuck Ave., Oakland, CA 94609. Include $3.80 for the first book and 75¢ for each additional book, to cover shipping and handling. (California residents please include appropriate sales tax.) Allow two to five weeks for delivery.

Prices subject to change without notice.

DO WHAT YOU LOVE, THE MONEY WILL FOLLOW

Discovering Your Right Livelihood

Marsha Sinetar

Paulist Press
New York/Mahwah

Also by Marsha Sinetar,
published by Paulist Press:
Ordinary People as Monks and Mystics:
Lifestyles for Self-Discovery

Copyright © 1987 by Dr. Marsha Sinetar

Library of Congress Cataloging-in-Publication Data

Sinetar, Marsha.
    Do what you love, the money will follow.

    Bibliography: p.
    1. Vocational interests.   2.   Job satisfaction.
3. Self-actualization (Psychology)   4. Work—
Psychological aspects.   I. Title.
HF5381.5.S53   1986   650.1   86-30390
ISBN 0-8091-2874-8

Published by Paulist Press
997 Macarthur Boulevard
Mahwah, New Jersey 07430

Printed and bound in the
United States of America

Contents

To the memory of my father

Personal Acknowledgements
and Author's Notes

Many people contributed to the production and publication of this book. For instance, my always cheerful, outstanding word processors and proofreaders, Joanne Gemkow and Pam Bacci, deserve my written thanks. They do all of their work for me after their regular working day, and have given this project many weekends and holidays. I'm indebted to their enthusiasm. To my two editors, I also want to add a word of thanks: Dianne Molvig patiently manicured each chapter after it was completed, and Georgia Mandakas, my editor at Paulist Press, steadily helped me all these months while meticulously readying the text for publication. Both of these fine editors greatly assisted me by freeing me to think about ideas rather than the details of manuscript preparation.

I also want to acknowledge all my supportive friends at Paulist Press—especially Father Lynch, Don Brophy and Hugh Lally—who have, from the start, encouraged me and made me feel a part of Paulist's highly professional family.

I am deeply appreciative to all those who consented to an interview for this book and who sent me follow-up letters and tape recordings to continue our discussions about work. All have helped advance the idea that people who love their work make a significant contribution to others while growing into selfhood. I must add that I have the greatest respect and affection for everyone who put his or her hand to this project.

Finally, I wish to add a note of appreciation and encouragement to readers—both to those who wrote to me after

reading my first book as well as to those who may write after
reading this one. Perhaps readers think that an author is not
interested in their stories, thoughts and opinions. But most
writers that I know are very moved by the letters they get. And,
feeling as I do that all humans hold much in common, if readers
have experiences or comments that they would like to share, I
will gratefully receive them. These serve as feedback to me and
as yet another source of ideas for future works. Readers may write
to me at Box One, Stewart's Point, California 95480.

Introduction

About ten years ago, I began to experience a great longing to change my life. The thought of letting go of what I had—a well-paying, secure job; a beautiful home; friends and family nearby—was truly terrifying. I who had always clung to outward forms of security, I who had wanted guarantees in every part of my life, also ignored the inner dissatisfactions and urgings I felt.

Years before, this prompting from within had started. And I had ignored it. I distracted myself with a respected career and with the inevitable promotions that came my way. I distracted myself even more successfully with an accumulation of material rewards and symbols of success. The unknown was too frightening to me. This, despite the fact that by all outward appearances I was a creative, spontaneous and enthusiastic person.

In reality, I did not truly trust myself. I was afraid to cross uncharted, unconventional waters to get to a more desirable place in life, afraid that—when truth be told—I would not have the requisite strength and competence to accomplish what I so dearly wanted. I could not even imagine how to start. While I did believe the adage "What man can conceive, he can achieve," I couldn't conceive of doing what I knew I would love. My mind clung so desperately to the familiar.

Then one day, as I drove to work along beautiful Wilshire Boulevard in Los Angeles, on a smogless, sunny California morning, a startling thought entered my head. It was as clear a thought as if someone was speaking to me: "Do what you love, the money will follow." At that very moment, I knew I had to, and would, take a leap of faith. I knew I had to, and would, step out, cut myself loose from all those things that seemed to bind

1

me. I knew I would start doing what I most enjoyed: writing, working with industry (instead of public education) and living in the country instead of in the city.

That decision transformed my life. Since that day, I have gradually expanded my role as an educator and as an organizational psychologist. I have added a depth and a complexity to my work which I had always hoped I could have—a dimension my intellect thirsted for, but which self-doubt made me believe could not be mine.

Paradoxically, I have also simplified my life. I have relocated to a quiet rural community where I had wanted to live. I am working on projects and with people that hold keen creative interest for me. All my material needs are met. I did what I loved, and the money did follow.

But in this regard I am not unique. Countless others have discovered the validity of the do-what-you-love premise. Over the years, I have met hundreds of people whose example and experience serve as added proof (and as inspiration) that it is possible to do work that is intrinsically fulfilling and also be able to pay the bills!

Do What You Love, The Money Will Follow is my acknowledgement to all people who do the work they really enjoy. It is also a handbook that hopefully will show readers "how" to follow their own hearts to the work of their dreams. And more: it is at its core a comment about the spiritual aspects of work—a book that suggests people can fulfill themselves as authentic, unique human beings through doing their right livelihoods. This book says that work, love, "play" and—ultimately—even devotion are unified into a cohesive activity for the fully developed, self-actualizing personality.

This final, larger dimension of the book stretches the psychology of work beyond mundane understandings of vocational theory into a developmental commentary about work. Work can be used, as can anything and everything we do, to communicate our love for self-and-other. For the rare person who is religiously or spiritually inclined, work even becomes a vehicle for devotion, a way of utilizing one's gifts and talents to serve others, a way of truthful self-expression. I suppose this deeper message categorizes

Do What You Love as a text in spiritual psychology, but I believe anyone can utilize the principles outlined herein for his or her own growth and development.

A word more about my background may be in order. A few years ago, as I began to say in the opening paragraphs, I was a public school teacher. For five or six years I taught all levels of students: primary, middle and even college level classes. Then for another five years I served as a public school principal. This soon became a demonstration school for the county in progressive educational programs. For another two years I was a "curriculum consultant," and a mediator/liaison agent for public school districts and the state board of education. I mention my educator's background so that readers can get a sense of the tradition and professional ethic of my own vocation. These early professional years were spent working for a public school district in California, and, simultaneously, for six years, teaching and designing management development programs for Loyola University's Industrial Relations Center in Los Angeles. At no time until my relationship with Loyola University did I have any business training. Despite this apparent lack in business background, I have been unusually successful in the private sector.

Today, I head my own small, vigorously healthy, private practice in organizational psychology, mediation and corporate "change-management." The problems I solve are in the management/leadership domain. I am privileged to work with, and advise, some of America's top corporate executives. These men and women are among the brightest, most ethical and creative people in the country.

Even though, prior to starting my own firm, I had no previous industrial experience, no business connections, no "right" to imagine that I had something to offer Harvard, Stanford, and Yale graduates—to name but a few of the superior universities from which my clients have graduated—growing into this advisory role has been as natural for me as breathing.

Perhaps I dared imagine having something to offer industry's leadership because I felt uniquely qualified for my work. My qualifications are not born of schooling, degrees or the right "political" or business connections, but of natural, intuitional talent. It was this talent which I believe urged me to leave the familiar, and this sort of talent which most people can locate within themselves. Advanced training and experience are important of course, but we should not put the cart before the horse. My own experience in adjusting my professional course in mid-stream to that of a more expanded, sophisticated and complex one, and the experience of hundreds of my own clients and interview subjects who have successfully revised their careers provides the foundation for the guidance I offer in *Do What You Love*. This book presents our stories—stories I have been gathering with increasing momentum over the last decade. It also presents a good deal of solid psychological background material about what is required to know and do one's right livelihood. Additionally, the benefits of such work are detailed at length.

Readers will be able to reflect upon their own situations and apply the principles of right livelihood to their own lives. They will recognize case illustrations of people like themselves. They will identify with people who worried about paying bills or pleasing parents, spouses or other authority figures, or with those who felt they were too old, too inexperienced or too undeserving to identify and do fulfilling work.

The case examples I use are not of persons who, by some magical fluke of fate, just closed their eyes to the necessities and demands of the real world. These are not people who woke up one day to find themselves rolling in a "fun job" and money. I am not suggesting that such outcomes are likely or even the most desirable. Nor am I suggesting in any way that doing what one loves means doing what one *feels* like doing.

In some cases, people who embarked upon finding, and doing, work they loved are still waiting for the money to follow. This is the case of one of my oldest friends who, years ago, decided to become an actress. She is still hard at work: studying, working at bit parts and off-Broadway roles, to make that dream a reality. Thus I maintain that hard, patient, disciplined long-term effort is required to do one's right livelihood.

Others I know are still in school. In some cases, an investment in tedious, often boring graduate or advanced studies may be necessary. Others hold down two jobs, as in the case of a woman I know who wants to be an artist, but who is not good enough yet to profitably sell her work. First she must paint, experiment, paint more, learn what works for her. This period will, for her, take years. Consequently, she works at another job, full time, while she spends all weekend time, almost every evening, painting. I write of this so that, at the outset, no one thinks I am suggesting that material rewards immediately flow out of the leap-of-faith which is made to do one's right livelihood. The reason that this book's title contains the phrase, "The Money Will Follow," is precisely because we must do the work first, invest of ourselves first, seed faithfully in the small, steady, incremental ways of our chosen work first, and then—as a harvest of abundant crops naturally follows the seeding, watering and constant caring process, of seeds—the fruits of our efforts result.

While the people I describe in these pages are working away at their chosen vocations, simultaneously they are growing successfully as human beings. And this is the beauty of right livelihood. As people honor the actions they value most—by *doing* them—they become more authentic, more reliable, more self-disciplined. They grow to trust themselves more; they learn to listen to their own inner voice as a steady, truthful and strengthening guide for what to do next and even how to do it. The example of such individuals points the way for like-minded others to plan their growth steps, as that growth specifically relates to their own life's work.

The examples I have used throughout this book are realistic; sometimes they "only" teach us how to be patient and endure. At other times, because of a specific success or enthusiasm expressed, the examples serve to inspire. The following pages contain stories, and a continual psychological narrative, about what it takes to build inner confidence, and self-esteem, and about how to listen to one's own self and hear one's own inner voice over the din and clatter of experts, society's expectations and media-hype. It is this inner listening that is necessary if one wants to follow "the way of the heart" to the work that is most enjoyable, most fulfilling.

Readers will survey what right livelihood is and how it leads people to personal health and personal development. They will examine what I call "The Big R"—resistance—in order to see how this phenomenon blocks energy and enthusiasm, robs them of satisfaction and reward. They will explore the subject of money and see how it relates to feelings of high self-worth—feelings which are so necessary to making life what we want it to be, as well as necessary to earning a decent salary or fee for our efforts. Readers will come to understand how increased self-trust and high self-esteem leads to increased material success, and, at the very least, to self-respect. They will read that high self-esteem only comes from confronting and handling life's challenges—not from taking an easy, contracted life position.

Additionally, readers will learn how to maximize their own resources while waiting for the money "to follow." They will discover how to prepare for the unknown and unexpected, how to enjoy whatever it is they must do until their goals are realized. Hopefully, they will realize that doing what they love provides rich inner rewards that include money but which also transcend money.

Finally, perhaps most importantly, *Do What You Love* reveals a well-kept secret: that there are hundreds of thousands of people who have overcome both internal and external obstacles to become successful doing work they love. If people can cultivate self-respect and inner security and develop a commitment to their own talents, they can earn as much money as they need, or want. This is true success, and this book describes what it takes to achieve it and even what it means to go beyond the goal of money to the goal of authentic self-expression, self-trust and actualization.

The task is easier than people imagine. All it takes is everything they have to give: all their talent, energy, focus, commitment and all their love. The rewards are worth it and are evident the minute one consciously chooses on behalf of his or her own values, inclinations and vision.

1

The Psychology of Right Livelihood

I'm looking for something more than money out of my work. I expect deep fulfillment and a little fun too.

Executive, Major U.S. Corporation

Work I disliked the most was work I wasn't suited for. Once, for example, I sold vacuum cleaners door to door. Now there's nothing wrong with that job, except I was painfully shy and basically introverted, and knocking on doors in strange neighborhoods was, for me, an unnatural act. But I was working my way through college and in desperate need of tuition money, so I silenced my fears and told myself I could do it. The money was good, and that somehow made it all right. The only catch was my heart wasn't in it. I lasted one day.

Looking back on that experience and others depressingly like it, I realized that I am not cut out for some occupations. I have a specific disposition and a given set of aptitudes that require an equally specific type of work. I know now that work needs to fit my personality just as shoes need to fit my feet. Otherwise I'm destined for discomfort. As an organizational psychologist and educator, I have come to believe that this is true for everyone. Our right work is just as important to personality health and growth as the right nutrients are for our bodies.

Almost any job has its benefits. "At least I don't have to take it home with me," "It's only five minutes away," "It pays the bills," are some of the advantages people identify in their otherwise uninteresting, tedious, or unrewarding work. Moreover, even in situations not particularly suited to them,

7

people are able to develop new abilities. A shy person can learn to be more socially comfortable by selling vacuum cleaners, cars, or Tupperware. An extrovert can learn to work in solitary, focused settings. A technical specialist can become a good manager of people. Clearly we can see that people do grow through "staying the course," through facing difficulty, through self-discipline, through toughening their resolve and perseverance.

Yet, even though we are all fairly adaptable, elastic, and multi-dimensional, we are not born to struggle through life. We are meant to work in ways that suit us, drawing on our natural talents and abilities as a way to express ourselves and contribute to others. This work, when we find it and do it—even if only as a hobby at first—is a key to our true happiness and self-expression.

Most of us think about our jobs or our careers as a means to fulfill responsibilities to families and creditors, to gain more material comforts, and to achieve status and recognition. But we pay a high price for this kind of thinking. A recent national poll revealed that ninety-five percent of America's working population do not enjoy the work they do! This is a profoundly tragic statistic considering that work consumes so much time in our lives. In a few brief decades, our working life adds up to be life itself.

Such a nose-to-the-grindstone attitude is not even a good formula for success. When you study people who are successful, as I have over the years, it is abundantly clear that their achievements are directly related to the enjoyment they derive from their work. They enjoy it in large part because they are good at it. A bright client of mine once told me, "I'm at my best when I'm using my brain. My ideal day is when my boss gives me lots of complex problems to solve." Another client remarked, "I like people, and when I'm involved with them, time just flies by. Since I've been in sales, I find everyone I meet interesting and fun to talk to. I should be paying my company for letting me do this work."

Right Livelihood is an idea about work which is linked to the natural order of things. It is doing our best at what we do best. The rewards that follow are inevitable and manifold. There is no way we can fail. Biology points out the logic of Right Livelihood.

Every species in the natural world has a place and function that is specifically suited to its capabilities. This is true for people too. Some of us are uniquely equipped for physical work, athletics, or dance; some of us have special intellectual gifts that make possible abstract or inventive thinking; some of us have aesthetic abilities and eye-hand coordination that enable us to paint, sculpt, or design. Examples are numerous of nature's way of directing us to the path that will support us economically and emotionally; this is the path that we were meant to travel.

Any talent that we are born with eventually surfaces as a need. Current research on child prodigies—youngsters who, from an early age, are mathematical wizards, virtuoso musicians, brilliant performers—tells us that they possess a burning desire to express themselves, to use their unique gifts. In a similar fashion, each of us, no matter how ordinary we consider our talents, wants and needs to use them. Right Livelihood is the natural expression of this need. Yet, many of us cannot imagine that what we enjoy doing, what we have talent for, could be a source of income for us or even a catalyst for transforming our relationship to work. But, indeed, it can be. Leaders in every walk of life (e.g. housewives, crafts persons, entrepreneurs, inventors, community volunteers, etc.) who have the drive, skill and compelling vision to advance their ideas, despite obstacles, need to exert their influence as much as their solutions, energy and enthusiasm are needed by others.

The original concept of Right Livelihood apparently comes from the teachings of Buddha, who described it as work consciously chosen, done with full awareness and care, and leading to enlightenment. I do not advocate saffron robes and vows of poverty, but I am keenly aware of the wisdom contained in the Buddha's concept. For many people today, alienated from both their talents and their labors, his injunction is food for considerable thought. We must begin to think about ourselves and our work in a larger sense than mere nine-to-five penance for our daily bread. However, this larger concept of work carries with it increased demands, demands not everyone is willing to meet.

Right Livelihood, in both its ancient and its contemporary sense, embodies self-expression, commitment, mindfulness, and

conscious choice. Finding and doing work of this sort is
predicated upon high self-esteem and self-trust, since only those
who like themselves, who subjectively feel they are trustworthy
and deserving, dare to choose on behalf of what is right and true
for them. When the powerful quality of conscious choice is
present in our work, we can be enormously productive. When we
consciously choose to do work we enjoy, not only can we get
things done, we can get them done well and be intrinsically
rewarded for our effort. Money and security cease to be our only
payments. Let me discuss each of these qualities to illustrate my
point.

Conscious Choice

The very best way to relate to our work is to choose it. Right
Livelihood is predicated upon conscious choice. Unfortunately,
since we learn early to act on what others say, value, and expect,
we often find ourselves a long way down the wrong road before
realizing we did not actually choose our work. Turning our lives
around is usually the beginning of maturity since it means
correcting choices made unconsciously, without deliberation or
thought.

The ability to choose our work is no small matter. It takes
courage to act on what we value and to willingly accept the
consequences of our choices. Being able to choose means not
allowing fear to inhibit or control us, even though our choices
may require us to act against our fears or against the wishes of
those we love and admire. Choosing sometimes forces us to leave
secure and familiar arrangements. Because I work with many
people who are poised on the brink of such choices, I have come
to respect the courage it takes even to examine work and life
options honestly. Many pay lip-service to this process; to do
something about the truths we discover in life is no easy matter.
However, more people live honest lives than we might imagine.

One young woman told me she had grown unusually
depressed about her career in finance, one for which she had
been preparing herself since high school. "Lately I've lost interest
in what I'm doing. I'm living more for the weekends; on Sunday

nights, I find myself dreading Monday mornings. Maybe I'm bored and need more responsibility." Yet, when her boss suggested she return to graduate school for an MBA, she began to feel even worse: what she found in herself was a host of conflicting desires.

After scrutinizing her enjoyments, motivations and values she admitted, "When I first started talking with you I thought I wanted to climb the corporate ladder. But I've come to realize that the idea of starting back to graduate school doesn't appeal to me at all. This is the first time I've been willing to see that.

"I realize I haven't been truthful with myself. What I really want is more flexibility with my time—not less. I dearly want to have children and to be a mother. I've entertained the graduate school goal so as to please other people.

"My boss—even my parents—would like to see me become a financial whiz. I know I have the capacity to be good in finance, and I guess I look like their image of the corporate brain who makes good. But I also know I have a great interest in raising a family, in being a good wife and mother, in trying my hand at some sort of crafts. That is what would really be satisfying to me at this time—not business."

She discussed her decision with her parents, and with her boss, and they were highly critical. But she was willing to pay the price of their possible rejection in order to stick to her choice. "I feel more together than I have in a long time," she told me later. "I feel an inner confidence that tells me things will work out just fine."

A Spanish proverb teaches, "God says, 'Choose what you will and pay for it.' " And so it is that as we weigh the yes/no possibilities of our choices, we learn more about our strengths and weaknesses and become more willing and able to pay the price of each choice. By *choosing* we learn to be responsible. By paying the price of our choices we learn to make better choices. Each choice we make consciously adds positively to our sense of ourselves and makes us trust ourselves more because we learn how to live up to our own inner standards and goals.

. But the reverse is also true: When we unconsciously drift through life, we cultivate self-doubt, apathy, passivity, and poor judgment. By struggling, by facing the difficulties of making conscious choices, we grow stronger, more capable, and more responsible to ourselves. Once we see and accept that our talents are also our blueprint for a satisfying vocational life, then we can stop looking to others for approval and direction. Choosing consciously also forces us to stop postponing a commitment. In this way we move one step closer to being responsible, contributing adults.

Choosing our work allows us to enter into that work willingly, enthusiastically, and mindfully. Whatever our work is, whether we love it or not, we can choose to do it well, to be with it—moment to moment—to combat the temptation to back away from being fully present. As we practice this art and attitude, we also grow more capable of enjoying work itself!

Work Is a Way of Being

As a way of working and as a way of thinking about work, Right Livelihood embodies its own psychology—a psychology of a person moving toward the fullest participation in life, a person growing in self-awareness, trust and high self-esteem.

Abraham Maslow, foremost to study and describe such healthy personalities, calls them "self-actualizing." The phrase simply means growing whole. These are people who have taken the moment-to-moment risks to insure that their entire lives become an outward expression of their true inner selves. They have a sense of their own worth and are likely to experiment, to be creative, to ask for what they want and need. Their high self-esteem and subsequent risk-taking/creativity brings them a host of competencies that are indispensable to locating work they want. They also develop the tenacity and optimism which allows them to stick with their choices until the financial rewards come. They are life affirming. For them, work is a way of being, an expression of love.

A friend of mine is a furniture maker—a true craftsman and artist. Of his work he says, "I get great satisfaction from making fine furniture—the process enriches me, makes me feel that I am somehow in each piece." He believes, as I do, that part of the unique beauty of a lovely, hand-made piece comes from its being part of the spirit that is brought to it during its making. He nourishes his creations with his care and attention, and his work, in turn, nourishes him.

Self-actualizing persons follow the often slow and difficult path of self-discipline, perseverance, and integrity. No less is required of those of us who yearn to trade in our jobs or careers for our Right Livelihoods—work that suits our temperaments and capabilities, work that we love.

Self-Expression

Work is a natural vehicle for self-expression because we spend most of our time in its thrall. It simply makes no sense to turn off our personality, squelch our real abilities, forget our need for stimulation and personal growth forty hours out of every week. Work can be a means of allowing the varied and complex aspects of our personality to act on our behalf, translating our attitudes, feelings, and perceptions into meaningful productivity.

It may help to think of yourself as an artist whose work is obviously a form of self-expression. His first efforts may appear to be experimental, scattered, bland, or indistinct. But as he applies and disciplines himself, as he hones his skills and comes to know himself, his paintings become a signature of the inner man. In time, each canvas speaks of the artist's world view, his conscious and subconscious images, and his values. He can be understood through his works, almost as if he had written an autobiography.

Though the medium may be different, physicians, carpenters, salespersons, bicycle repairmen, anyone who uses his work as a means of self-expression, will gain the satisfaction of growth and self-understanding, and will single himself out from the crowd. Even entrepreneurs, who comprise a large part of my client base, tell me that there is "something within" which finds outer expression through their businesses. This expression allows their ventures to thrive. The remarkable thing about such self-expression, they say, is that it breeds confidence—both in themselves and in their customers and employees, who quickly recognize someone whom they can count on.

Commitment

When we are pursuing our Right Livelihood, even the most difficult and demanding aspects of our work will not sway us from our course. When others say "Don't work so hard" or "Don't you ever take a break?" we will respond in bewilderment. What others may see as duty, pressure, or tedium we perceive as a kind of pleasure. Commitment is easy when our work is our Right Livelihood. As social activist and former Secretary of Health, Education, and Welfare John Gardner once said, the best kept secret is that people want to work hard on behalf of something they feel is meaningful, something they believe in.

I met with a young man last year who had drifted into a far from satisfying, but lucrative computer career. After much inner struggle he decided to leave his secure niche to return to school and study psychology. Recently, I received a letter from him and a copy of a straight-A transcript of his first semester courses. He was elated about his grades, but was having a hard time making ends meet, a condition he had never before encountered. Yet his certainty that he had found the right path for his life allowed him to excel and also gave him the power to respond resourcefully to the trials his new choice presented. He used his former skills and contacts to find part-time work and eventually decided to take a semester off to earn the lion's share of his tuition. "Once upon a time I would have quit when the going got rough," he reflected, "but now I'm eager to do what I must to stick to my choice." Because he is committed to his choice, he has gained a new level of vitality which fuels his ability to see it through to completion.

Successful people not only have goals, they have goals that are meaningful for them. They know where they are going and they enjoy the trek. Like this young man, when we are excited about what we are doing, when we are progressively moving toward the realization of meaningful goals, the difficulties become solvable problems, not insurmountable obstacles. I know that nothing will stop him from becoming a psychologist, and he will probably be a fine one at that. I knew it when he wrote in his recent letter, "The courses have been difficult and challenging, but I feel at home in this work and I am experiencing great joy for the first time in my life."

Mindfulness

If we think of what we do every day as only a job, or even as only a career, we may fail to use it fully for our own development and enrichment. When we are bored, frustrated, constrained, or dulled by what we do all day, we don't take advantage of the opportunities it offers. Moreover, we don't even see opportunities. The kind of relationship to work that is manifested in drifting attention, clock watching, and wishing to be elsewhere also robs us of energy and satisfaction.

In contrast, anyone who has ever experienced active, concentrated attention knows the truth of the statement by well-known Quaker writer Douglas Steere: "Work without contemplation is never enough." You may have played a game of bridge, read a book, gardened, pieced together a ship in a bottle. Afterward, you realized that you had lost track of the passage of time and forgotten your cares.

A friend's experience of a tennis game illustrates the power inherent in mindfulness during work: "It was a slow-motion game—everything lost its ordinary quality, everything seemed more vivid. I could almost see the threads on the tennis ball, that's how fully I was in the moment. I was entirely free of caring whether I won or lost. I played without my usual ego and emotion. I just played with total attention and my game was unsurpassed. More than that, I felt completely happy and fulfilled."

What can be achieved in such momentary pursuits is the result of a quality of mind—a mind fully absorbed in its task, in the present—that can be available to us daily when we are working at our Right Livelihood. Absorption is the key to mindfulness, the deep involvement in the work itself and the way in which each task is performed. Mindfulness puts us in a constant present, releasing us from the clatter of distracting thoughts so that our energy, creativity, and productivity are undiluted. You become your most effective. Attention is power, and those who work in a state of mindful awareness bring an almost supernatural power to what they do.

If you are asking, "How can I do what I love when I'm afraid . . . when I'm uncertain of the outcome . . . when I have to make ends meet . . . when I don't even know what I love to do?" read on. You, too, can find your Right Livelihood, and when you do, it will enable you to pay the bills and will richly reward you with a sense of meaningful participation in the one life you have.

2

The Belief System
Called "Myself"

It's too late. I've spent too many years doing exactly what was
expected of me: being a good son, a good husband, a good father. In my company I'm known as a "good soldier." When I
ask myself what I am about, I'd have to say I don't know anymore. I've tried for so long to fit in, I've held back for so long,
I don't know what or who I am.

Middle-Aged Executive,
Multinational Corporation

High self-esteem provides the power to know what and who we
are. It gives us the courage to live out that very personal
knowledge in our daily actions, choices and way of interacting
with the world. Conversely, low self-esteem cripples the ability to
"make waves" on behalf of what we know is right and truthful for
ourselves. In extreme cases, it hides what the individual wants.
In striving to achieve emotional security, acceptance and a sense
of belonging, people who don't think well of themselves violate
their own life and its directives in favor of the wishes and
expectations of others.

People with high self-esteem have many advantages when it
comes to choosing their right livelihoods. Thus, as a first step in
our discussion of this topic, it is helpful to examine the critically
important skills and characteristics that such individuals share:

● They know what they want because they hear themselves, are
able to pay attention to the silent, indwelling push to pursue

one career or life-path over another. In this way they
acknowledge their unique life's purpose.

● They have the sense or feeling that they deserve to have a
life—including work—that makes them happy. They feel
deserving because they have experienced themselves as being
in their own corner, rather than abandoning what they know is
right and fulfilling. They are not weighed down with the
heavy, extraneous baggage of fear, guilt and nameless self-
defeating thought patterns.

● They solve problems creatively and assertively, acting from a
consistent base of self-trust. Their self-statements tell them
that they have what it takes to figure out what to do. They
have learned that they must respond to trouble, and so they
face squarely whatever challenges they meet.

● They are self-disciplined and willing to take time to get what
they want. Not compulsively motivated to have everything
"instantly," people with high self-esteem are willing to pay the
costs of being in charge of their own lives. This means they
behave in consistently disciplined, patient, concentrated ways,
as opposed to hoping that someone will do the difficult chores
for them or rescue them from the tedious, demanding task at
hand. This characteristic further bolsters their self-esteem.

By contrast, those with low self-esteem do not know what
they want out of life. They have lived protected, restricted,
perhaps indulged or abused lives so much that their day-to-day
behaviors are constricted, fear-motivated and timid. The person
with a healthy self-view knows how to fend for himself, in work as
well as in other areas of life. He places great reliance upon
himself in determining the course of his life and in deciding how
to act. Active, creative and enterprising, this individual initiates
more activities directly related to his own life's goals than does
the person with low self-esteem. As a result, his subjective level
of comfort and satisfaction is higher, too.

A young man who fits all the characteristics I have just

described wrote me a letter in connection with this study. In it he described how he found a work that was perfect for him, even though his parents and friends expect him to enter another field. He writes:

> I am a full-time college student, working part-time. But my job has basically changed the course of my life.
>
> I am a student assistant teacher substitute at my university's campus child care center. I am on call Monday through Friday, and have been assigned to all age groups, but mostly I work with the infant/toddler group . . . The main responsibility of the job is to make sure that all the children are taken care of. This includes their supervision, feeding and even diaper-changing. I also have additional supervisory responsibilities. My feelings for this job are difficult for me to put them into words, but here is a try:
>
> First of all, in case you haven't guessed from my "handwriting," I am a male. This has made for some interesting situations. . . . My own reactions to the job were mixed at first, because I had never been around children of this age, and I wasn't sure whether I would be able to get the hang of "all that maternal stuff." After my first few days, however, I was adapting so well and having such a great time I couldn't imagine why I'd been apprehensive.
>
> I find that when I'm working, I become so totally involved that I forget everything else. That has never happened with any other job I've had. I also find that I have "unlimited" energy while I'm working, but as soon as I get home, I discover that I'm exhausted.
>
> I feel that if I weren't getting paid, I'd rather be with the kids than doing anything else.
>
> As I mentioned, this job has helped change my life. . . . I was a rather frustrated, unhappy computer science major for a little over a year. At the beginning of the school year, I knew that I had to change, but I had no idea to what.
>
> In high school people didn't ask me what I was go-

ing to major in, they asked me where I was going to major in computer science. Working with children had never been an option for me. But after discovering that I was good with children, and more importantly that I loved working with them, I was able to plan out—with a career counselor—a basic set of goals, the main one being to graduate with a degree in child development.

This is a typical example of how people who believe in themselves "listen" to themselves about things that count. It also shows how work can liberate energies, emotions and a developmental life-path when one is rightly situated. And it illustrates another related characteristic of the mature personality—a maturity, discussed more in depth in the third part of this book, which has little to do with chronological age—and that is the tendency to experience work as play.

"I cannot imagine not doing this." "I'd pay them to let me do this." "I get so engrossed I don't know where the time goes." These are all attitudes of people who have resolved the work/play split; for them there is no difference between their life's work and a recreational pursuit. In part, this attitude stems from their keen involvement with their work. They also feel this way since their attention is not divided between thoughts of what they are doing and what they would rather be doing. Unlike the bumper sticker, "I'd rather be sailing," which some people put on their cars, these individuals would not rather be doing anything else.

How can it be that some people have so many real and subjective advantages? The answer is found partially in their idea of self—their verdict about their likeability, their competence, their "powerfulness" or ability to handle life. In other words, the answer rests in their self-esteem. People who like themselves allow themselves to succeed in all aspects of life—even in their work.

Self-esteem is, of course, not a static thing, not a black-or-white, concrete issue. It fluctuates and adapts to whatever we happen to be doing or feeling at a given time. On some days and in some situations, we are more confident that we can do what we intend. Sound health, a good night's sleep, familiar surroundings and supportive people all help us feel strong and capable. On other days—for example, after a rough day's work or after a confrontive meeting—we may feel spent, fatigued, perhaps even fearful. As Coach Vince Lombardi said, "Fatigue makes cowards of all of us."

From everyday life experiences, we perhaps know what it means to feel cowardly inside. We probably know how it feels to be courageous and strong too. The point, however, is that when we talk of self-esteem, we are really discussing a person's dominant way of being, his life's posture, his overall tendency with respect to the important issues of personal power, competence and worthwhileness. These clusters of attitudes color everything he does: how he relates to others; whether he feels he has the option to speak up for what is of value to him (despite fears, rejection, criticism, etc.), whether he believes he deserves to live in a fulfilling, personally meaningful way.

Because feelings fluctuate and because we often choose to ignore or act against our feelings, I am not discussing self-esteem as a feeling. Rather it is a *total belief system* that predictably sets up choices and experiences for us and thus continually reinforces itself through our habitual ways of acting. It is our total way of experiencing life, the context or filter through which perceptions are screened. In other words, it is a major belief system that helps shape our reality.

While it is not my purpose in this book to discuss the nature of reality, a few words may be in order about how we "set" our reality—especially since this mindset follows us throughout life (if we do nothing consciously to alter it). The tone, plot and outcomes of our life flow out of this original belief we have about our personal worth, capability and power.

Self-esteem is our earliest self-verdict. It can also be described as a self-judgment. It is our primary idea about that abstraction we call "myself." Formed early in life, perhaps even before birth, our self-judgment becomes our world-view shaper, the mold or context from which other perceptions flow. At birth, we either connect to, or may somehow be rejected by, our mother: a mother whose body, touch and verbal/non-verbal cues become our matrix (or primary connection) with the world. Ultimately this matrix (i.e., our idea about ourselves in relationship to it) becomes our sense of the world.

Added to the shaping influence of this original subjective impression are other cues that we get from significant adults—any adult to whom we repeatedly turn for security, praise, nourishment, guidance and love. We take in the obvious and not-so-obvious messages that adults in our midst give us—their verbal and silent communications, their domination or passivity, their fair and respectful treatment or abuse. We examine the way in which they encourage us to live forceful, self-affirming lives or the way in which they thwart us toward self-abandonment in order to please or protect them.

Do they show us respect? Are they fair or unjust? Do they listen to us when we tell them our needs? How do they act when we ask for what we want? Do they help us solve our problems? Or do they rush in to solve them for us? Do they avoid us, abandon us? Do they die? Are they predictable? Do they enter into a deep, trustworthy relationship with us? How we interpret these messages, and perhaps the messages themselves, quickly form the stuff of our self-opinion. Everything these cues convey helps us create our conception of self, world and other people. Solidly, consistently and "forever" our beliefs are shaped, unless we consciously decide to reinterpret matters in later years.

Ultimately everything experienced is screened through the filter of our self-view. We screen out evidence that contradicts our initial self-opinion and selectively take in evidence that supports it. Our thoughts, choices and attitudes form a relationship with things, others and events. This tapestry weaves in and out of all impressions, experiences, feedback and injunctions, turning out to be the fabric of our very self. What we *think* we are evolves into what we in fact become. Thus, our infant minds are structured both from within ourselves and from without. To understand how deeply our belief system affects our life and how it develops, it may be helpful to examine three key questions that we answer in early childhood. These involve our sense of power, our sense of competence and our sense of worthwhileness.

1. *The Power Question*

As human beings, we must know whether or not we can handle life's difficulties. While still young, we look for evidence that we can survive by our own resources. Children who learn to deal and cope with difficult situations feel they have the wherewithal to tackle life. Those who have not had the opportunity to see what they can do usually lack information about their own power. In extreme cases, they grow up believing they are "helpless." Helplessness and powerfulness are both learned.

Children who survive a rough childhood, for example, often become exemplary adults. Research about such youngsters indicates that about fifteen percent of those who make it through the most taxing, abusive or fearful childhoods become highly able, competent adults. In successfully surmounting the trials of their youth, they develop a powerful, resourceful self-image. It's easy to imagine why they also inspire others and why others like to be around them. They believe they are able because they have seen themselves able in real-life situations.

A friend, a successful business woman, whom I interviewed about this topic, talked about her childhood and her ability to get out of a small, poverty-stricken southern town:

I don't really know what gave me the initial idea that I could make it out of that horrible situation. I had no education, no advantages of any kind. But I recall that as one of nine children I was able to get the attention I needed. As bad as things got, I always knew how to manipulate the situation so that I was taken care of, so that my needs were met. Even when I got attention negatively, I always got my parents to involve themselves with me, with my problems, my concerns. All I knew was that I had the ability to get what I needed—and I needed out.

Another, a man whose schizophrenic mother created havoc at home, reported:

> It was so bad at home, I withdrew into myself. I day-dreamed constantly about how I could make money and leave. I also turned to adults outside of my home who were sane. That's the only way I could feel hopeful. They were the ones who taught me life could be worthwhile and pre-dictable. I found teachers or the parents of friends who were there during the really scary times, such as when I found my mother had cut her wrists and was bleeding all over the bathroom floor. Or, when I would try to talk to her and all she could do was talk out loud to the "voices" in her head. That's when healthy adults saved me.
>
> They counseled me, they encouraged me, they were my role models. With the combination of my own daydreaming and planning, my ideas of what I would do, and the healthy, reliable adults who got me through those years, I felt that I could survive. That sense got me through my first fourteen years. Shortly after, I left home. I've never returned. Nothing later in my life was as diffi-cult as that early chamber of horrors. Surviving that, I knew I could survive anything.

Through positive relationships with adults, through artfully managing the environment so that their needs are met, children who make it through traumatic beginnings learn how to deal with trouble. They do not (perhaps because they cannot) run away from the problem; rather they adapt ingeniously. By doing so they discover their capacity to cope, to solve things if only temporarily, and to be superbly creative.

Their discovery of personal strength is accompanied by feelings of hope and inner confidence. In adulthood they then tap a vast reservoir of resourcefulness, energy and creative skill, because as children they earned the right to believe in these aptitudes.

By contrast, persons with low self-esteem must learn—if they are to grow whole—that they have power, and that they can surmount difficulty. They usually do this in two ways. The first way is by growing more aware—learning something about the dynamics of the issue, by reading, attending lectures, studying and thinking deeply on the subject. The second and perhaps the more important way is by dealing with the very things they find most difficult. At some point, they must face their own difficulties related to goals they may have long ago discarded as impossible or undesirable. They have not seen or experienced themselves as capable of going after even the small things that they've wanted.

A young managerial drop-out sat in my office not long ago, lost and bewildered. Her eyes were dry, no longer able to shed tears for the wasted life she believed she had led and that she considered ending.

> I've always been afraid, always anxious, that I wouldn't be able to do what everyone wanted me to. It happens every time I want to do something—like get a good job, live on my own. I always seem to screw things up, just when I'm on the right track—like doing too much, overdoing things from the start. When I first started college and had to make all A's from the start, I put everything I had into my studies. When I received my first C grade, I was completely deflated. Then my behavior swung to the opposite, and I stopped studying at all. When I knew I should be actively studying, I just watched television or ate or went out with friends. It wasn't the grades that really mattered, just like it isn't the failures now that really matter. What concerns me is that I feel so horrible all the time. You know, inside. I feel like nothing really matters. I even hate to hear myself talk about this to you. But it's all I talk about these days—how unhappy I am. I'm sick of that, and I'm sick of myself.

A closer look at her life reveals she had a dominating, strangulating mother, whose injunctions were, "Be socially acceptable," "Meet the right people," "Be something." These messages carried with them another message: you are not socially acceptable, you are not something in and of yourself. While the other two individuals quoted above had concrete and visible problems against which to fight (e.g., poverty, a mentally confused and sick parent), this woman's early life was, on the surface, more physically comfortable. What she needed to do was extract herself from the belief that she was somehow blemished and helpless in controlling her destiny. In order to do that, she needed to identify the grain of the person she really was, deep within herself, and begin to let that person out in her daily choices and actions.

Because it is unlikely that parents who are themselves strangled by low self-esteem and negative self-worth can love, part of her job was to disentangle herself from her mother's "voice." This turned out to be a long process requiring much therapy. But whether an individual needs or chooses to go to therapy or selects some form of self-ministering, personal power can only be gained by choosing to act on behalf of our own inclinations, potentials and distinction. In this way, by seeing ourselves actively in our own corner, we earn the right to believe in our own power.

2. *The Competency Issue*

Each child also wants to know, "Am I competent?" By this we mean, do we have the capability, perhaps even the brightness and wherewithal, to learn, to solve practical problems, to reach our own solutions?

Children watch to see if significant others "step in" to rescue them during new learnings, or if they are trusted enough to learn how to do something on their own. If successful in meeting the demands of simple, growing-up experiences (such as learning to read, playing a new game, riding a bike, dancing, getting along with bullies and so on), they conclude they are capable people who have what it takes to perform successfully and effectively later in life.

If, however, they watch themselves fail, or if parents, teachers, siblings and peers tell them they are failures, then they carry that message of failure with them into adulthood as well.

A child may decide she is woefully incompetent if her

parents rush in to do things for her time after time. When a parent's attitude is, "Here, let me do this for you; I'll do it quicker and better and I won't mess things up," the child learns something about her own competence, or lack of it. A repeated string of such "let-me-do-it-for-you" dramas carries with it the message, "You are stupid and slow." Whether a parent scowls with displeasure at the child's inability to fight his own fights or talks things over with him while helping him stand up to playground bullies, the child collects data for his mental scrapbook about his competence.

People who are overly dependent on the expectations and directives of authority figures (say, superiors at work or doctors or lawyers) seem to have an inordinate need to be liked by those people. Often they take jobs that are too easy for their innate talents or intelligence, and seem to act out of a belief that they cannot do any better. This frequently is because they do not believe they can do any better.

On the other hand, those who are tough-minded, independent and responsible believe they can master things. They demonstrate their competence in daily performances. Not only does this help their ability to progress in a way that honors their uniqueness, but it also strengthens the belief that they are competent. In other words, they increase their belief in their capabilities as they mature.

3. *The Likeability Issue*

The opinion, "I am a likeable person; people accept me and like to have me around," is also formed early in childhood. We look for evidence that we have significance and worth in the eyes of others. We watch what they (i.e., our parents, teachers, siblings, etc.) do while we are around. When we speak, do they look into our eyes and listen, or are they preoccupied with more important things? Are we disciplined in a way that tells us we are good persons—in spite of our mistakes—and that we are capable of understanding what to do differently next time? Or are we taught that we cannot do anything right? Do others speak to us calmly and openly, communicating that we matter to them? Or do they talk at us, as if we were sheep, telling us what to do and exactly how, as if we hadn't minds of our own to figure things out? Do we sense we have "permission" to speak up for what we want, to know what we want? Or is there a silent, unspoken game being played in which we are supposed to act out the role of Stupid, pretending we don't know the answers to certain questions, pretending we don't want what we do want? All these questions, if answered honestly, help us see how we have come to our own conclusions about our likableness.

These questions and our highly subjective, individual answers determine our level of self-acceptance, our sense of having or not having a rightful place in the scheme of things (which relates importantly to our adult sense of having a place in the world of work), ultimately a place in the world itself.

Those who feel likeable and worthwhile in childhood learn that they can state their honest opinions and needs, that they can think of what their preferences are, that they will not be rejected if they ask for what they want. This is a vastly important lesson and gift. For when people sense they will be rejected if they speak up for what they want and need, they learn to swallow these requests, stuff them down into themselves. Eventually, if they are too timid or if the rebuke they get at speaking up is too severe, they forget what they want—as did the executive whose comments opened this chapter.

I remember when I was a child, I learned well from my European born and bred parents how not to ask. When we visited friends, I was instructed not to ask for a drink of water, not to ask to go to the bathroom, not to accept cookies if they were offered. "Only take one cookie. Just sit there, like a polite, good girl." Readers may identify with my overdeveloped sense of politeness that evolved over time because of such instructions. My thought was that "good girls" didn't speak up. Fortunately, I also learned—in other situations—that it was all right to know what I really wanted. Had this other significant lesson not been learned, identifying my own vocational directions might have been more difficult.

It takes some doing to speak up for what we know is right for ourselves, especially when we are youngsters, living in a family of frowning others who "know" what is right and wrong for us. This is even more true for the child who is naturally timid, or who interprets things, people and events as fearsome or unmanageable. In all fairness to parents, it must be said that children differ in their interpretation of what their parents do and say. Some children take the slightest criticism as a heavy, profound rejection; others are more sturdy. Some are aggressive from birth; even before birth they kick and pound away in their mother's womb. Others are silent, quiet types.

A large part of how we think about ourselves comes from the way we think our parents saw us, or, more precisely, from the way we think they treated us. More than likely it is during this sensitive period that we get our mottos, scripts and maps for our life's choices. We literally ingest the messages we get from our childhood, metabolizing them into words of personal strength and capability, or weakness and ineptitude. Then these ideas, strung out into repetitions reinforced by experience, form the architectural framework for all of our life experiences.

If early messages tell us that we are "okay," then we believe, "I'm pretty good." "I guess I'll have a pretty nice life." "It looks as though I'm going to have fun." On the other hand, if the messages received tell us that we're lacking in some way, we may decide that we're not very likely to have a personal shot at true happiness. We may believe we don't deserve to reach out for the things we want. Thus, we tell ourselves to get used to being on the short end of things, to adjust to dwelling in anxiety or in drab, lusterless experiences—wondering, always wondering, why suffering is so much a part of our life. Or we may believe—as did the woman who managed to leave her poverty-stricken home— that we deserve better. And so we strive for and finally attain it.

The above discussion all leads to one essential point: it is from the business of childhood that our adult working life takes shape. This includes our ability to identify what it is we want to do in life, the happiness we allow ourselves to reach for, the way we solve or avoid problems, our willingness to stand apart from the crowd, our ability to take responsibility for our decisions, and our ability to be responsible for the goals we set. Persons with high self-esteem feel a connectedness to their own inner drives, images and objectives. At the same time, they feel related to others, and their values are typically life-supporting. Indeed, they enhance other people's lives as they enhance their own.

3

Expressing Your
Distinctive Self

What seems different in yourself; that's the rare thing you possess. The one thing that gives each of us his worth, and that's
just what we try to suppress. And we claim to love life.

Andre Gide (from an unknown work)

Before we can express ourselves distinctively through our work
we must take several important steps. These steps combine
synergistically to improve our self-esteem, and in fact people with
high self-esteem seem to have learned them automatically. First,
we must come to know, and accept, our dark side—our "shadow"
as Swiss psychiatrist Carl Jung called it. Along with that, we must
learn to fully accept ourselves as we actually are.

This embracing-of-self has several life enhancing ingredients,
not the least of which is learning to treat ourselves with love.
Truly, we are three people in this process: our own Prodigal Son,
who has misbehaved, especially when he chooses wrongly, yet
who wishes to return to the love, safety and comfort of his home;
the father who accepts him back without questioning, with a
generous loving spirit; and the second son who questions, judges
and opposes this loving welcome. It seems to me that the work of
our adult lives—if we have not learned it in childhood or
adolescence—is to quiet the voice of the "second son." Instead,
we can act out the father's role so as to fully absorb ourselves into
the loving center of our own being and consciousness.

Until we accept ourselves, it is unlikely that our vocational
uniqueness will reveal itself through us, since vocation is nothing

more than a way to live productively and uniquely. We also learn that breaking up of old habits and behavior patterns takes time. We allow ourselves whatever time is necessary to grow and see that entrenched ways of being—however hurtful—do not vanish overnight. So, instead of expecting instant results, we discover that it is healthful to befriend time and work with it. Instead of vainly wishing to be magically transformed, we grow in patience for the needs of our own inner self. In this manner also we grow into the good parent role, as the parable of the Prodigal Son teaches us to do.

Finally, we continually learn to treat ourselves as if we counted in our own eyes. In this way, too, we break our adherence to a conduct code that discounts and negates what we really are, what we really enjoy and value. As we slowly achieve mastery in each of these areas—even turning to a guide or counselor from time to time to help us learn what it is we are to do next—we unloosen our interior knowledge of what we must do with our life. These two steps—becoming familiar with our own learning/growth process and our life's purpose—are intertwined.

1. *Using Our Flaws, Idiosyncrasies and Faults*

People who function effectively in their work know their limits. They use them in the service of their lives, managing to integrate these limitations into the way they work best. Rightly, they have discovered that somehow they must attend to their own physical and psychological makeup, emotional tendencies and concentration patterns, and that these are good helpmates in getting a job done. In fact, a person's combined limitations form a complex of attributes that has meaning beyond anyone's current understanding—even the individual's. This complex is the essence of one's expressive life.

A client of mine is a hall wanderer. By nature restless, he thinks best when strolling around. Because he has come to accept this about himself, others have too. After many years of working with him, colleagues now expect him to walk the halls. Of course, his superior thinking has made millions of dollars for his company, and he has earned the "right" to stroll as much as he wishes.

Another person, a scientist, prefers to work in isolation in a company that values an open door policy. She regularly closes her door at work, even though at first she was soundly criticized for doing so. Stubbornly aware of how she needed to work in order to produce quality results, she stuck to her favored work-style. Others eventually came to accept it.

All of these people have adopted a way of working that harmonizes antagonistic tendencies: the desire to concentrate with the need to walk around, and the desire to fit into a corporation with the need to act out a personal working style.

"Use your faults" was the motto of French songstress Edith Piaf. Perhaps this matter of understanding and using our limitations revolves around just such a slogan. I'm not sure whether the traits I'm discussing here are "limitations," but certainly they can seem to be when measured against the behavior stereotype that others have for our way of being.

For instance, a writer friend of mine and I often discuss our "laziness." Each of us realized years ago that part of our creative process encompassed a period of complete torpor, a sort of resting or idea-incubation. This seems unattractive, even "bad," when looked at on the surface, when compared with how we have been taught to work. The Puritan work ethic of my own upbringing strongly opposes resting during the day. Yet after some creative projects I find that this is what I must do in order to go on to the next project.

My friend laughingly tells of staying in bed all day, watching soap operas on television, while she unconsciously builds up a new storehouse of images and ideas for her next books. "I used to hate seeing myself lie there. It went against all my pictures of what I 'should' be doing and how I 'should' look. In my mind's eye, I felt that I was supposed to be a starched and immaculate vision in white all day, a Betty Crocker of the typewriter, constructively producing neat and clean copy twenty-four hours a day, like perfect cookies from the oven." She gradually realized that if she didn't give herself time out when she needed it, her next project was contrived, forced, never truly original.

I take long drives into the rural countryside where I live, listening to music as I drive. I have always loved barn and church architecture. A couple of days of looking at old, weather-beaten buildings of this type, traveling up and down dusty roads or along the Pacific Coast's rugged Highway One, is for me both a rest, and a symbolic visual journey. It mirrors the subjective, spiritual route that my creative side needs to take as I summon up energy to produce yet another chapter or article.

No other part of our personality reveals our basic temperament, our fundamental way of working, more than does our dark side—the part of ourselves which illogically unfolds at its own time and which has its own requirements. I'm referring to our uncontrollable impulses, the habits we simply can't break; the unacceptable, contradictory tendencies moving us in opposition to the way we intended to go. These are the opposing thrusts that give our life richness and mystery. These impulses, habits and contradictions even supply the dynamic energy that gives our lives distinction and drive. Jung described it this way:

> Conscious and unconscious do not make a whole when one of them is suppressed and injured by the other. If they must contend, let it at least be a fair fight with equal rights on both sides. Both are aspects of life . . . and the chaotic life of the unconscious should be given the chance of having its way too—as much of it as we can stand. This means open conflict and open collaboration at once. That, evidently, is the way human life should be. It is the old game of hammer and anvil: between them the patient iron is forged into an indestructible whole, an "individual" (p. 288).

This attitude does not mean that we continue to harm ourselves, or that we ignore or escalate addictive, self-limiting behaviors. It means that we stop warring against ourselves. We try to take an objective, aerial view of what each behavior is saying about us, what it means in the big-picture of our self's journey unto itself. Here are some helpful questions to use in spotting the potential value of our "bad habits."

● Do you have work-habits which you may have rigidly suppressed in an attempt to conform and be more like others?

- Do you have personality traits which you, like my writer friend and myself, initially struggled against, thought were wrong and tried to change or hide?

- Have you stopped trying to achieve something in some "non-significant" areas of life because you were once told these weren't important enough to warrant attention?

- Is there a "time-out" activity (like sleeping, watching TV, fishing, listening to music, daydreaming, etc.) that gives your work efforts renewed vigor, but which you feel you shouldn't do?

If we can examine ourselves as constructed to express a total creative statement with our life, then our habits, daydreams, fantasy life, values, the dualities of our personality can all be understood and used in the service of this statement. It is not only our words, works and relationships which say something about us as individuals. It is what we are that makes a statement. As such, the controversial aspects of our personality may be adding a needed color, tone or impetus that energizes our movement toward selfhood and the life/creative statement of our very selves.

2. *Self-Acceptance: The Second Reconciliation*

Yet another resolution is needed after, and while, we come to know our limitations and personal "quirks." This is a larger assignment, for it demands that we accept what we see our life is meant to be, regardless if that purpose and essential self "fit" our conscious sense of right living. There are many examples of this: the would-be artist who realizes he hasn't the talent to make a go of his art work and who must create another occupation if he wants to eat; the lawyer who wanted to be a fisherman and discovers that if his life is going to mean anything to him, he will have to give up a lucrative practice for something more humble and "ordinary"; the woman who sees she must choose against having children if she is to live out the truth of her being; the man or woman who realizes that business is not for him or for her, and that only a home and children will give his or her life fulfillment.

Each of us must eventually submit to the meaning and purpose of life as we are destined to live it from within ourselves, even when such submission calls for a sacrifice of unfulfilled potential which may seem to us a personal loss or defeat. We cannot reject ourselves and hope to have high self-esteem or happiness. Yet often—because of the power and influence adults have over our minds and choices early in life—we learn that what we really want is wrong or shameful. This is certainly the case for so many who were taught that they must become "professional" people or gain a certain credentialed standing in the community, but who—deep within themselves—longed for something simpler and less complicated as an occupation. This is also the case with those who inherit their parents' unfulfilled ambitions. If we long for total creative transformation and an authentic life, we may face a crisis in which we come to see ourselves truthfully, and then not really like what we see.

Until we can communicate full self-acceptance, our lives will lack healing. People have a curious and regrettable way of siding against themselves. They align themselves with others' appraisals. A client who dreamed of starting her own business felt that to do so would be too aggressive. She believed that her entrepreneurial instincts were "masculine," and would—if played out with full force and enthusiasm—cut her off from her friends and even limit her chances at marriage. Another person, a well-to-do merchant, feared that if he told his father he didn't want to be a partner in the family business, his father couldn't survive. "I don't want it to be this way. I want to do what my mother and father have expected me to do. The only thing is that I am unable to find any emotional satisfaction in it." Upon further exploration he also realized that he had married the woman of his parents' dreams, and that his whole life up until that time was really an acting-out of his parents' expectations, values and ideas of success.

Another individual clung to the notion that she could only achieve self-worth if she became a corporate vice president. She had worked her way through college and graduate school with the single purpose of one day being successful, which to her meant being a well-paid executive. Somewhere along the line, while struggling to get through graduate school, she had taken a job in a trend-setting restaurant. She found she liked the varied dimensions of the role: she liked cooking, serving people and playing "hostess." She enjoyed decorating the tables and lightly socializing. Yet she believed that owning a restaurant was a social disadvantage. In terms of the status she craved, she felt that it would be beneath her to wait on tables or be a small shopkeeper. Nothing could convince her that having a restaurant could be a way to unlimited financial opportunity, creative expression and pure delight. At this writing, she is in a corporate headquarter's environment; she awaits a promotion to the vice-presidency of her unit, a promotion that may never arrive because she is perceived as overly-brittle, humorless and stressed. My impression is that this woman lost a spontaneous, lovely part of herself when she sided against her real vocational preferences in favor of what her logical, rational self told her was "acceptable."

When we cling stubbornly to outmoded, media, parental, or peer-group inspired ideas of what we "should be," the ultimate effect is that we cast ourselves out of our own house. The fear of what we really are is not only a conscious choice—if we can but become aware of having made it—but also stems from years of suppressing unacceptable elements of ourselves, since vocational preferences are only part of a cluster of preferences which have to be quelled if we force ourselves to embark upon choices that are unnatural to us. For example, the woman who would have liked to own a restaurant also enjoyed having a flexible working environment, where she could wear many functional hats. She likes decorating, making small talk with people she doesn't know; she enjoys music, dressing up and the whole battery of performance-type activities which are a part of the theatrical side of the restaurant business. By contrast, the job she has chosen relegates her to a single floor of a large, somewhat austere corporate office. She can perform most of her day's work by sitting behind a desk in a small colorless office. She has a staff of functional specialists, and she rarely needs to converse with those she doesn't know. The company that she works for is

conservative, and expects executives to dress appropriately, so
any flair that she may have for color, costume, decorating and so
forth must be suppressed. While this is one of the best
corporations in the world to work for if one is naturally suited to
such an environment, it is the kiss of death for those who aren't,
since its standards and corporate culture are so well defined and
cohesive.

Being reconciled to ourselves as we are is a first mark of
personality health. Whatever we see as our "self" must have a
place of dignity in our own hearts and consciousness before we
can become individualized as personalities.

Of course, if we take just the tiniest incremental steps in line
with what we see as our essential values and goals, we will move
healthfully in this direction. But in order to take these little steps
we must pay attention to the way we "speak" to ourselves
mentally, sub-vocally. We have already seen that work-habits that
do not conform to the way we see others working can be a clue to
some larger self-and-life statement. Our habits, vices and
attachments are but a language through which we can more
clearly understand ourselves.

Similarly, if we listen to the way we speak to ourselves when
we make mistakes, we may be able to hear whether or not we are
nurturing or destroying ourselves and our self-esteem.

One man, who was in therapy when I met him during a
business project, admitted that he wept for the boy he had been
when he realized how brutal he had been with himself during his
adult life. "I have held myself to an impossible standard, always
criticizing myself, always striving for a stainless perfection and
holding back any feelings that would have pitted me against
people I felt to be important to my career. When I recently came
across a picture of myself as a teenager and saw how sensitive and
sweet that boy's face was and how tough-skinned and callous the
man has become, I cried bitterly. In a way, I felt that I—the real
me—had died at my own hands."

Many people suffer abuse at their own hands. They feel
ashamed and embarrassed about how they look or what they
need. They keep their true feelings secret because they fear
others will not approve, or because they themselves do not

approve. They blame themselves when others criticize them, or when they haven't measured up to self-imposed standards of perfection that they think they must achieve to be worthwhile. Their self-statements consist of criticisms, fear-provoking warnings and threats. And then they wonder why they feel depressed, tired, and hopeless!

Depression is the single most common complaint of those who seek therapy. It has been described as a national epidemic. Writing about this phenomenon, psychologist Claude Steiner says:

> Therapists who bother to ask their clients why they are depressed will find that most people (except for the few who are couch-broken by previous therapists and have come to disbelieve their own common sense) will say that they are depressed because they have no friends or loving relationships or that their loving relationships are not satisfactory. . . . in most cases of depression it will be found that the person readily sees how her or his depression would be lifted if she or he could get a certain specific kind of stroke from a certain, specific kind of person or persons. Thus, the appropriate strategy for depression is teaching people the procurement of the strokes that they want (p. 271).

While I agree that people need to be taught how to procure the strokes they want (i.e., a stroke is defined as a "unit of human recognition"), I believe it's also essential that people learn how to improve the way they treat themselves. Because this is such an integral part of the do-what-you-love philosophy, our next chapter is devoted to this topic. Suffice it to say at this point that we can't penetrate depression until the individual hears what it is he continually says to himself—until he becomes awake to the sound of his own internal voice. Without understanding how we separate ourselves from our own approval, we cannot make inroads into our healing. Here, in the words of one woman who learned to listen inwardly in order to know how she defeated and discouraged herself at every turn, is the statement of someone learning to accept her Prodigal Son into the fold and safety of her own home (i.e., her own heart).

I now hear myself when I discount myself for whatever it is I'm feeling. I hear myself saying, "Oh, don't feel that way," or "you'll never amount to much," or "you shouldn't want that." All through the day I realize that I discount my most tender emotions, that I take responsibility for other people's anger—thinking in some self-inflated way that I have the power to make them angry instead of realizing that they are grown-ups who are responsible for their own feelings. I'm actively cruel to myself in my own head, and this cruelty sounds to me like the voice of my parents long ago who wanted me to be something more than I was.

What I realize is that I want to turn this cruel voice into something gentler and more loving. So I have started being gentler with myself. When I hear an abusive self-statement, I revise it into something sweeter, more accepting. In my mind's ear, I try to hear how I would sound if I were actually talking to a little, lost child. This way it's easier to produce a bit of compassion and kindness toward myself.

Another way to listen to ourselves is through our dreams. Dreams can help us understand our inner workings, solve life's problems and see what it is our unconscious is working on at the moment. Dreams can point us in the right direction when we are lost and can let us see the emerging self. They let us become familiar with our emerging self through our own images and dream-language.

There are now a number of excellent books about using dreams to become open to ourselves. One helpful text, *Living Your Dreams,* by Gayle Delaney, a noted dream therapist, suggests that, prior to sleep, people ask themselves for the kind of dream they wish to have. They thus actively engage their dreams in solving life's problems. Delaney calls this pre-sleep request "dream incubation," and believes it is the process of eliciting at will the dreams we need to help us know what to do

in daily life. I also recommend a systematic tapping into our
nighttime processes by writing down our dreams whenever they
generate an emotional response, and then reviewing the pattern
of our notes over a period of time.

One woman who had recurring dreams of being stranded in a
high place (e.g., in trees, on top of tall buildings, on ladders, etc.)
saw over time, that she was learning to ask for help. In her early
dream notes, she would wake up (or the dream would end) while
she was still stranded, unable to get down to safety on the
ground. In later dreams, although she often was still stranded,
there was someone around to help her. More importantly, she
was able to ask for help, and whoever was around would always
cheerfully oblige. This independent woman, who had never been
able to ask for anything in daily life, saw through her dreams that
it was easy and permissible to ask and that others enjoyed helping
her. She was learning to connect with the rest of the human race
through her honest admission of her needs and limitations.

Another person, this one a man who was fighting against his
own self-defeating hostility, was angry at himself and everyone
around him. He intimidated friends and business colleagues alike.
He describes his dream:

> I am befriending, patting and even feeding lots of formerly
> unfriendly, vicious dogs, especially one big, black one,
> which after growling at me finally lets me pat its head. To-
> ward the end of my dream the dog and I are playing and I
> wake up with these words in my head, "The thing in us
> that we fear just wants our love."

The sentence he remembered upon waking was a piece of a
poem we had discussed several months earlier. Apparently, he
had been digesting the poem's essence unconsciously, thereby
assimilating it in his mind and understanding, and allowing the
words to help him make welcome a previously rejected part of
himself.

There is no end to the questions we can ask ourselves about
our needs prior to going to sleep—much depends on our ability
to enter into "conversation" with our interior self, and some

people are better than others at this sort of thing. But to fully tap
into the inner, unconscious resources, we must become familiar
with the special, personal, symbolic language of our own mind.
And we must also be open to the language of symbols in general.

I have found that my own dreams take on an individual
stamp. Each one has a unique imagery, but the sum of my
dreams has a recognizable landscape. They all have signs, specific
routes, creatures, and people that I have come to know,
remember and understand. After just a few weeks of notating my
dreams in a structured, systematic way—say, upon arising each
morning, or perhaps even when awakening during the night—this
landscape became very coherent.

Our unconscious creative reality is mysterious, but it is not
incomprehensible. Whether we first turn to dream therapists,
books or other references, it is important to finally "own" our own
symbolism and thus further strengthen our bond-to-self.

Another secret behind self-acceptance is learning to accept
others. A good practical habit to start this would be to notice,
non-judgmentally, what we say mentally when others are foolish,
unkind or deserving of criticism. When we find ourselves
downing others mentally, and especially if we say anything
unkind or negative to them, we should make a point of saying
silently to ourselves, "They are doing the best they can right
now."

Then we must mentally forgive them—and also ourselves—
for having been so judgmental and reactive. This is most difficult
when we are emotionally involved or heavily invested with the
other. A spouse, parent, or sibling can trigger the most profound
negative feelings in us. But, as we forgive them, as we forgive
ourselves for what we feel about and toward them, we heal
ourselves and learn to accept ourselves in the process.

Forgiving ourselves dissolves all kinds of unhealthy
attitudes—about ourselves and about the other. We are released
from brutal, self-downing emotions when we stop criticizing
others. In a very real way, there is no one else "out there," and
our criticism of others often is nothing more than self-criticism:
we cannot accept or tolerate in ourselves what we get angry at in
others. But sometimes our anger is an appropriate emotion. If we

hate ourselves for our own healthy responses, then there is a never ending cycle of suppressing what is helpful to our well-being.

When people insult, threaten or discount us and we don't allow ourselves any angry reactions, thinking that we must be saint-like and sweet all the time, we relegate ourselves to an unnatural, artificial way of being. Better to tell people what we need, feel and want, in a plain-spoken, forthright way, even when we think we "should" be sweet and unruffled, than deny perfectly natural feelings from being expressed. In time, as we accept our own anger, we may indeed find that we are able to take the stupidity or hurtful remarks of others in our stride and turn the other cheek. This more elevated response does arrive in time, but it is unlikely to be a sincere, heartfelt attitude when we pretend to be something we are not.

As we permit ourselves these unacceptable feelings and reactions, it is easier to stop criticizing others for doing something senseless, mean or cowardly. As we catch them in the forbidden or stupid act, it is easy to forgive them. We know how to do it because we have experienced self-forgiveness.

Whatever the other has done, if we can express love back to him or her, we will be the ones who are helped. Sometimes it is helpful for people to say inwardly, "I accept the fact that I do not like what they are doing (or that I don't like what I am doing) and even though I would like to understand, forgive, be patient with them (or with myself) I am not yet able to do that." Or, "I may not like that I'm being critical, cowardly, reactive (and so on) now, but that's where I am in my development, so I accept myself as I am, much as I would accept a child who was not yet fully mature."

If we can be such good parents to ourselves, in time we will become mature, loving individuals who can accept others when they are less than perfect. In other words, we say we accept whatever it is we hear or see ourselves doing, stopping the action if it is something undesirable, but not discounting or downing the person behind the act. Putting it another way, we embrace what we are at the moment (e.g., angry, critical, fearful, jealous, etc.) and make it "O.K." By doing so we practice the role of the generous parent who is fully capable of teaching a child, by example, how to act.

Self-criticism increases our fear and belief that living a blemish-free existence is necessary. The only cure is to help ourselves feel secure within ourselves, so that we eventually come to see that no matter what we do, we will not cast ourselves out of our own hearts. The more demanding and self-critical we are, the more likely it is that we will continue (unconsciously or consciously) to heap bad feelings upon ourselves and suppress parts of ourselves we feel are despicable.

For some, self-acceptance may be the first experience of approval and security they have had. From this unusual form, through it, we can reduce resistance to ourselves, decrease distrust and increase love of self-and-others. It heals our own psyches to put our arms around ourselves, if only figuratively and emotionally, and say to ourselves within our heart-of-hearts that we are all right as human beings even when we are imperfect, even if we regress, or need safety and security. This is a sure route, although an unusually difficult one for some people, to a consecrated feeling toward the self; it is also a sure path toward enhancing self-esteem since nothing can be gained by negative self-judgments. It is one thing to stop our self-defeating actions and habits. This is a very helpful practice and can aid our growth and self-respect.

On the other hand, a sure way to defeat ourselves is to hate ourselves for what we feel and for what we see ourselves doing. A woman I know said that she would not accept the fact that she disliked her mother. She felt she "should" love her mother, take care of her, see her and minister to her—as if she were already a saint, forgetting that at this time in her life she hadn't yet earned saint's status or even emotional maturity. As we talked about her early life, it was clear that her mother had abandoned and emotionally abused her.

She had been rejected at a tender, young age—although this may have been the kindest thing her mother could have done at the time, given the fact that she was incapable of loving her child and that what came most naturally to her as a mother was destructive to the youngster. Still my client was filled with shame for her own feelings, and this kept her stuck in many untenable life situations: she was rigid and critical in social relationships, she had few friends, she drove herself at work and felt like a second class citizen, undeserving of true happiness or success. She believed she had to stay at an unfulfilling job rather than look for another position. She dressed blandly, much more blandly than the interesting person she was, and in all ways seemed to be living through the framework of a self-deprecating, pessimistic world-view.

I suggested she monitor her dreams and keep a notebook recording what her dreams said to her about these feelings. Not long after that, she phoned me and was elated to relate one of her dreams:

> I was gardening outside my house. A young child came by—she was hungry and cold—and I asked her if she wanted me to help her find her mother. She started to cry and said no, she didn't want to go home. I asked her if she wanted to stay with me, and she nodded. She was clinging to me, as if she were afraid, and when I asked if she was afraid to go home, she said she was, indicating that her mother had scared her badly.
>
> My counsel to her was that in order to stop fearing her mother, she would have to forgive herself for being scared. I also told the child that she would forgive her mother more quickly if she did not force herself to go home. I told her she could stay with me, that I would feed her, and that all she had to do was stop hating herself for being scared to go home. Her fear, I told her, was entirely natural and probably was the prudent thing to feel, helping her get the protection she needed.

"I understand," she cried, "why I have been so fearful, so reluctant to return and visit my mother, and why it was perfectly natural to have those feelings as a child, and even now." Seeing herself in the image of a frightened child, and hearing her own nurturing, supportive advice to that child, she was finally able to treat herself more humanely. This was the first time she had treated herself so kindly, since she had not learned such treatment as a child from her own parents.

We can only help ourselves feel safe within ourselves by making it all right to be as we are—even when our actions are not what we think they "should" be. The sooner we accept ourselves, the sooner the detestable actions will cease, because most of these stem from our insecurities and angers.

Our insecurities are also the reason we keep other people at a distance and off-balance. A friend of mine calls this the "accordion syndrome." He says we expand when we feel safe— usually when there is an absence of intimacy in the relationship (as with new acquaintances or friends who aren't too close to us) and we contract when we feel more vulnerable. The insecure person is always proving his or her world-view and self-idea to be *right*. If he has created himself to the image of someone unlikable, then he will act in such a way to assure that this self-idea stays intact.

The best solution for this dilemma is to make sure our insecurities fade so that we can strengthen ourselves from within. Then the helplessness, worthlessness and unlikability will gradually fade as a new idea (i.e., the idea that we are safe, strong, etc.) is born.

It is ironic but true that too often we must take care of ourselves as if we were a frightened child. At some level of our being, of course, that is what we still are. It is pointless to throw a child who is afraid of the water into the deep end of the pool. Much better to work calmly, gently and firmly with that child in the shallow waters until he sees that he won't drown. This more loving manner needs to be exercised within ourselves if we would be whole. Perhaps I am really saying what the German poet Rainer Marie Rilke said so many decades ago when he wrote:

> Perhaps everything terrible is in its deepest being some-
> thing helpless that wants help from us.

Not only does a more supportive, loving attitude toward ourselves help us heal, but also our growth requires that we step away from the crowd, even if it scares us to do so. When we love ourselves as we are, we give ourselves the strength and confidence to move in our own directions, leave the safety of what has been called "the herd," and grow into what we really are.

Growing toward the expression of our true way of being requires mastering a number of new skills—such as experimenting with novel behaviors, attitudes, meeting new people and situations. Brutal force or punitive self-messages in the face of these lessons—during which we tell ourselves "can't" make it, or that we don't know what to do—are bound to recreate habitual avoidance patterns. These self-statements can only do us harm. How much better it would be if we could accept the part of ourselves we see as hesitant or threatened. Like a kind and stable parent talking to a child, we can also tell ourselves that, step by step, little by little, we will learn how to deal with the unknown. How much wiser to accept the part of ourselves we have long felt to be loathsome and by doing so incorporate even this into our consciousness of what we are.

As Jung correctly taught, this shadowy self of questionable courage or virtue is our dark brother, without whom we could not be whole. If we cannot accept this unacceptable, limited, frightened and frightening part of ourselves, there can be no healing in self-esteem. Hence, we will pay a very great price if we continue berating ourselves for having these qualities. It is the very thing in us that we now consciously hate which, were we to accept and embrace it, would make us whole. I have observed great benefit come to those who read the following scriptural passage upon arising every morning, reflecting upon it as they read:

Love is patient, love is kind, and is not jealous; love does not brag, and is not arrogant, does not act unbecomingly. It does not seek its own, is not provoked, does not take into account a wrong suffered, does not rejoice in unrighteousness, but rejoices with the truth, bears all things, believes all things, hopes all things, endures all things. Love never fails (1 Corinthians 13:4–8).

And so it is in this matter of enhancing our own self-esteem: love never fails.

3. *The Pace and Personal Tempo of Our Growth*

Another constellation of issues relating to healthy self-esteem is the pace with which we work at growing. The insecure, neurotic person is often crippled in his or her ability to be patient with self-development. He visualizes grand and flashy progress through many idealized goals. His real desire is to impress others, not to improve the quality, tone and character of his life. He may want people to see how quickly he can move through an ordeal. Or he may want others to be impressed with his total, instantaneous transformation.

This individual wants surface, noticeable changes quickly, an instant "fix," a magic formula for whatever ails him. Perhaps he needs to handle a given problem rapidly because the pain and discomfort is so unbearable that he must avoid the feelings that would surface if he were to take his time and substantively solve the matter. That would mean he would have to face a part of his personality he hasn't seen before; it might mean he would have to deal with the shadowy, hidden, ugly parts of himself. Hurrying to improve is disruptive to the natural growth process of human development. Thus as the person seeks a quick fix, he also circumvents his own growth.

The human way of growing is unique; it has no rules, and can occur in many ways. Sometimes people realize something— for good or bad—instantaneously. They get a flash of insight that changes their lives forever. Sometimes growth is slow and cautious, as it is in the case of the one who knows what he must do to heal and improve, but who isn't ready for many years to act upon that knowledge. I have had clients tell me that they've known for ten or more years that they would take a certain life step, but that they were waiting until they were emotionally able to do that.

Sometimes people experience a mix of both: they receive an insight about how they must change, and then spend years acting out that burst of awareness—years which teach them the importance of steady, disciplined effort or meticulous, careful planning.

Rushed, forced, pre-programmed formulas for growth are unnatural and do not consider individual temperaments, needs and styles of changing. We can't force a child's tooth to grow through its gums; neither can we hurry along a budding flower. Each entity has its own tempo and its own requirements for its labors. Wishing, cajoling or threatening will do no good. To a large extent, our own maturing, improvement and transformation is also an organic, natural process. The very fact that we desire a change is a sure sign that, in time, we can change—especially if we intelligently and responsibly choose to act in ways that honor this new direction.

The inner self requires ample time to pass through each of the steps it must take to assimilate experiences, memories, former irritations or addictions into the not-yet formed behavior. Rushing headlong into some pre-conceived, intellectual notion of what we "should" be not only implies disrespect for the self, but we then wrongly assume to know what we need better than the inner self. Weekend seminars which promise miraculous transformations sometimes encourage this attitude, and I have seen participants try to be charismatic personalities much like these seminars' leaders when in fact they were not that type of person at all. This has led me to wonder if our conscious minds know best what it is we need. Perhaps we can better know our life's direction if we become sensitive to our dreams, slips of the tongue, incomprehensible inner images and intuitional leanings than if we assume an "expert's" idea of what is right is right for us.

Whatever our growth path, if one of our goals is to integrate our personality so that its many sub-selves start to work together as a whole, it surely will take time—and a different amount of time for different people.

When choosing between growth and inner safety, people must select safety—they must secure the ground they stand on before they can take strides into the new ground. Abraham Maslow's example of the child exploring a new environment is my favorite to explain this phenomenon.

Imagine a child desiring to explore a room. At first he clings to his mother as he scans the room with his eyes. After a bit, he tentatively moves away a short distance, always reassuring himself that his mother is nearby. His exploration grows more bold as he becomes more certain that she will stay nearby, ready to comfort and protect him if he needs her. If she were to leave suddenly, he would cease being interested in the excursion and would immediately begin to look for her. He needs his mother more than he needs to explore. The longer she is away, the worse his need for her becomes. He might even regress to an earlier stage of development; he might start crying, suck his thumb or—if she still didn't return—even soil his clothes, returning to an infantile response. His anxiety would produce these reactions, whereas his security (i.e., when mother was nearby) produced growth and curiosity.

Adult growth moves forward in much the same way. Adults cannot be pushed or bullied into their development—not even by themselves. Usually, as with the child, the converse is actually true: the more we try to coerce ourselves into "changing," the more entrenched our habits become. This may at least partially account for the fact that people who try to diet often quickly gain back the weight. It is as if their physical body isn't used to a lesser weight. This may also explain why battered and abused wives continue to stay with their tormentors. Although they consciously want to leave, it may take many years until they are ready to do it. By the same token, the more their emotional and physical safety is assured, the more likely they will have the courage to explore unknowns. In their case the greatest unknown is learning how to be treated well, but each person's unknown territory is uniquely frightening to him.

Just as we must move ahead slowly in our personal growth, we must also not rush ourselves in finding the work we love. First, we can simply ask ourselves what we love to do in a general sense, rather than in a work-related one. Our more gentle conversations with ourselves about the things we love to be, do and have allow us to identify what we love in an investigatory, mental excursion, without ever doing anything about it. We venture in our imaginations, through memory, emotions, the senses, into the potentiality of growth, all the while behaviorally

satisfying our need for safety. Part of this first series of
exploratory images may well include finding role models of people
who are acting in ways we might like to act. We teach ourselves
"how" to be simply by looking, by studying, by watching others,
much as we taught ourselves to walk by observing adults walking
about when we were crawling around as infants.

Next, by taking some small, inconsequential steps in the
direction of what we need and love, we explore the novel
feelings, conditions and consequences of these choices. For
example, a person who wants to become more athletic, but who
has always been sedentary, might first just buy a book about
athletes, or about the benefits of walking. A next step might be to
take frequent strolls around the block, until the novelty of this
new habit wears off. Only as an advanced part of the whole
scheme would he join the YMCA for a physical fitness program,
or attend an aerobics class, or begin to jog regularly. The idea is
to respect his feelings of timidity or anxiety, all the while moving
in the direction which would help his self-esteem.

Another example, and this one of how to structure emotional
growth: A client wanted to leave his wife, but found he simply
could not do so. He had left her years ago, and—upon her
threatening suicide—he had returned only to continue living,
despite therapy, in a toxic, unhappy marriage. During our
conversations he once asked me if it was easier for me to leave
someone, to reject someone, or to be left. I quickly answered that
it was probably easier for me to leave, and that while it was very
painful to know I had hurt someone, I had no real difficulty
leaving first. He immediately answered that he found it almost
impossible to leave first. During that same series of conversations
I noticed that he always waited for me to say that our time was
up, that he never started to close the conversation first even
though he might feel a sense of completion before I did. I asked
him if, in social situations, he waited for others to get up and
leave first, and he said that he probably did. Thinking about his
primary need—to get the courage to leave a toxic relationship—I
suggested that, in social situations, he start leaving first, that in
this simple, low-risk way he would symbolically be teaching
himself what it was like to "reject" another not because he didn't

like that person but because he had a need to leave. This is the type of small, yet related, choice that I believe helps us to increase our self-esteem. These small steps are practical and instructive and move us in the direction we truly need and want to go. Yet they are so seemingly innocent that, on the surface at least, we have very little to lose by taking them. Beneath the surface, however, these actions are tremendously powerful as they are symbolic—indications that a new self-idea is taking hold. In time (and it may require a great deal of time) we become strong enough to take the larger steps that will insure our happiness.

The more we respect our own pace, the more likely it is that we will be far less dependent on structuring safety into our developmental program. In other words, we grow to be capable of taking larger steps more easily. We will trust ourselves to "know" what we really want, need, are capable of doing and so on. It is also likely that we will be far less dependent upon outside critics whose opinions we used to seek out before starting a new venture. This dependence, at some level of our being, breeds hostility (i.e., against the other, if not ultimately against ourselves). The source, tempo and measure of our actions will increasingly be an internal one. This, of course, is the beginning of real freedom.

Self-acceptance does not come about in practice overnight. Neither does learning how to be patient with ourselves. But if we have any hope of finding a dream vocation or career, we must be on good terms with our hearts, so that we can discover what it is that our inner-man of the heart (to use St. Peter's term) wants to do. For this, patience and self-acceptance are required.

A way to begin grappling with this often complex, lifelong set of issues is to take an uninterrupted period of quiet time to do some reflecting.

With pen and notebook handy, we can periodically take stock of our true life's purpose.

Ask yourself:

1. What is my real life's purpose? (What do I want to have accomplished when I look back upon my life in old age?)

2. How, specifically, would I have to think, speak and act in order to bring that purpose into being? (What habits would I need to cultivate and what would I have to delete from my present life to live out my true purpose?)

3. What activities—what actual daily choices, attitudes and concrete accomplishments—would I do if I lived as if my purpose meant something to me?

4. How would I live, on a day to day basis, if I respected myself, others, my life's purpose?

Work is integral to the whole tapestry of our lives. If we have no happiness or joy within ourselves how can there be any at work? "The world is as we are" is the old Hindu saying. As we enhance our self-esteem, so we enhance our working lives.

4

Treating Yourself
As If You Count

It's amazing that I have not given thought to rewarding myself
before. The usual "reward" I give myself is something I don't
really want—like having another drink or going out with people I have absolutely nothing in common with. Those are
really punishments, yet I tell myself they are treats.

Workshop Participant

Certain long-standing habits may inhibit our self-esteem and our
ability to be distinctive. In an overactive bid for security,
approval, comfort or belonging, people learn to "reward"
themselves in self-defeating ways. One person goes on spending
sprees whenever things are going well. Another eats too much if
he's tired, bored or depressed. A third rewards herself by staying
out late at night, even though it means she cannot function in the
morning. The list is endless. Clearly these "rewards" are not the
activities which promote high self-esteem, but are designed to
further injure an already damaged psyche.

To reward means to repay or give a prize for good conduct or
merit. But each of these activities, and others like them, actually
inflict punishment on the person doing it. The one who goes on a
spending spree ends up in debt; the next few months are spent
paying off credit card bills. The person who overeats hates himself
in the morning when his clothes don't fit or when he steps on the
scale and sees he has gained back the weight he has been trying
so hard to lose. The woman who stays out late feels tired and
listless the next day, even though she had wanted to be alert to

perform well at the office. Turning these habits around can be difficult, because we have grown so used to thinking of these acts as "rewards."

Habits are hard to break. Certainly a first step is to identify what we do to thwart and limit ourselves, instead of rewarding ourselves as we had intended. A next step is to start another habit—the habit of treating ourselves as if we count, by doing the things that enhance our dignity, daily intentions and most cherished values.

Treating ourselves well is a step that can rapidly build self-esteem. Research studies show that people who have high self-esteem regularly reward themselves in tangible and intangible ways. Their tangible rewards consist of concrete items they enjoy—e.g., purchases, activities, "time-off" for vacations. Their intangible rewards may be in the form of self-statements that say they have done the best they could, or that they are happy with themselves. More importantly, their rewards carry with them messages, both symbolic and actual, that say they are worthwhile, that they deserve good things, and that they have succeeded in their own eyes. By documenting and celebrating their successes, they insure that these successes will reoccur.

The individual who fails to reward himself usually backs away from saying and doing what intuitively feels right. More specifically, he may choose the wrong friends or select the wrong job—perhaps one that is easier than he can handle, or one that is in the wrong field. He may give in to the pressures of other people's thinking, especially those in authority (like parents, teachers, lawyers or other "experts") or tell himself he "should" feel one way when in fact he feels another. The sum of these behaviors and choices is that he does not do the things that would convey to him that he is worthwhile. Sometimes, as we will see, he may not even be able to identify what it is he really wants to do.

This individual usually will not identify what he really wants because he is aiming for what he thinks is possible, rather than for what he genuinely desires. Thus, he limits his goal-setting. If he wants to be a contractor, let's say, he may feel he cannot achieve that goal, and will settle for being a carpenter instead. He might secretly long to ask out one type of woman, but will settle for another. Similarly, in the lesser areas of his life, he can easily talk himself out of products he would like to have, art work he wants to purchase, or friends or hobbies that could fill his leisure time with pleasure and enrichment. "This is not the way I'm 'supposed' to act," he may tell himself. Or, "Why would I want to buy (or: be, do, have, experience) that when others do not seem to?" Since his habit is to withdraw from saying and doing what is organically correct for him, it is easier to lower his standards than stick up for what he knows he needs to do. This self-defeating pattern starts in childhood, and can be hard to break or even identify. The practice of assuming authority figures know best what one needs, for example, is a mark of someone whose self-esteem is vulnerable. In this case, parents, teachers, and the opinions of others will matter more than they should. By contrast, when one possesses a strong sense of self, the expectations or prophetic remarks of authority figures are more objectively received.

In this connection, let us examine briefly how a person with high self-esteem might use psychological tests for his own enlightenment rather than—as so many do—submitting mindlessly to the results and predictions of these often misused instruments.

If we examine their typical response, we find that secure, inwardly confident persons use psychological tests for their own objectives, rather than allowing themselves to passively be at the effect of the results of these tests. We see that confident individuals use only the most helpful data, and ignore the rest—this is true even when the individual feels intimidated or insulted by what the test result may say. Its predictive value does not have power over the person's life.

Although in years past the use of psychological testing of one kind or another was in vogue as a way to determine employment, academic potential or college placement, by the end of the 1970's the use of tests had radically decreased in popularity. For one thing, mass produced, mass administered tests were felt to be impersonal, screening out individuality. For another thing, tests missed such aptitudes as creativity or intuitive skills; they reduced the human being to types and to a number on median scales. Also there has grown increasing controversy over such things as the socio-economic bias of most tests: they are written in a language and utilize problem-solving devices for which many persons have no background. A common criticism of academic testing is that it favors the person who has been raised in a standard middle-class, white setting and that it discriminates against minorities who may not have the experiential and language background to do well on these instruments. One consequence of the rising tide of negative feeling about academic testing is that a growing number of colleges are abandoning these as sole determiners of academic success. Despite this trend, many still look to tests and to experts who use tests as a way of gaining clarity about themselves and about their potential.

In the career counseling field, a slightly different issue seems apparent: that no test can identify what is in our hearts to accomplish with our lives. Some tests, like the Myers-Briggs Personality Indicator, are helpful to an individual in providing feedback as to what he or she is best suited for. These are very general, archetypical patterns, and can be taken as but one of many other inputs. The Myers-Briggs is one of the most widely used "tests" in career planning circles, the results usually given only to the person taking it (i.e., not used to determine placement potential or management aptitude). This instrument can give an individual some productive insights as to his dominant way of thinking, solving problems and sorting data.

One educator, responsible for helping his staff know themselves so that they can be more responsive to their students, says Myers-Briggs has been helpful to him and teachers. But another person, a client of mine whose company administered the test as a part of a career-planning workshop, called the test little more than a psychological horoscope. Thus even when it comes to career planning, paper-pencil tests are received differently by different people. This is as it should be since the individual himself must always retain authority over what such data means to his life.

Some career workshops survey personality traits by taking

into account how one is perceived by others. A secretary whose supervisor had undergone an intensive self-awareness seminar, designed to give individuals enhanced interpersonal skills and help them grow as persons, was troubled to find that this nationally-known workshop's approach was to send confidential questionnaires to co-workers and friends of participants so as to determine how the individual was seen by others.

"I want to learn how to be stronger as the person I truly am, not learn to be more sensitive to what other people think of me," this woman said. "That's been the problem women have had anyway. We're much too vulnerable to the cues and feedback we get from others, especially from men. What we need to learn is how to strengthen ourselves from within, not abandon our own perceptions while we pay greater attention to what others think." In her case, she rightly wanted more distance and protection from "what others think." Her supervisor, on the other hand, felt he had been insensitive to the opinions of his staff and so wanted their feedback. Here again, it is the individual who—when he knows himself—knows what he needs by way of feedback and information.

Also, more than a few people have been counseled away from college by well-meaning but misguided and narrow-minded teachers. My own experiences as a classroom teacher, later as a public school principal, horrified me in this regard. At the beginning of each year, even before meeting their students, teachers and administrators alike would pore over cumulative records to see who the "good" and "bad" students were. In this way, they insured having a predisposition toward their charges, putting a ceiling of achievement upon the less able youngsters.

In the upper grades, career and college counseling sessions tended to put students in "boxes" rather than to pursue what they were most interested in. Usually male students, who were more mechanically than intellectually inclined, were directed to vocational schools rather than on to college. No one knows how many would-be engineers and inventors have been steered away from their own potentials in high school career counseling sessions. When aptitude tests are used to reinforce a teacher's biases, the matter becomes even more insulting to human talent.

A friend told me this story about his high school career counseling experience:

> My English teacher in high school was so impressed with my writing skills, penmanship and spelling that she suggested that I consider not going to college. After I got my MBA I was going to look her up and let her know that I had survived without becoming a car mechanic or a carpenter as she suggested. The poor dear had passed away that summer.

Another individual, who had a Ph.D., and was an accomplished, successful entrepreneur, recalled that a physician had advised him that he was not "constitutionally equipped" for accomplishing the goals he had in mind:

> He told me I was too weak, that I would hurt myself physically and die young if I tried to do what I longed to do. He said that my sights were set too high for the body and the mind that I had been born with. While this information concerned me for a short time, I then decided—quite consciously—that I would live my life as I'd intended. If it meant that I would live a shorter life because of my body's limitations, then so be it. What I refused to do was treat myself as an invalid just because I had low energy or some physical weaknesses. All people have something that they can use as an excuse to stop them from living life fully. In the end this doctor's remarks only gave me more determination.

The dilemma is no different for the gifted student who wants to become a craftsman or work in a non-traditional, non-professional setting. Those who would do what they love must listen and march to their own drumbeat.

If the information we get from tests, teachers and other counselors can be used objectively to enrich and clarify our own decision-making process, these can be a helpful assist. In no case should we abandon responsibility for our own choice-making or

give someone else's conception of what we are more weight than
our own sense of self. This principle is not only useful in career
matters, but in all the areas of life as well.

The person with low self-esteem who is aware that he needs
to spend time alone to think, read or sort out personal issues, but
who sees that most other people busy themselves with parties,
social activities or community projects, may talk himself out of
time alone in order to fit in. The woman who doubts herself and
who does not wish to have sexual relations with a man may allow
herself to be "talked into" such relations when he intimidates her
into asking herself, "Why not? Everyone else is doing it. What's
wrong with me?"

"Why?" means justify, and the person who continually asks
himself "Why?" is responding to earlier, parental questioning in
which he had to justify his behavior to some authority figure. For
example, those who are unhappy with their work often ignore any
evidence that they would be better off in another type of job.
They have absorbed the injunctions of a parent, a peer group or
even a corporation about the type of work they "should" be doing.
They will pretend that what is right for them is not, rather than
make waves on behalf of what they really need. On the other
hand, through assertive, self-respecting behaviors, people with
high self-esteem do exactly the opposite. They support their own
happiness, even though in the short term this may be difficult
and problem-provoking for them and their loved ones.

Before being capable of selecting a type of work that fits us,
we have to be persons who behave daily in ways that support and
enhance our lives. Often this means doing the opposite of what
we would think we "should" do or feel like doing. A fitting
exercise for understanding what sort of activities would be true
rewards for ourselves is simply to list the things we *could* do that
would validate and express our most cherished values.

A value is something intangible or tangible that we esteem
highly, like health, truthfulness, beauty, courage, goodness,
playfulness, self-sufficiency, wealth, time to spend as we like and
so on. Some rewards listed by clients and workshop participants
include the following. I have listed possible values in parentheses

to illustrate how our reward activity can point us in the direction of our values.

● To organize my home and garage so that I can find things, so that things look and actually are more manageable, neat and orderly. (Orderliness)

● To spend time giving my baby a bath. I enjoy spending time with him, playing with him and getting to know him, and his bath time is one of the few quiet moments we have together. Instead of working late at the office, I would like to leave on time so that I can have more time for this. If I get home too late, he is already asleep. (Love; parenting; intimacy; playfulness)

● To buy a few pieces of truly fine art instead of squandering my salary on things that do not matter to me. (Beauty; aesthetics)

● To learn how to play the piano. (Music; art; beauty)

● To spend a weekend alone, uninterrupted, so that I can read, work in my garden, listen to music, etc. (Solitude; time to spend as one wants)

● To go hiking more often. (Nature; beauty; silence)

● To take long walks with my child. This is a perfect way to build a closer relationship with her, but I rarely manage to put aside time for it. When I do, I'm filled with satisfaction, love and tenderness—not only for my daughter, but for all of humanity. Somehow the walk softens my attitude, opens up all sorts of "heart places," shows me feelings I didn't know I had. (Parenting; relationship; intimacy; love)

● To balance my checkbook and do all the bookkeeping I've been avoiding. (Order)

As I have tried to indicate above, after they list their favored rewards, I also ask people to go back to their lists to identify what value the reward would enhance. Such things as health, orderliness, beauty and intimacy frequently come up, and people realize with a touch of irony that many of the "rewards" they have been giving themselves are nothing less than negations of the values they really prefer. Their true rewards show them that more self-discipline, self-affirmation and self-assertion are needed to gain control over their lives.

When people realize this and find ways to bring their values into being, they feel more worthwhile. It is as if they raise their self-worth "set point" for themselves, increase their self-respect, raise their expectations for themselves, and lessen the gap between their aspirations and the fulfillment of those aspirations.

Such habits as laziness, smoking, disorganization and other over-indulgences come to be seen as blocks to their creative capacities, their ability to learn new things, their intelligent life-responses, their true success and happiness. Self-discipline, in the form of acting out the rewards they really want, becomes their first step in controlling excesses and self-defeat. But rather than "try" to become more self-disciplined in a variety of unrelated areas (like getting up every day at 4 a.m. in order to exercise, or going on a rigid diet) people find that it is easier to understand discipline in the context of the rewards they want to give themselves.

One computer saleswoman, who habitually drank too much after each successful computer sale, discovered that when she made up her rewards list, what she really longed for was to soak in a bubble bath while listening to her favorite records. By doing this instead of going out with her friends for a drink, she formed a new, more worth-promoting habit. She grew to understand that her old "rewards" were actually punishments designed to stave off negative self-feelings of guilt. Gradually she became more consistent in the helpful, positive rewards she gave herself and thus sent herself more concrete messages that she was valuable and that she deserved good treatment at her own hands. At the same time, she grew in the ability to control her behavior as well.

Ironically, her sales results improved as she increased her feelings of worthiness and self-respect.

Ironically, just this single exercise begins to instill in people an ability to tolerate tension—a tolerance that people with low self-esteem do not usually possess. For example, when frightened by something, persons with low self-esteem want to withdraw and avoid confronting the difficulty. When there is some task that must be done—e.g., one that is demanding and asks them to really apply themselves—they habitually back away. For instance, people who speak up for what they want in the face of conflicting peer group expectations must endure a period when others become rejecting, angry or critical. They must sustain themselves during the tension of these days (or months or years), while continuing to move in the direction they have decided is good for them. They must be strong enough within themselves to persevere and know that, even though others may be critical, they are acceptable in their own estimation.

People who start genuinely rewarding themselves often find that they too must go against the wishes of peers, family or friends. One young man, an auditor for a large company, worked in a regional office whose staff had a tradition of going out together in the evenings during business trips. All the auditors were expected to have dinner together each night—a dinner which lasted late into the evening. My client was a long-time meditator and preferred to take time before dinner to meditate. After this, he preferred to read.

At first he abandoned his own meditation program in order to conform to the expectations of his regional manager, who was single and who used the traveling audit team to accompany him to dinner each evening. Later my client realized that by abandoning his favored way of using his free time, he was letting himself down. In order to return to his preferred behavior, he had to tolerate the resulting tension when he told his manager he wasn't coming to the group dinner—a tension that lasted many months and that threatened to damage his career goals. However, my client realized that his meditation program supported an important personal value—that of self-realization and spiritual growth—and so he stuck to his original intent. In time, his manager came to accept his decision because (as in the case of those with idiosyncratic work habits mentioned in a previous chapter), this man was extremely good at his job.

However, this man's choice illustrates what I call a "high risk" area of confrontation and tension. There are many important low-risk ways in which people can first learn to tolerate the discord that often comes from doing what is best for them. These actually are safer ways to learn how to take risks—because the low-risk way does not directly impact our major relationships or our jobs. Such things as learning a new sport or hobby, using our weekends as we prefer, or gradually speaking up to family or friends about things that matter are some examples of low-risk self-rewards.

Even in these areas, there may be higher and lower risk steps. Perhaps it is easier, at first, to speak up for services one wants at the cleaners or at the gas station than it is to confront a parent or spouse. Perhaps it is more prudent to learn how to say, "No, I'd rather not do that," when talking to acquaintances than when speaking to our families. The first area for learning these new skills should be safe and somewhat inconsequential. The primary objective is to change the "I-don't-count" response mechanism. In time it becomes easier to think, speak and act as if we count because we have gained practice and because we realize we do count! As soon as we believe this, others usually do too.

Also, when people lack self-confidence and self-esteem the challenges of day-to-day life are demanding enough. A "small steps" approach will do. For example, one of the hallmarks of self-defeat and self-loathing is to try to do things in a grand manner and "show others" how great we are. Thus, people with low self-esteem often idealize themselves by seeing themselves achieve in a flashy manner. They are unconsciously setting themselves up for the bad feelings that will come when their behaviors and relationships do not work. Instead of learning the new skill of asking for what they want on a lesser level, they bite off too much and fail. The person who confronts his boss, instead of learning more adroit assertion skills during off-work hours, is a good example of this. He defeats himself in an important high-risk area as yet another way of insuring his low self-idea remains true. By this defeat he can then say to himself, "I knew I was a loser," and avoid seeing that he is responsible for sustaining his poor self-image.

We do not need to exercise self-control over everything at once (such as giving up smoking, going back to graduate school, and ending a toxic, yet major, personal relationship all at the same time). It is more helpful and decidedly more intelligent to strategically plan some small, consistent, coherent steps in line with the new behaviors we want to develop. All that is needed at first is some smaller symbolic gestures that we count in our own eyes, not a huge, overblown manifesto.

Another reason to take small, incremental steps toward more productive rewards is that, at first, some people feel guilty for doing what they really want to do. Guilt is that feeling of culpability or remorse that we feel when we think we have done something wrong. It is a complicated feeling. Some believe it is not a "genuine" emotion, but that it results from holding in anger for so long that it turns against us. Others believe that guilt is helpful as a communication from our own conscience and feel that it can keep us out of trouble when we heed its warnings. Whether it is real or not, guilt certainly manifests itself in our behavior.

Guilt feelings may block our ability to follow through with actions we really want to take. For example, we may feel it is "wrong" to buy ourselves something luxurious that we can easily afford, but that we have been taught is a foolish purchase. Guilt feelings can cause people to experience severe depression after they have been successful in some work or personal project. Chronic bad luck accidents or impoverished social relations can stem from self-imposed guilt. People can distract themselves with hard work all week long so that they do not realize they feel guilt-ridden, and then—on the weekend—they may feel anxious and irritable. They drive themselves all the time in order to avoid their own negative feelings. It is as if the individual's non-conscious self will not allow him to be happy or successful, and continually blocks his true peace of mind. The way Freud described this phenomenon was that the ego does not dare become successful because the strict superego prohibits it. As we will see in a later chapter on our personal injunctions or "shoulds," part of growing up is consciously choosing which actions and attitudes we wish to discard and retain in our life. Often as they mature, people find they must question some of their guilt-feelings as well.

People who stay in underpaying, thankless jobs for years more than they need to admit that they would feel "selfish" leaving their boss to do what they truly want. This attitude may be a throw-back to earlier times when the individual's dominating, sometimes brutalizing, parents were severely unloving, competitive or punitive. The child may have been subjected to ridicule for his creative efforts, or for trying to become independent. A supportive text in this regard (if a person feels that he "cannot" strike out on his own, cannot move in toward a better, more wholesome life) is *Self-Realization and Self-Defeat,* by Dr. Samuel Warner. This is an excellent reference work on the subject of self-defeat and corrosive guilt feelings.

If, however, we are able, but just resistant, then a helpful posture to take is simply to stop *acting* as though what we don't feel (or what we don't want) is what we do want. We need to stop pretending in the least significant areas of life before tackling more significant ones. In this way, we learn how to exert our will in the direction of our values and creativity. The person who, for example, can stop agreeing with opinions of others if their opinions are not ones he really finds himself in concert with moves toward self-respect with each honest statement, however simple it might be.

David Viscott, M.D., whose book *The Language of Feelings* is also very helpful in this regard, offers this valuable advice:

> Your ultimate goal in life is to become your best self. Your immediate goal is to get on the path that will lead you there. Why should you feel guilty if you refuse to be intimidated by [someone] who persists in standing in the way of your being that best self or who is "hurt" when you finally manage it? . . . The highest love a person can have for you is to wish for you to evolve into the best person you can be.

No one owns you, no matter what your relationship. You are not here on this earth to fulfill the unmet dreams of a frustrated parent or to protect another person from facing the reality of himself or the world. You are here to develop and grow, to do your share to make the outside world a better place to live, to make the immediate world in which you live, the world that is you, as honest and as true to your feelings as you possibly can (p. 127).

Thus, before we can liberate ourselves for true vocational fulfillment, we may need to encourage ourselves in smaller, more subtle ways. We must demonstrate a higher standard of decency toward ourselves, exercise more kindness toward others and encourage ourselves in the direction of lesser goals. In all these ways, we will start to feel more worthwhile in our own eyes—and as we begin to communicate that positivity to the world, we will stand out more and more in the process. From these "inconsequential" but powerful actions, we can insure eventual, outer success. But even the tiniest action can be grounds for being rejected if it is an authentic one.

Each time we speak or act in ways that differentiate "us" from "them" (i.e., everyone else, or the idea of our parents that we project onto others with authority) we run the risk of alienating ourselves from others. This can be very frightening for the individual who doesn't have the inner strength to stand apart. Because of the loneliness and despair that results from being an individual (i.e., a unique human being, rather than one of the herd, the crowd, the majority culture), many opt against themselves, annihilating their vocational best-interests as they cling to the safety of belonging.

In this way, they preserve a sense of safety and avoid having to take responsibility for their own selfhood. The quiet person tries to be more outgoing, even though he is by nature reserved. The extrovert attempts to be reflective, even though she prefers an active, lively social life. The man cultivates a "macho" image, although he really would enjoy more feminine pursuits, such as cooking or poetry or tending to the house. The woman shuns her gentler side, as she strives to be the son her father wanted, or she abandons her entrepreneurial interests to live up to her mother's idea of what is "lady-like."

Whatever the scenario, our need for love and belonging can be so strong that it blinds us to our most valuable talents and qualities. We then live a life of pretense and self-negation. Of course, our working life will suffer also, because it is but a part of our life as a whole.

"Holding back," denying creative expression of what we find most inspiring, may result from a fear of rejection. While this is a rational fear in childhood, in adulthood it can warp the entire personality. Some people have censored so much of themselves for so long that they forget what it is they do feel and think. They have consistently turned to others to gain love, acceptance and safety. In adulthood, when they need to be authentic, they cannot recall how. They have not developed the requisite skills for distinctiveness. As a result, they are less than they would be—bland shells of what they were meant to be.

Not only do such people cut themselves off from their own vitality, but holding themselves back also causes them to continue to defeat themselves in other ways. As they observe themselves thwarting their own thoughts, opinions and true desires, they eventually lose self-respect. Soon they know themselves to be cowards, and this further contaminates their ability to be unique. In extreme cases, their preferences and values are so completely suppressed that they do not even know they are out of sync with life.

Happily, the reverse also works. The more we see ourselves as courageous, even in the tiniest choices, the more self-respect we gain and the more distinctive we become. In addition, acting out our authentic desires and values quickly erases a history of holding back and self-abandonment. It results from our believing that we can be self-affirming, speak up for ourselves, and handle rejection or the disapproval which comes from "not fitting in." This belief—that we can survive if we express our real self—is a major step in the development of high self-esteem because it is based on our actions, not just on "positive thinking." Moreover, the ability to express ourselves truthfully can easily be learned through practicing *indirectly significant choice-making*.

Indirectly significant choice-making is a way of healing a wounded self-image and learning to be more distinctive at the same time. It entails locating several low-risk, positive actions and choosing to do these things on a regular basis. In time these actions—symbolically a way of speaking to non-conscious selves about our self-worth—make it possible to behave self-affirmingly in larger arenas: in relationships, in the world of work and in other major areas of life. Because it is through the symbolic that our unconscious is always approached, symbolic behavior can be a safe, systematic and effective route to healing the personality.

A mother of five (whom I will call "Virginia"), sounding like so many other people, confessed, "I've been doing what others expect me to do for so long that now, even though I have the time and money, I don't know what I want to do." Virginia had to learn how to make healthy, responsible choices that permitted her to say "Yes" to the life within her.

During her earlier life she had been a fragmented personality: making decisions without any organized core of values behind them, looking to outside sources for direction and approval. She wanted to know and accept herself unconditionally as she was now, instead of telling herself she would only be worthwhile when she did some certain thing. By practicing indirectly significant choice-making she was able to say "Yes" to things that didn't directly impact her relationships or life in a major way, while still giving expression to what she valued.

In our first session I asked Virginia what she enjoyed doing and what she enjoyed having around her. At first, answering that question proved almost impossible for her. But in time, with further questioning, conversation and my own disclosures of what appealed to me, she realized that she loved flowers—freshly cut ones—and music, especially Bach.

An initial assignment for Virginia was to keep her home—and her desk at work—full of fresh flowers. Also, she was to listen to as much Bach as she desired. I told her that I wanted her to treat herself lavishly whenever possible, explaining that her treatment of herself carried a symbolic message to her unconscious mind (as well as to her conscious self) about her own worth. Initially she doubted my sanity, but she said she would try.

This assignment, although it seemed on the surface to be trivial, was difficult for Virginia to carry out. "I find it almost 'wrong' to spend money on myself—it seems so frivolous. I forget to play the records I love most, or I tell myself I should save them for a time when I have company. It feels strange and selfish to be listening to music when I think I 'should' be reading or getting ready for work." However, she made the effort. As she acted in line with her own favored way of being, she reinforced a new idea: "I am worthwhile." With each self-affirming choice she felt better. This simple technique, perhaps best taught and perfected by Dr. Champion Teutsch of Los Angeles, author of *From Here to Happiness*, carried out over a period of time, can reprogram negative internal messages, making an individual feel new again on the inside.

One day Virginia "remembered" that she had always wanted a massage. She cheerfully told me that she had a massage at Elizabeth Arden's and described the experience as "delicious." Her new conscious choice to do something nice for herself (something that meant Virginia had to invest time and money in herself) was a major victory. It marked a turn in her self-view and in her ability to treat herself well. Virginia herself realized this.

I noticed after my massage that I carried myself differently. People on the street reacted to me in a new way— perhaps it was my perception of myself that was different. What I realized was that we say a lot about ourselves by the way we hold our bodies and that I had been holding mine in a cowering position for a long time. Even my shoulders are rounded and bent over—something that I'm going to try to change.

For a few hours after the massage, I walked around as if I belonged, as if I mattered. I experienced a whole new set of reactions from people. For a little while, I saw what life could be like to me. Although it was an odd, unfamiliar feeling that made me feel self-conscious, I liked it.

Next, Virginia chose to sign up for some deeper, more intensive body therapy. This decision and the subsequent massage-therapy further stimulated her growth as a person and altered her way of seeing herself. As we choose, for good or bad, as we act, we make statements to ourselves about ourselves.

Saying "Yes, I will do this," or "No, I do not want that," teaches us what we think about ourselves. When we change our choices and thus change what we do, we also change our self-view. When we deny ourselves, for example, we notice it. Rewarding ourselves can come through self-denial; what matters most in our actions is the motive behind the action.

Self-denial (e.g., dieting, saving money or whatever) is certainly helpful to high self-esteem much of the time. Often we make a positive statement to ourselves when we say "No" to something we want, as in the case of the former alcoholic who turns down a social drink. The point here is that everything we do makes an impression on us, for good or bad, and learning how to choose healthfully in the direction of our long-term interests, self and most cherished values can start us on an enhanced life path. This path frequently begins with the most innocuous actions, and so it is helpful to be aware of what our actions are saying to us about ourselves.

Using self-observation as a guide or even memories of previous satisfactions and former successful actions, we can note our answers to questions such as these:

● What makes me happy? What activities, what possessions, what daily actions—however small—fill me with delight, make me feel energized and optimistic? What actions make me feel as if I count in my own eyes? (Often my clients find it helpful to keep a running list of their answers for a week or so to questions such as these.)

● What memories fill me with joy? What important goals have I always wanted to achieve, but haven't made time for? What have I done in the past to bring myself optimism, good feelings, or positive reactions?

● Which of my traits or characteristics, when expressed, make me glad to be me? What kind of person am I at my best? How do I act and look when I am that person? (Even if someone cannot recall having acted "his best" he may have an image of himself as he would ideally like to be. A caution at this point: I am not talking about an "idealized image"—i.e., how we feel others would like us, or be impressed by us—but rather how we would feel fulfilled when expressing some inner quality, talent or virtue that means something special to us.)

● What "top" five values do I strive to live by and/or do I admire in others?

By choosing to act in accordance with our own values we grow in insight and understanding. We also strengthen our muscles of self-respect and self-understanding. As was said in the first chapter, with each conscious choice to live out our best, most ethical, most generous self we become more fully human. With each blind, mechanistic or programmed-by-other choice, we negate our rightful human and most genuine personal qualities.

Choosing rightly, and in direction with what we truly want, we learn about our strengths. We also notice our weaknesses. As we choose what is most helpful to us, we feel our power growing. Every time we consciously choose something, however insignificant it might seem, in line with what we feel is highest and best in ourselves, we support our true life goals. Also, we reinforce the idea that we are good, valuable and worthwhile. This reinforces our next proper, healthful choices. Thus, a more positive cycle takes hold of our habits, thinking and outcomes.

When our actions affirm what we love we grow—as did Virginia, who was willing to buy herself flowers even though that felt illogical, foolish and "unnatural." We grow by moving step by step, choice by choice, in the direction of whatever it is our inner self tells us we need at a given time or in a given situation. Again and again we must affirm our essential self through our choices. If we can cultivate an "ear" for the subjective delight, ethic and preferences of our own inner self and move responsibly toward that, we grow whole.

The shape and spirit of each honorable, truthful act changes us; these transform and express us as we are at our best. We are thus gradually given the will and power to break the bonds of our self-defeating, self-negating habits, fears and robotic attitudes. In this way all choices, all day-to-day decisions have the energy to transform our lives if we are but open to the messages and cues from our inner, creative power and the way in which this power relates us to outer life, relationships and work.

No book, seminar or evangelical expert can choose these directions for us. Nor is there a pill to swallow which will bring about the uplifting effects that healthful choices can have on our lives. Self-honesty, awareness and an ongoing inward listening can open our hearts to our inner predispositions and talents, and thereby help us with our growth and development.

By and large, if we continue to choose healthfully, we end up trusting ourselves. Thus, recovering the skill of tuning in to our own inner world transforms the simplest acts so that eventually the outer world more positively mirrors our inner world. In this way we find an important key to recovering our lost vocational capacities. Even in late adulthood this recapturing process, this more elegant and concrete expression, is possible. In fact, this course may point to the primary work of adulthood, since the work of childhood has other requirements and lessons. Our "formula" then, if there is one, entails these steps:

- That we identify the values, ethics and behaviors we cherish, toward which we are predisposed and which have a creative power that is generally beyond our intellectual, logical comprehension.

- That we plan a small, safe, gradual and perhaps even conservative approach to bringing our essential inclinations into being. In small steps we choose to demonstrate whatever it is we genuinely value.

- That at least part of our energies and attention be focused on the question of how we reward ourselves, that we listen inwardly to locate those actions that are attractive to us, beneficial in a long-term, holistic sense, and that we discover which actions, although actually repugnant, we do mechanistically in order to "fit in," gain approval, conform or defeat ourselves.

● That we learn to tolerate some tension, discomfort or pain (if that is required) so as to actively "stand in" for ourselves and treat ourselves as if we counted in our own eyes. This way we slowly break the vise-like grip our unproductive, habitual response patterns have over us, and we learn how to make meaningful choices, even when these are not easy, or "comfortable."

● That we locate a competent therapist, support group, minister, rabbi or counselor if we feel overburdened, blocked, threatened, inordinately guilt-ridden or isolated when undertaking any of these steps so as to responsibly attend to the pain, risks or discomforts inherent in our own growth into full personhood.

Although we may dearly want vocational self-expression, it will elude us unless we are open to the creative power contained within. In the final analysis, nothing less than scrupulous honesty with ourselves is called for. More than that, the daily, acting out of our "highest self" promotes our wholeness—vocational and otherwise. Our own choices and daily actions decree whether we will be able to act out the essential truth and meaning of our lives in our vocation.

5

Dealing with the Big R: Resistance

> The direction of change to seek is not in our four dimensions: it is getting deeper into what you are, where you are, like turning up the volume on the amplifier.
>
> Thaddeus Golas,
> *Lazy Man's Guide to Enlightenment*

Lest anyone be under the illusion that this book just beamed itself into existence, let me set the record straight: the Big R always lurks.

The Big R is what I call *resistance:* the subtle inner mechanism that urges us to back away from life's difficulties and demands. The Big R exists in most people, to a greater or lesser extent, even in those people who love what they do. It intensifies the difficulties of problems, tasks and routines. Each manifestation of the Big R undermines enthusiasm, energy and our finest intentions. Because it is so subversive and pervasive, it is worthy of discussion here as we delve into growth and work-related topics.

Tarthang Tulku, a lama from Eastern Tibet, says that resistance is a habit we learn as children. "When a child encounters something he does not want, he has all kinds of maneuvers to avoid it, such as crying, hiding or fighting. . . . Unless we are taught to face our problems directly and work through them, the pattern of avoidance will be repeated . . . it can become a natural, accepted way to act" (p. 62).

Another way to look at the subject is to reflect upon some of the differences between successful people and those who continually get in their own way. However one defines success, it's a fact that those who experience more of what they desire in life seem to be people who do not back away from problems, growth or difficult tasks. We have seen that adults with high self-esteem often came from early childhood beginnings wherein they had to face their problems alone. Moreover, if we observe the behaviors of those people we think are successful (e.g., healthy, creative, materially and professionally fulfilled), we see that they do things willingly that others only talk about doing, but avoid. The healthy ones willingly watch what they eat, exercise, meditate and don't burn their candles at both ends. The creatives protect their time for projects that stimulate them. The materially or professionally fulfilled study, invest wisely, and turn a sharp, focused eye toward what most keenly concerns them. They, too, protect their time, resources and talents so that their energies are not scattered or diminished. All these sorts of activities also demand that such persons discipline themselves. Discipline becomes a powerful tool for getting what they really want out of life. They build habit patterns that allow them to communicate and act with vigor and courageously face whatever must be done. Their habits allow them to use their talents rather than blocking them.

Such is not the case for the unsuccessful or the unfulfilled. Their habit patterns help them avoid challenges, demands and the use of their talents. They prefer comfort over challenge, safety over growth, invisibility over visibility. The ideal set of circumstances for such persons is a womb-like environment: warm, safe, secure, with all their needs met. They avoid confrontation and risk at all costs. Thus, professionally and personally, they back away from what would help them become more useful to themselves and others. Public speaking, confrontational communications (now called assertive), community leadership projects, decision-making, commitments of all kinds, meeting new people, taking new jobs, and taking a stand on difficult or unpopular matters are all forbidden to such persons:

their own comfort-seeking tendencies insure their lack of fulfillment.

But, as I wrote earlier, there are degrees of withdrawing. Even productive, energetic people often must deal with their own resistance if they want to grow. To illustrate: I know the Big R has me in its grip when I—a person who loves to be active and working—eat junk food, talk on the phone, sleep or fill the hummingbird feeder instead of working. When under the influence of my resistant side, I would do anything to escape the frustrations of my work.

In our last chapter we saw that our work-habits can be unusual and non-conforming and "look" unproductive. We also discussed how we must learn to use these so-called "limitations" in the service of our overall goals, because they can be a strong ally to us and to what we need to do. However, I want to distinguish between these odd work habits and resistance.

The need for rest, privacy or a change of scenery (e.g., closing the office door, driving down a beautiful country road, strolling down the office corridor) is a mechanism we may use to help ourselves concentrate or solve problems. These habits are not necessarily a sign of resistance because during these idiosyncratic ways of taking "time-out," we are actually working, albeit on a subterranean level of awareness.

Another personal example: writing is for me both a creative activity and one of strict discipline. When I am just about to embark upon a new project, or when I have just completed something tedious, I find it helpful and renewing to rest, change the scene or alter the way I'm working. I do not interpret this as "the Big R." Rather it is a regrouping of ideas, or a storing up of new energy, an incubation period for my next outpouring of ideas and concentration. Similarly, when I am troubled by something— say a chapter is not falling into place or something in my practice of management psychology is puzzling to me—I find that active time-out does me good. Sometimes I will go to a movie (preferably a comedy), or take a long drive. These are wonderful outlets for stimulating my imagination and motivation. Long walks are equally beneficial for me. The point is that I am working during these time-outs, but in a way that may not look like work to others. I even used to have difficulty giving myself this type of time-off because I was so used to a certain form of "work." But, by contrast, when the Big R has me, I cease to work at all.

When, for example, it is time to put my tax materials in order for the end-of-the-year wrap-up, I find it amazingly easier to do other things. I hear myself not wanting to deal with the taxes. I see myself procrastinating or becoming preoccupied with trivia, engulfed by mesmerizing distractions. Under the Big R's more severe spell, I simply cease to function: a human houseplant, with longish hair, seated glazed-eyed in front of a typewriter or adding machine.

Resistance is an inner device, and because everyone is unique, it has many disguises. In some ways it is a form of flight, a running-away from whatever needs to be done. Others might say it was a type of "fight"—an obstinate refusal, albeit covert, to do whatever is expected. It is a superb vehicle for defeating ourselves and others. Resistance, for example, is what makes us late with projects or puts us into a fearful, anxious or muddled state when doing something new or complicated.

Resistance makes us inert, restless and apathetic, and, as Jung once wrote, "it begets meaninglessness." Apathy and restlessness are the opposites of the traits; we need to be enthusiastic, focused and purposeful. The person who is always flitting from one thing to another, who cannot concentrate on any one of life's courses, is a resistant person. So is the person who is too tired or lethargic to put his attention on what really must be done, or the one who is always dependent on the thinking or strength of others. These people avoid being responsible participants in life; eventually they avoid finding any meaning in life.

The economist Fritz (E.F.) Schumacher once wrote that because work is so central to life, what people do is more significant to understanding them than what they say, how they vote, how they spend their money, or their social class. I would take that thought a step further: *how* people do their work uncovers hidden truths about them and their way of meeting life's challenges.

We have already said that persons with low self-esteem avoid being powerful; they have learned to be helpless. They withdraw from the simplest demands in a task, as well as from life's opportunities. Author and counselor John Sanford describes these tendencies in his wonderful book, *The Transformation of the Inner Man*, with these words:

> The first and deepest malformed condition is called by psychologists *amniosis*. It means an inability to come out of the amniotic fluid and be born, or flight by regression to return to the safe hiding place of the womb. . . . Amniotic people want to be taken care of. They want to find strong people—ones in whom they can nestle, upon whom they can become dependent, and by whom they can be mollycoddled. Paula and I have grieved to see some children and adults, from well-behaved families who do everything properly, walking about dead-eyed with no bounding energies for anything. Their stance says, "If I can just get through life without making any ripples . . ." We want to throw them off a high bank and say, "Sink or swim, buddy!" We wouldn't; we know that's not the way. But we want to (pp. 227–229).

When such a person is bright enough to work at a complex job, he may not try for it, or he may give himself and others numerous good reasons why he "cannot" do it. Or he may give it a try and after a short time start to make disastrous decisions and fail. Thus, he proves once and for all that he is not capable. Others, upon receiving a promotion, find themselves quickly overwrought with anxiety and fear—emotions that create so much inner turmoil for them that they soon become dependent upon their co-workers or their managers for help. Managers or peers who spoon-feed them eventually learn that no amount of help is enough, and those who are insightful realize that these individuals do not really want to assume responsibility at all.

A woman who began to work for a corporate accounting department had enormous potential for much more than her first-line supervisory job. Each time she was given tasks that required her to work independently and make her own decisions, she

would lean heavily on her supervisor—asking many inane, petty
questions and creating more work for him than he could handle.
In this way, she discouraged him from recommending her for
other promotions and also reinforced her deeply entrenched idea-
of-self that she wasn't able to handle responsible, complex work.
Her own anxiety blocked her ability to become more than she
was. Yet, because anxiety is often viewed as only a natural
response to new challenges, she never examined the other
messages this emotion was saying.

Often people turn away from the chance to be more than
they are because this contradicts their early idea-of-self. Not only
does a new activity or responsibility unbalance the homeostatic
quality of their belief system, but many people also have a
cunning way of avoiding being responsible for themselves. In
effect, they are unwilling to stand on their own feet and prefer, as
the Sanford quote indicated, to use others to do for them and to
define them.

It is easier to ask the boss for his or her opinion than to have
our own. It is easier to have our spouse, parents or children
support us than it is to support ourselves. It is easier to
manipulate, blame or seduce others into labeling us or doing
things for us than it is to define ourselves or to do things for
ourselves in our own way. In all these ways and so many others,
people avoid taking authority and authorship for their own lives.

In addition, people turn away from growing and from seeing
their own potential, because this too contradicts their early
programming. To make matters worse, most people have a secret
prejudice against their own strengths, talents and greatness.
Perhaps this is because by being strong, they must be willing to
take the consequences of that power and let go of the pretense,
however unconsciously buried, that they are helpless. Perhaps it
is easier to believe we have little potential than to admit our
talents. In this way, we avoid the jealousies and demands of
others. Some women, for example, have told me they do not wish
to act as intelligent as they are because their brightness cuts them
off from others—from both men and women. Some creative
engineers and gifted thinkers I have known are actually timid and
self-deprecating about their intelligence—as if this pseudo-

humility will stave off their colleagues' or friends' resentment and hostility. There is even a cultural bias, in most societies, against those who try to be enlightened and successful. This bias has its roots in early mythological stories that teach that ultimate knowing or perfected being is, and should be, reserved only for the gods.

We are also afraid of any feedback that would make us seem small in our own eyes. But we are equally fearful of information that demands that we stand tall and become visible and powerful in the eyes of others. There has always been a conflict between the powerful, knowing, "enlightened" individual and society.

Society is made up of logical, rational laws and orderly processes. The powerful individual, the creative thinker, artist, poet or inventor threatens this order, unmasks narrow, limited thinking, and is disruptive to the status quo. Every really serious writer, inventor or artist testifies to the solitary, lonely process of creative work. Creation takes courage, just as it takes real courage to be an individual.

Psychiatrist Robert Lindner, famous for his research on the benefits of "positive rebellion," believed that adjustment was a synonym for conformity, and that society conditions each human infant away from his or her own uniqueness. Through a variety of mechanisms (e.g., the need for love, care, belonging, approval), each child slowly but surely adopts the cultural overlay of perception and thus is schooled away from his own interior wisdom, from his own self. Lindner categorized as successful rebels "all those who managed, by their own efforts, to transcend the barriers society erects for the controlling over the non-conforming."

> Among the group are those who have surmounted . . . the barriers that any society erects for the containment of the rebellious. In this group, apart from the few rare, soaring souls who are members of the estate from birth forward—Socrates, Lao-tse, Christ, Gandhi, and others—we must include those who have somehow recovered from a negative condition—be it a neurosis or even a psychosis—and re-entered the evolutionary stream in such a manner that

they have given it impetus. This subdivision of human beings is very small; but compared with the rest of us, its
members are literally supermen because of their ability to
express their human potentiality to an extent and in a manner hardly conceivable by the remainder (pp. 225–226).

I want to dwell for a moment on Lindner's discussion of the
positive rebel, for this individual has much to teach us about our
own right livelihood and the qualities we must adopt, in order to
practice it with vigor and commitment.

First, the positive rebel is essentially a catalytic agent whose
very manner and mode of being energizes others by calling forth
and stimulating their own non-conformity. This characteristic has
much to do with resistance, for the truly whole individual cannot
and will not tolerate his own resistance, specifically because it
robs his personality of needed vigor and vital, focused energy.

The individual also must, by definition, be what Lindner
termed "psychologically successful" within himself. This means
that while he functions at any level and in any role of society (as a
business leader, housewife, community volunteer, student, or
whatever) his undergirding sense is that he is living out his own
life's purpose through his own efforts and creative will. This
compelling inner vision is part and parcel of the mature, self-
actualizing personality, and has everything to do with resistance
as well. To the extent that we accept our own greatness, the
mission and charter for our own life, we want to work against
anything—either external (in society or through the actions and
efforts of others) or internal (our own "enemies within")—that
would hold us back.

Maslow also understood the connection between the healthy,
self-actualizing, whole personality and the necessity to work
against one's own resistance and blocks:

The timid man also may tend to identify probing curiosity
as somehow challenging to others, as if, somehow, by being intelligent and searching out the truth, he is being assertive and bold and manly in a way that he can't back up
and that such a pose will bring down upon him the wrath

of other, older, stronger men. So also may children identify curious probing as a trespass upon the prerogatives of
their gods, the all-powerful gods. . . . Something similar
can be seen in the exploited, the downtrodden, the weak
minority or the slave. He may fear to know too much, to explore freely. This might arouse the wrath of his lords. . . .
In any case, the exploiter or the tyrant, out of the dynamics of the situation, is not likely to encourage curiosity,
learning and knowledge in his underlings. People who
know too much are likely to rebel. Both the exploited and
the exploiter are impelled to regard knowledge as incom-
patible with being a good, nice, well-adjusted slave (p. 59).

Low self-esteem—giving in to our resistance to excelling,
living out our potential, living out what we know to be true
within ourselves—is a much more comfortable route to follow. In
this sense, the fear of knowing what one is capable of doing, the
anxiety that comes from doing our best and living out our
potential greatness—even if that greatness is less flashy than we
had expected, even if it is "only" living out the truth as we see
it—is directly connected to the fear of having to do something
about what we know. Again, we come up against the fear of being
responsible.

From all sides, therefore, it is much safer to give in to our
lethargy, our belief—which we have engineered—that we "don't
know" what we should do with our life's energy, our restlessness
and lack of commitment, our fatigue and so on, than it is to know
what to do and do it. It is much safer to limit our vision of what
our life could be.

I recall a woman client, married to a known drug abuser,
who struggled for three years to decide whether to leave him. It
was not so much that she was worried about whether to divorce
the man, but that she felt that she would be "wrong" in letting
him down—this despite the fact that he never came home,
misspent their funds, was obviously having affairs with a host of
other women, and gave her every evidence that he wanted her to
leave him. She continued to dwell on what their relationship had
been many years ago, refusing, actually unable, to see that the

man had turned into someone quite different than the man she had married. At the same time—through her inordinate need to assume more responsibility for the continuation of the relationship than was appropriate—she was unwilling to see her situation as it really was.

In some ways his daily abuse and neglect was his only way of telling her that he wanted a divorce. Still she clung to the hope that they would reunite, that things would be as they were. The woman's therapist, minister and parents could not understand what she was waiting for, and in her more lucid moments she could not understand either. "It is as if I am fixed in this indecisive place," she explained helplessly.

Three years later, after taking many small glances at her husband as he actually was, she came slowly to grips with what she had to do. She "suddenly" realized that at the very least she had to make a life for herself—that she had to put her own house in order.

While part of us clings to our fantasies and wishful imaginings, another part longs for a stronger way of being, and a resolution of problems that are often largely of our own making. We yearn for the ability to take the growth step that will mean a better life. The net result is that both these drives—the holding back and wishing to go forward—are at work in us simultaneously. When faced with new opportunities, we resist acting as firmly and boldly as we could.

As we resist, our own personal pattern of avoidance comes into play. Some people grow confused. Others procrastinate decisions, or they act in ways that greatly stall their best interests. If we wish to control and manage our resistant nature, then a simple, excellent way to do so is to observe it objectively and without judgment when it shows up in our day-to-day choices. I stress the importance of non-judgmental observation, because the general rule regarding our inner workings is that anything we can detachedly observe, we can eventually control.

Eventually, as we awaken to our peculiar way of avoiding difficulty, we then can choose to turn our energies in a more positive, self-supporting direction. We become free to choose because our awareness (and the subsequent energy that is freed by our non-resistant, non-critical observing activities) is freeing. Awareness is energy. When we are under an unconscious habit (e.g., apathy, restlessness, procrastination), our awareness is caught up in either the slothful or the over-active, frenzied project. We do not notice our resistance. What is "real" is the emotion or attitude pulling us away from focusing on what must be handled. When we become aware, we simultaneously liberate our attention from the distracting emotion or activity and become free to choose another path.

The easiest way to observe our avoidance patterns is to look at our response to anything demanding: a new task, something tedious and repetitive, a co-worker's request, deadlines or routines, rules or restrictions, or the demands of the job at hand. Eventually, most will notice their individual and quite reliable way of avoiding things. Some exhibit resistance in a highly charged emotional form, through fear, self-doubt, and hostility. This pattern seems especially true for those with buried, suppressed resentments against authority figures. They are just waiting for an opportunity to release these feelings with impunity. In this case, the Big R shows up as work slow-downs or the inability to meet deadlines. This is most noticeable when someone in authority makes demands.

Others develop chronic physical "symptoms" that cause dysfunctioning. They get headaches, they cannot concentrate, they grow confused, and find they cannot understand the simplest directions. By watching *how* our job gets done, each of us can discover his favored way of subtly non-cooperating with his own best interests.

Given our all-too-human reluctance to see ourselves as we are, it isn't easy to spot our own avoidance patterns. "Put a snake in a box," an old adage goes, "if you want it to learn its shape." This means that as the snake hits itself against the sides of the box, it begins to discover its own form. I do not know about snakes, but people can teach themselves about their peculiar brand of work avoidance and resistance by observing themselves objectively as they go about their daily routines. Routines are our own "boxes," and often these will bring to the surface valuable information about the Big R.

Those whose work results in crafts, products or sales may have an easier time seeing themselves than those whose work is more intellectual and thus harder to track. But anyone can, with some practice and sincere intention, become an objective observer of himself. In this way, we can learn how we hold back our own good and that of others. Because it is simpler to describe, I will use craft-making as an illustration of how we can see ourselves as we work, as we resist, as we function smoothly.

"The object is a mirror," writes potter and weaver Carla Needleman in her book, *The Work of Craft*.

That I took so long to recognize it is a telling commentary on the fact that I don't know myself. . . . I suffer from what I see. It, the object, contradicts my ideas, my illusion of what I should be producing and it wounds my self-love to see it. But it is me. It could not be better—I have worked as well as I could and this object is the only possible true representation of that work (p. 51).

In a few short lines, Needleman helps us understand how the object—everything that is done—expresses what she *is*.

This observation is called "mindfulness" and is an objective awareness of ourselves as seen through our thoughts, actions, products or services. Each of these has the power to show ourselves our potential, as well as our dark side. By being aware of ourselves, through a detached, moment-to-moment watchfulness, we are able to see the direction we should follow to improve ourselves.

For example, if we suffer from feelings of worthlessness, we can see that while we observe ourselves at work. In that case we might avoid—in the simplest everyday execution of tasks—real tests of what we can do, giving ourselves excuses and ways out instead of facing these challenges boldly. We might say to ourselves or to others, "I'm too old/young/educated/over-educated/special/ordinary/tired/hyperactive/etc. to do this." We hope that others believe us, as we try to convince ourselves that we "cannot" do more. We give less than our best, or we avoid the tasks completely, skirting the fact that were we to settle into it and confront its demands, we might understand what to do. We justify our contracted efforts with some ingenious rational excuse that gets us off the hook of being responsible to our own potential.

In this way, through our self-idea and our excuses to support that idea, we save our battered ego from further humiliation, which would certainly be ours if we saw ourselves fall short again. Unlike Needleman who says she suffers from what she sees, we suffer from the fears of what we think we might see. So we don't really look at ourselves at all. The excuses and strategically useful resistance pattern we have taught ourselves save us from seeing what we could be.

Interesting, is it not, that the way we work, and the work itself, might be a camera that produces pictures that never lie? It could be—if, that is, we choose to view the snapshots produced by our own consciousness as it looks unemotionally upon our functioning, our unique use of energy, and our daily, ordinary conduct.

Thus, those who want to get rid of debilitating resistance can start by observing themselves, mindful and non-judgmentally, at work. Some things to observe include:

- The ease or difficulty of getting out of bed in the morning.

- The length of time we can work at one thing without interrupting ourselves to do something else (e.g., go to the bathroom, take a coffee break, talk on the phone, walk over to the water cooler for a conversation or a drink, look out the window).

- The posture of our body: how it leans to or away from the thing we are doing, how we use our energy, breath, and attention in the service of the task or in avoiding it.

- The way our mood, the weather, or the task itself affects our results. Ideally, we should have no "mood," the weather should not interfere or influence us in any way, and all tasks are just tasks demanding our attention and careful handling.

Our energy should flow, unobstructed, through us in the service of the job at hand. I have known people who, although ill or arthritic, have been fully transformed and robust during their working day. Norman Cousins gives a beautiful illustration of this in his book *Anatomy of an Illness*. Cousins describes with feeling visits he had with two masters, Pablo Casals and Albert Schweitzer. At that time, both men were octogenarians, fully alive, creative, and committed to personal projects of such great value to them that any physical limitations they had disappeared while they worked. A particularly poignant and revealing passage about Pablo Casals helps us understand how a person uses energy when he has no resistance to his work. Casals had various infirmities that made it hard for him to walk, dress himself and breathe. His body was stooped over, his hands were swollen and clenched. However, prior to breakfast each morning he had a ritual of playing the piano. Cousins writes about the transfiguration that took place as Casals started to play:

> I was not prepared for the miracle that was about to happen. The fingers slowly unlocked and reached toward the keys like the buds of a plant toward the sunlight. His back straightened. He seemed to breathe more freely. Now his fingers settled on the keys. Then came the opening bars of Bach . . . he hummed as he played, then said that Bach spoke to him here—and he placed his hand over his heart. Then he plunged into a Brahms' concerto and his fingers, now agile and powerful, raced across the keyboard with dazzling speed. His entire body seemed fused with the music; it was no longer stiff and shrunken, but supple and graceful and completely freed of its arthritic coils (p. 73).

Cousins goes on to say that because Casals was completely caught up in his own creativity, in his own superordinate goals and life's purpose, the effects of these desires on his body chemistry were health-promoting to an amazing degree.

Many people might react to this example by saying that they are "ordinary" people who do not have the necessary genius or creative drive to transform their energy, attention, and body in this way. My response, however naive, is that even "ordinary" people are affected this way when they do what they love. The young man in Chapter Two who was so charmed by his pre-school charges—"I become so totally involved that I forget everything else"—is but one example that upholds my idealistic bias.

All of us can take steps—no matter how small and insignificant at the start—in the direction we want to go. One of my clients, a college student, realized that if he wanted to get his life in order, he had to clean and organize his apartment. The apartment had become a disastrous mess. In order to feel better about himself, in order to move in a direction he wanted, and needed, to go, this young man knew he had to do something first about his living space, starting with the relatively easy objective of acting against his usual lethargy which blocked his life from moving forward at every turn. By overcoming his slothfulness on a moment by moment basis, he was taking steps to improve and tone up his entire life.

We do not have to be or have *all* that we want in order to choose to act on behalf of what we value. Taking small, gradual steps leads the way to taking larger steps later on.

Right here, right now, we can act. And each time we do, we gain some measure of increased self-esteem, some measure of control over the Big R. As common and pervasive as the Big R may be, we do not have to let it sabotage our life's goals.

Gradually, we find a relatively "safe" way to get to a higher level of health without abandoning the familiar, the known, and the safety that are so important to our well-being and growth. What little actions, what small possessions, what nearly invisible characteristics do we enjoy expressing? These can help us move into more fulfilling ways of being. Even locating others who are inspiring to us and understanding why they are inspiring can help us identify what we want to do for ourselves—even though such information might normally be threatening.

We can take safe steps toward the larger goal of being our best self and discovering what it is we want to do in life. The point is to identify the things that light us from within. Then we can think of some small, inconsequential ways to live out that enjoyable activity in everyday life.

We can begin by simply listing the things that we enjoy doing; this will direct us toward our "next steps." If we enjoy riding on a subway train, love to watch the city zoom by, feel at one with the life and vitality of the city during these rides, then subway riding is what we can treat ourselves to whenever time allows. If we love music, then perhaps a concert is the requirement of our off-work hours—even if, as was true for one elderly woman I knew, we can't afford to buy the tickets and must become ushers to earn our way in. At the very least, we can listen to the type of music we most enjoy.

If we enjoy living in lovely, orderly surroundings but cannot imagine how to afford a better apartment, then wherever we are, whatever our economic situation, we can start choosing in that direction, even if our choices are merely symbolic. Right here, right now, today, we can act out what we value by straightening out or painting our apartment. One fresh flower can represent beauty for us and help our unconscious mind feel supported, valued and dignified.

One man, who deeply wanted to be more courageous, realized that he could act more bravely with his spouse and neighbors before taking on life's larger challenges. He did not have to banish all his fears at once. All he needed to do was say "No" to those things that intruded upon his time and privacy or which undermined his dignity. This was difficult for him to do at first, but as he practiced saying "Yes" to those things that were important to him and "No" to the things that discounted his values, he found that he grew in self-esteem. Within a year he was taking more control of his life in significant ways. He found that he had the wherewithal to spend his weekends the way he really wanted. He stopped socializing with people who had little to offer intellectually. Most important, his relationship with his wife improved remarkably because she was very attracted to his new self-affirming manner.

I'm also reminded of the energetic author and philosopher, Eric Hoffer, who was both a practicing longshoreman in San

Francisco and a research professor at the University of California at Berkeley. Hoffer's home, as I saw it when he was interviewed on television, was a tiny, one-room apartment above the docks of San Francisco. His small, immaculate room was simple and neat. Because it was so small, it was not spectacular. However, the room was aesthetically pleasing in every way. It was full of light. Piles and piles of books were stacked up everywhere in an orderly and well-balanced way. The sight of this feverishly passionate thinker, sitting quaintly in the midst of such visual richness, was greatly impressive, and the memory of Hoffer's living environment has stayed with me through the years.

We need not be formally well-educated to live well: to be knowledgeable or committed to long-range, substantive goals. Nor need we be affluent to live elegantly and beautifully, as the apartments of artists or designers who are just starting out in life show us.

We do need inner affluence—that quality of being that enriches us in all the really important, life-affirming ways—in order to live well. We do have to live out our highest values and aspirations in safe, unobtrusive ways, ways that symbolically (at the very least) show us that we care about ourselves, and that, emotionally, we are in our own corner as well.

We do not have to be, do or have all the things we say we want before choosing to act on behalf of what we want, value and are inspired by. In fact, our initial, gradual steps, taken consciously and long before we have what we want, make it possible to take the larger, riskier steps later.

6

Dealing with the
Big S: "Shoulds"

> Your health is bound to be affected if, day after day, you say
> the opposite of what you feel, if you grovel before what you dis-
> like and rejoice at what brings you nothing but misfortune.
>
> *Dr. Zhivago*

Our personal "injunctions"—as psychiatrist Eric Berne termed
those internalized commands that run our daily lives—are deeply
embedded in us. Not only do many superficial dictates drive our
conduct and attitudes, but also we are powerfully governed by
the more serious, deeper injunctions of our culture, families,
religious organizations, and the media. While each person has a
unique moral code, and must stick to it or suffer the
consequences of real and painful guilt, it is also essential that each
uncover the false rules by which he is emotionally imprisoned.

As an individual becomes aware of who he is, he begins to
evaluate which injunctions are important and which are not. This
is part of the work of all maturing persons. As later paragraphs
will describe, this work probably has little to do with where we
were born, our age or even our gender. It is simply one of the
essential tasks of growing whole as a human being.

Most Westerners follow at least some of the guidelines in the
Judaeo-Christian ethic (e.g., the Ten Commandments) as a fairly
reliable set of rules for their daily lives. Even with these
guidelines, there are times when we must make personal
decisions that force us to confront what we really believe. These
crisis moments, when we come to a fork in life's road requiring us

to take a stand, help us to re-evaluate what we want to say with our lives and actions. For example, someone who firmly believes in the principle "Thou shalt not kill" may realize that he must put aside this injunction to protect his life or the lives of those he loves.

Others, for instance dedicated pacifists, might make no exception to the "Thou shalt not kill" injunction. For them, even saving their own lives is not sufficient reason to kill another human being. In the final analysis it is what we do that tells us and others what kind of person we are and what are our deepest values or antipathies. Our moral code of conduct, the values, ethics and laws we live by, are helpful allies in ordering our lives. Thus when I speak of dissolving our "shoulds," I am speaking about examining all types of external injunctions which tell us what we ought to be and to do. The purpose of this examination is to live a progressively more authentic, vital life.

In this chapter I wish to explore a secondary, though no less powerful, category of "shoulds": those somewhat less dramatic, but nonetheless significant rules of living that we learn from parents, teachers, peer groups, religious dictates, the media and a variety of other social sources. These commandments have the power to hammer into our minds a constant barrage of images and subtle, subliminal programmings that strongly condition what we think we are supposed to be, do, have and look like. This program often has little to do with a moral code; rather it is sometimes a confining, constricting prism through which we see ourselves as limited, defined and controlled by others.

Eric Berne taught that our lives are pre-ordained from childhood by what he called scripts. A script is the parental/ancestoral blueprint for an individual's life, much like the blueprint that a builder follows when constructing a house. We are scripted (another term now commonly used is "programmed") primarily by our parents, who—verbally and non-verbally—instruct us on how to be happy, successful, and pleasing. A script is our "handbook" for getting along in the world.

It is from our parents that we learn how to think for ourselves or how not to, how to have relationships or how not to, and how to succeed or how to live a life of "quiet desperation."

Claude Steiner, a West Coast psychologist and an early colleague of Eric Berne, helps us understand how we are programmed by our parents' injunctions in his excellent book, *Scripts People Live*.

> The main injunctions . . . tend to come from one of the parents, and the parent of the opposite sex is often the source. The parent of the same sex then teaches the youngster how to comply with these injunctions and attributions. Thus, if mother dislikes assertive behavior in men and boys and enjoys sensitivity and warmth, she will enjoin her sons not to be assertive, will attribute warmth and sensitivity to them, and . . . will provide her sons with a father who gives them the proper example (p. 85).

In other words, our parents' behaviors, choices and attitudes model and shape our childhood perceptions, world-views and beliefs. Each of us then lives out countless "shoulds" which, if not evaluated as adulthood approaches, can cripple our zest for living, thwart our ability to know what we want to do with our lives, and render us impotent in matters of creative, independent thinking. Therefore, an essential assignment of what I call "psychological homework" for any adult wanting to become a fully functioning, conscious person is to root out and evaluate the "shoulds" under which he lives. For some, this process requires therapy. For others, deep reflection, reading and experimentation may be enough. All that may be required is to elevate the understanding of what kinds of injunctions drive us to act in certain patterned ways, in compulsive, limiting ways, and to see what prevents us from acting as we would like to act. Many who feel depressed and hopeless and whose self-image is closed and narrow find, upon examining their personal injunctions, that they have been taught to be overly self-conscious—that they have learned to care too much about what other people think or will say, and that they have robbed themselves of power as a result. Others find they have learned not to be emphatic enough. Each person's script is unique and this makes the investigation highly personal.

There are "Being injunctions" that program a whole life of actions, attitudes and decisions. Some examples of what parents tell their children are: Be Perfect, Be Careful, Be a Winner, Be Polite, Be Docile, Be a Risk-Taker, Be a Loser, Be Smart, Be Dumb, Be Pleasing, Be Irritating. And there are negative commands as well: Don't Trust, Don't Expect Much, Don't Argue, Don't Live, Don't Think, Don't Take Chances, Don't Give Up, Don't Worry, Don't Be Sexual/Humorous/Charming/etc. The list goes on and on.

We are programmed by externals in almost all the areas of our life—in our social conduct, in business relationships, in personal interactions, in political beliefs, in financial habits, in our way of thinking and in our appearance. In order to discover these highly personal "shoulds," we first must know that these "shoulds" operate in constellations. They are grouped and linked together much like a child's erector set. One "should" holds up others. This interlocking network is beneficial: our world-view and conduct are thus held securely in place. It is also easier to liberate ourselves from a constellation of beliefs because if we locate one "should" and start to break its hold over us, other "shoulds" will naturally fall away too since they are connected.

An example of the constellation phenomenon is seen in many gender-related "shoulds." In our society, for instance, men are usually programmed to be fairly active. They are taught that they "should" overcome difficulty, that they "should" be strong, capable and competent, that they "should" take care of their wives, children, employees and parents. Also, men are taught that they "should" protect their country, that they "should" be brave, honorable and strong. Along with these injunctions, another group of related ones fall into place, supporting the primary "shoulds." Men are taught not to show—or even acknowledge—their soft, vulnerable side, not to give up when the going gets rough, not to abandon their responsibilities—no matter how life-damaging these may be. Men are supposed to be competitive, and this word can mean they "shouldn't" become too friendly with peers or colleagues. In fact, I know some men who are strong competitors with their friends yet who manage to preserve the friendship. But to accomplish the dual-role of friend/ competitor, they have had to do serious soul-searching and conduct an ongoing, truthful dialogue with their friends—

especially at times when it would be most natural to withdraw or become enraged by their friend's triumphs. This is not easy to do because it requires the ability to be intimate in the truest meaning of the word, which suggests close, essential relationship.

Most men are still conditioned by the traditional "avoid intimacy" should. For them this creates damaging psychic overloads when they are faced with thankless, emotion-laden jobs. For example, men who cannot express their feelings or who believe that they must cope alone with conflicting emotions are ideal candidates for fatigue or burn-out. In my professional practice, where I deal almost exclusively with male clients in corporations undergoing wide-scale, rapid change, I often have occasion to talk with men about highly sensitive personal issues. Often they admit that they are tolerating unhappy jobs and sexless, barren marriages and impoverished personal relationships. They feel lost. Even some of the young managers, in their thirties or forties, worry that they are getting old, and that it is too late to change.

Organizational psychologist Harry Levinson, who has made insightful contributions to the study of burn-out among effective managers, describes the problem as follows:

> People suffering burn-out generally have identifiable characteristics: (1) chronic fatigue, (2) anger at those making demands, (3) self-criticism for putting up with the demands, (4) cynicism, negativism and irritability, (5) a sense of being besieged, and (6) hair-trigger display of emotions (p. 76).

Levinson is not referring only to men. However, from my professional observations I see men more at risk here than women. For one thing, men, taught to "be strong," often withdraw from their wives and co-workers just when they most need their support and friendship. Also, men are less likely to give themselves permission to speak about their fears, emotional binds or sorrows. While women clients openly cry, complain, express and work through their worries in the course of a single counseling session, male clients take much longer to disclose their real emotions. It is not unusual in many consulting sessions for men to wait until the tail-end of our session before presenting the real problem they wish to discuss. Some do not even know what they are feeling: their emotional world is a foreign language to them.

Of course, this traditional male-programming is changing even as these pages are being written. However, the net result of generations of men who have bought into our society's successful male image is that men often are confused and disconnected from themselves, their emotions and their best inclinations. Psychologist Herb Goldberg outlines the self-defeating "success syndrome" and describes the typical masculine script as something that cuts men off from their own development.

> The male's inherent survival instincts have been stunted by the seemingly more powerful drive to maintain his masculine image. He would, for example, rather die in battle than risk living in a different way and being called a "coward" or "not a man." He would rather die at his desk prematurely than free himself from his compulsive patterns and pursuits (p. 3).

Goldberg reminds us that men stunt themselves by closely identifying with the culturally-defined male image, and that they cut themselves off from their wives, their children, and their inner, emotional selves and even from their sexuality. For example, many men, once they are married, deny their own ambitions and dreams in order to try to live up to their wives' demands and expectations of what a man "should be." In a similar manner, there are endless career expectations for men in management positions—expectations that create socially rigid roles for the corporate or community leader. They are not permitted to fail, retreat, or even rest when they have had enough.

The burn-out syndrome described above is just one price men pay for this unconscious limitation they place upon themselves. Perhaps an even worse price is that they forfeit their true identity—and consequently their real masculinity—by a servile surrendering of all that is most human, noble and decent

within themselves. Gradually, under the constant barrage of
social, corporate and family pressures, men give up their natural
urge to protest, revolt and grow.

Women are no better off. While women today have been
liberated from the social requirement to stay at home and while
they can be admired both for their feminine, home and family-
related interests and their more masculine business/career-related
interests, the majority still remain relegated to the "shoulds" of
society. Being a woman in today's society is more complex than
ever because they—like men—are being asked to grow into fully
human beings. But I caution anyone from thinking that the
women's liberation movement has made a woman's task of
developing her true personhood easier. One woman told me:

> As adults, we women are often influenced more than we
> should be by our family, the media or friends. We switch
> on TV and see Jane Pauley on the "Today Show," with her
> beautifully coiffed, made-up countenance. We hear of her
> wonderful, perfect family of twins, her successful hus-
> band, and how she gets up at three in the morning to do
> her career. Then we think, at least I do, "If she can do it,
> why can't I?" Men must have it rough in exactly this same
> way. Everywhere we turn there is someone telling us, if
> only by example, that we should be more, do more, have
> more.

Such comments lead me to believe that while all gender-
related "shoulds" help us identify our governing injunctions, and
help us see what drives our lives, the work of liberating ourselves
from these commands is clearly a genderless, human task. The
issue is not, as psychiatrist Thomas Szasz tells us, whether or not
we have found ourselves, but whether or not we have taken
responsibility for creating ourselves. Women have not taken
responsibility for defining and creating themselves as individuals
any more than men have. Each is pitifully defined by others, by
society and by a pathetic dependence upon externally-written
ways to be a "success" as a person.

For instance, simply achieving Super-Mom status is no

indication of self-definition. A recent study revealed that women comprise almost two-thirds of the general psychiatric, psychological or community mental health users. An estimated eighty-four percent of all private psychotherapy patients are women. Sixty percent of the new psychotherapy patients each year are women. Seventy percent of people using medically prescribed, mood-altering drugs are women. And eighty-five percent of these drugs are prescribed by family practice and internal medicine physicians, not psychiatrists. Even more alarming, the same report indicates that seventy-five percent of all physicians are men, and that eighty-six percent of all psychiatrists and eighty-four percent of all psychologists are men. Thus, women are allowing themselves and their "conditions" to be defined largely by men.

We are all lessened as persons when living according to unexamined, unconscious "shoulds." While it may be impossible to be totally free of parental or societal conditioning, it certainly is possible to increase our capacity to consciously choose a life that we value and that is supportive of the best in us. And it is possible for men and women to define themselves.

All of us owe it to ourselves to examine our own lives, the rules by which we live and the values inherent in our choices. We must decide for ourselves who we are, what our conduct should be, and how we wish to use our lives. This is a difficult assignment for everyone, because it forces us to confront the "shoulds" and the "shouldn'ts" that run our lives. And yet this confrontation is entirely right and essential, because it aids the growth in awareness that unites us with our own potential. The easiest thing is to do nothing; yet the harder task of self-scrutiny and truthful living is the only way to raise our self-esteem and self-respect.

Because this is so complex, we may need help from a competent therapist, especially if we feel incapable of plowing alone through the resistance and injunctions that victimize us. However, we do not need a therapist who is bent on helping us cope or adjust to the world, so that we simply become happier, more bland conformers.

Most psychologists or psychiatrists are just average people.

As such they may not have done their own self-defining work, much less be able to help others do theirs. Moreover, as I have written elsewhere, therapists easily see almost everything as a psychological problem, as neuroticism. Some problems simply persist because we are cowards, because we have avoided living as we know we ought to and want to, because we have avoided the harder (but truthful) choice. Perhaps the best guide here is our own intuition. Even a trusted friend, minister or rabbi can sometimes help us gain objectivity. When choosing a therapist, I urge people to be discerning about the person that therapist is.

Before selecting a therapist, I recommend visiting several for at least one evaluative session. This way we can find out what methods or approaches they prefer and, more importantly, we can appraise our own feelings about these professionals. In the final analysis, as with all choices, we are responsible for choosing a helpful, enlightened guide. We are responsible for staying with, or terminating, a therapist. We are responsible to evaluate the efficacy of treatment, and we alone are responsible for getting better.

Another approach to this shopping-around process is to consider that therapists have different objectives. Some psychotherapists try to help people cope with ordinary reality—with marriage, career-changing, various phobias, neuroticisms and so on. Others want to help the individual with what has been called the "transpersonal" level of reality. (See my book, *Ordinary People as Monks and Mystics*, Mahwah: Paulist Press, 1986.)

Transpersonal simply means the superconscious, true or "higher" self. In truth there is no "higher" self in actual space or location, but the word means the deepest aspects of the whole self, both conscious and unconscious. One long-range objective in ridding ourselves of constricting "shoulds" may be to locate and work with a guide who can communicate with us about our transpersonal self, all the while helping us also become persons who can act responsibly in day-to-day life. Anyone who calls himself a "guide," however, needs to demonstrate his own aptitude for effective living.

Of course, some will not wish to consult a therapist or helper. They may prefer to work alone in a journal, with a trusted, objective friend in conjunction with (or without) more formal therapy. Journal work is an excellent approach to uncovering hidden truths about ourselves, and I heartily recommend keeping an autobiographical, private log of both triumphs and tribulations along this path.

Another route to discovering our specific "shoulds" is to learn to listen to our bodies, minds and feelings about what we are experiencing day-to-day, moment-to-moment.

One woman who was able to hear her body and feelings said she realized that guilt pinpointed many of her significant "shoulds." By keeping in touch with her frequent bouts with self-imposed guilt (which she felt at the smallest provocation), she realized that she assumed inordinate responsibility for her husband's and parents' happiness and comfort. Her parents had taught her that she was "supposed to keep them and all people in authority" happy, cared for and safe. She typically denied herself time to work on important work projects whenever her husband asked for her help in his business. What finally brought the whole matter to a head was the increasing resentment and inner turmoil she felt whenever she tried, but failed, to tell her husband that she was busy with her own work.

Another person discovered how henpecked and dominated he was when he learned to listen to his own feelings. He had been brought up to "respect" women, which in his case meant that he felt compelled to keep his mother and his wife happy. Afraid to get a divorce, even though he experienced himself to be in a spirit-breaking marriage, he drifted physically and emotionally away from his wife until he found a mistress. However, as often happens, the mistress eventually assumed a progressively dominant role in his life until she also demanded that he "respect" her needs. His own increasing frustration and resentment and the various cues that his body gave him (i.e., backaches that physicians couldn't help with any kind of medication or surgery) finally brought him face-to-face with his own docility and, as he put it, "blind stupidity."

The woman who feels that she must always look pretty can locate her "shoulds" by becoming sensitive to her feelings. She may feel anxious when she looks in the mirror and sees a wrinkle

or gray hair. Perhaps she feels a gripping in the pit of her
stomach when a prettier woman comes into her presence or
competes for the attention of the man in her life, because, as we
have seen, "shoulds" and "shouldn'ts" travel in constellations, and
this woman can uncover many other "shoulds" just by being
sensitive to what her body and nervous system are saying to her.
Our physical pain is an excellent guide to the diseases of our soul.
More important than examining wrinkles or gray hair is the
examination of dis-ease, for this is a silent, but powerful, language
capable of telling someone how he may be hurting himself.

Once we recognize how we are dominated by our "shoulds,"
we can start to break, or at least lessen, their hold over us.
Combatting the tyranny of our "shoulds" is a twofold process.
First, we must act in responsible, creative, and safe ways to move
in the direction of what we truly value and feel we must do.
Simultaneously, we must accept responsibility for the
consequences of these new actions as well as of our existing
habits.

Let's take a closer look at each part of this process. First, in
regard to taking action, I must emphasize again the wisdom of
taking small steps. Keeping in mind the advice of William James,
who said, "What should be preached is courage weighted with
responsibility," we must remember that some people are so bent
on self-destruction that they misinterpret all suggestions, taking
them to the extreme. Thus, they find one more way to do
themselves in. These are the people who jump into deep water
without knowing how to swim—the reckless, self-and-other
defeating. We must develop the ability and courage to become
positive rebels, not to commit suicide! Thus, I encourage people
who are ready to defy their old "shoulds" to start with small,
cautious steps, rather than with gigantic leaps by which they
might hurt themselves still further.

For example, the man who felt dominated by all the women
in his life—and realized that in subtle ways he even encouraged
their dominance—began to simply refuse to answer their phone
calls immediately. He waited until he was ready to call them,
thus honoring his schedules and his own desire to communicate.
By so doing, he learned how to add his own needs into the

interpersonal equation. From this minor step, he was able to extend his new-found self-control into other areas of his life. Gradually, he was able to take more major steps that attested to his growing courage, self-affirmation and self-respect. He found that, within six months of beginning this kind of "paying attention to himself," he could take many other steps, large and small, which symbolically taught his mind, subconscious, nervous system and emotions how he ideally wanted to act. As he felt more respected in his relationship, he came to see that he wanted to solve his marital relationship. Soon it was possible for him to tell his wife what he needed from her. To his surprise and delight, she listened. Ultimately, he was able to terminate his extramarital relationship and have a strongly committed married life. This process took several years, each of which brought him into more accord with himself. I mention the length of time his growth required because usually it is a lifelong process.

Next, as we learn to take responsibility for the consequences of our behaviors, all of us must define for ourselves the actions we need to take. Two factors influence our ability to find our own correct, most useful actions. First, we have to be capable of tenacious creativity. Tenacity is essential because, as shown in our chapter on resistance, we resist much of what is good for us. Creativity is important because we will be acting in new ways and so may need to experiment. It is easy to act correctly once or twice and then forget to continue, returning to our old habits. We may need to keep track of the habits we are trying to start and reward ourselves each time we behave productively. Here again, a notebook, diary or journal is a helpful tool.

One way I suggest dealing with this recording-process is to write down the positive things we do each day. The best time to do this is right before going to bed, so that our minds can register our productive actions before and during sleep. This is when creative learning is at its peak—when our minds easily absorb new attitudes and ideas. It does not matter how many actions we have to list. One day we may have only a few, another day as many as twenty. The point is to focus our attention on the productive, self-affirming actions we took during any given day and then mentally acknowledge our small victories. I have found this technique very helpful to clients in raising their self-esteem and freeing themselves from old behavior patterns. Just a silent positive mental acknowledgement before bed is often enough to start building more constructive habits. One client of mine said she used her driving-home-from-work time as a "quiet period" in which to reflect upon her day's positive happenings. "I mentally reward myself at the end of each working day," she said, "and this helps me reinforce the good things I am learning to do."

Another very helpful technique is to increase our concentration abilities so that we can remember, moment-to-moment, what our new intention is. TM, Zen or other classical meditation techniques are excellent training devices for developing a stronger focus. These ancient, classical systems are natural partners for any self-improvement program since research shows that these also enhance self-esteem and bring order into life.

In addition to tenacity, we also need ingenuity so as to devise positive actions that will train us in new self-attitudes and behaviors. One commonly suggested device that can help us be more creative in thinking up actions is to list our goals. Then, for each goal, we can also list ten to twenty activities that will help us reach the goal. A goal is not "do-able"; only an activity can be done. Through this process of listing the steps which will take us toward our desired objective, we help ourselves to move through our "shoulds" and "shouldn'ts": the activity list forces our minds to grapple with how we want to get to our goals. The short questions listed in Chapter Three show "how" to go about identifying activities which relate to our key goals.

One of my clients was terrified about looking for a new job, after losing a job that he had held for years. He expressed his feelings about facing job-hunting:

I don't mind telling you that I'm filled with trepidation. I feel like I'm too old to be going out on interviews, that I don't want to have to "prove" myself all over again. And I'm pessimistic about my chances "out there" in the job market world.

As he started looking for another management position, he realized that he was under the control of an old lifetime injunction: "You shouldn't boast about yourself." His fear of job interviews was intense, because he felt thwarted in his communications. He wanted to tell prospective employers about his many strengths, but he felt uncomfortable "selling my wares," as he put it.

To clarify what he needed to do, he began by writing down his goal: to locate another upper management position with a Fortune 500 company. Then he listed several activities that would help him reach his goal:

- Prepare my resume with the help of a top executive placement firm.

- Write personal letters to all the contacts I've identified in the area of my interest.

- Follow up letters with personal phone calls, so as to get interviews whenever possible.

- Positively present myself during the interview. This means talking about my accomplishments, what I've achieved for this company, and what I've accomplished nationally in my professional organization.

- Follow up all high potential interviews with a note, when appropriate.

Listing goals and activities is one way to discover the actions we need to take in order to chip away at our "shoulds."

Another method is to identify role models—people who are already doing what we want to do (or who are what we admire)—and then list the characteristics they have that we want to emulate.

For instance, one of my clients identified several well-known musicians as inspiring role models. Since childhood, she had loved music and had wanted to be a musician. But she didn't

believe that she had the talent, so she went to business school
and abandoned her first love. By identifying her role models, she
realized that music had to be a part of her life, at least in her free
time. She also discovered that all her role models possessed great
tenacity. One was a blind singer, another was a handicapped
violinist, and another was an acclaimed concert pianist who had
faced many personal difficulties as a child. Upon further reflection
she admitted that she had given up music because she lacked
perseverance, and that there were other areas of her life that
suffered because, as a rule, she gave up too easily. Thus, here
was another viable attribute she could work into her "action
plan." The trait she admired in others was already in her, needing
only to be developed.

A third way to discover our own individual action plans is to
list our values, and then determine how we can demonstrate
these clearly and consistently in our lives. A sculptor friend of
mine took a part-time job as a carpenter to pay his bills. But he
soon found out that it was essential to include sculpting in his
daily life. He had to keep the value of art alive for himself and
stay committed to what he really was in his own eyes—an artist.

> If I don't sculpt each day—and I usually manage to do this
> late into the night—I feel I am abandoning something that
> has deep significance for me. When I first started my part-
> time job, I felt relieved at first because it helped me finan-
> cially. But soon I felt uneasy—as if I had rejected something
> very critical to my happiness. As soon as I disciplined my-
> self to work at least three hours each night on my sculpting,
> I felt my life was back in balance again.

The other facet of gaining control over our self-limiting
"shoulds" is learning to accept the consequences of those actions.
This is rarely easy. By acting as we want, we may stir our parents'
anger and friends' rejection. We run the risk of bringing upon
ourselves financial difficulties or society's disapproval. Indeed, it
is the consequences (not the action that precedes the
consequences) that we really fear and want to avoid. And it is the

fear of consequences that keeps us stuck in our old "should" programming.

If we intend to move through our "shoulds," then we must learn to face the consequences of each action. The man who began to stand up to the domineering women in his life had to face his fear of doing something "forbidden." At first, he felt reluctant and incapable of saying what he really wanted. He made excuses for not calling back his wife and mother right away. Later, he was able to tell them it hadn't been convenient or possible for him to call immediately. In time, months and months later, he had some heated, confrontational discussions with his mother and wife. He told them he was changing, that he didn't like being phoned so frequently at work, and that he would prefer they not phone him there at all, except in an emergency.

This was a major breakthrough for him. "I felt as if I were facing my own death," he admitted, smiling nervously at the hold his "should" programming had over his behavior and his nervous system. But, because he persevered, he knew the next time would be easier. And it was. In time his relationship with his wife improved, as she actually liked and even respected him more for standing up for himself. They were eventually able to go into marriage counseling; in time, they managed to save their marriage—something they could not have done if the man persisted in obeying his fearful instincts and tendency to withdraw.

The person who wanted to find another job also needed to face the consequences of his actions:

I schedule appointments for myself to get out and meet people who have a position open. During my interviews, I feel frightened. But I've found the best medicine is just to bite the bullet and talk anyway. The bad news is it doesn't seem to get much easier. The good news is that yesterday I received a call from an excellent company. They want me to come back for a third interview, and I think if I want the job, it's mine.

Similarly, my sculptor friend has had to deal with the consequences of taking a part-time job to survive financially, while doing his art at night. Disciplining himself enough to fit in three hours of sculpting each day meant giving up some other things in his life. But once he acknowledged how important his art was to his life, he knew he had to accept any inconveniences. "I never knew myself as one who could work this hard, but my love for sculpting has made me certain that this is the right course for me," he said in explaining his ability to have two jobs.

This whole idea of accepting consequences compares to an experience I had years ago when I had to have some acupuncture treatments. Early in the treatment series, my tendency was to flinch, to pull away from the anticipated pain of the needle. Indeed, my anticipation of the pain was worse than the pain itself, and it also made the pain more severe. Because I, in fear, tightened my muscles, I made it harder for the needle to penetrate the sore spot. My Asian doctor would tell me, "Let it go. Move toward the pain. Don't resist the needle." I came to see that the needle was a perfect metaphor for the problem situations of life. As I went toward the needle, teaching each muscle to welcome it, I also learned to invite the costs of my choice—in this case, a little sting. With the sting came healing. By accepting the consequences of our choices, by facing our opponent, our pain, our difficulty, we increase our self-esteem and self-respect.

We do have to pay for our choices. Some of our choices bring a deep and more prolonged sting than that of a mere needle: sacrifices, deprivation or troublesome situations, ongoing self-discipline, risks. The sooner we "go toward the sting," the sooner we are able to get on with the demands and greater challenges of our lives which the consequences of our acts deliver. In moving courageously toward the results we want, we transcend many of society's limiting "shoulds"—simultaneously liberating ourselves for the life and the work we really want.

7

The Money Will Follow

Giving and receiving are one in truth.

A Course in Miracles

A young entrepreneurial friend of mine, in response to my saying that I was writing a book titled *Do What You Love, The Money Will Follow,* asked eagerly, "How long do I have to wait?" We both laughed, knowing that he seriously meant that at his stage of business life, money was sparse and that he was tired of "waiting" for it to follow.

He, like almost everyone who is not independently wealthy, wanted some positive reassurance that he would not be broke forever. He won't be. Judging from his tenacity, his strong, driving work-ethic and his excellence in his field, he is sure to be materially successful soon. But, as my title suggests, there is a waiting period. The waiting period is certainly different for different people.

Three aspects of "the money will follow" are discussed in this chapter: "letting go," "waiting," and "inner wealth."

First, people who try something new—perhaps they take a hobby or keen interest and turn it into a viable business, or they change careers and move from one field to another—have to be good at "letting go." They must be capable of sensing when it is the right time to move and when it is best to wait. Some people are naturally intuitive about their risk-taking. Others use risks as a way of doing themselves in: their self-defeating scripts, their low self-evaluation and their lack of experience can create poor judgment calls about "letting go." Almost everyone, good risk-taker and not so good, wants a formula to help him take risks. Unfortunately what works for one may not work for another. Nothing can take us off the hook of being individually responsible for our life decisions.

Next, there is a "waiting" period, as the title to this book and this chapter suggest. What we do while we wait is also a matter of judgment, choice and faith. It is during this waiting period that we must, individually, learn to "read" the situation. This is when many people, after a period of evaluation, decide that they do not have the talent or temperament to continue. Perhaps they, like a client of mine who started her own business, realize that they prefer the excitement of working with a large company instead of the solitary, lonely atmosphere of being the chief cook and bottle-washer, the head, hands and tail of the organization:

> I miss the chemistry of working with lots of people in a large company—the group meetings, the lunches with my friends. This business of doing everything myself isn't for me. I thought it was, but I was wrong. I didn't realize how much I would long for someone to talk to about my victories and defeats. I didn't know how difficult it would be to keep my emotions in check while I waited for this business to "take." I suppose I just don't have the personality for this entrepreneurial venture. I still love the work. But I'm aware and honest enough, to see that I can't do it . . .

Another part of waiting, along with having the material and emotional resources to persist, is knowing how to judge external feedback, the environment and the results of our work itself. This, too, is part of the evaluation process, a process which is natural and necessary in changing careers or our work focus. Those who evaluate correctly, those who persist in their efforts, are almost guaranteed success.

The third aspect of "the money will follow" is the ability to think well of ourselves and our capabilities, even without money. This is such a large subject that I will spend two chapters discussing it. In our next chapter, I discuss the key role of being resourceful during times of uncertainty and waiting. However, in this chapter it is important to acknowledge that each person who embarks upon a new vocational path may be subject to strong negative self-opinions if money is not forthcoming quickly or in ample supply. This is certainly true in America where we typically equate success and money. The successful person, in our society, is the one who has a great deal of money. The unsuccessful person is the one who is poor. Our own self-evaluation—our subjective comfort and discomfort—is critical during the early stages of waiting for our financial security because it can trigger unproductive actions during this period.

Let us take a closer look at each of these three aspects briefly described above. First is the matter of "letting go." This issue is likely to stimulate strong emotional responses in us that can overshadow and color our judgment in other areas of life as we "wait." One man wrote to me about his experience in leaving a solid, tenured position as a teacher in order to pursue an insecure position as a potter. In addition to his letter, he sent me a tape that included these remarks:

> I voted with my feet to leave a very successful teaching career and become a potter which, in 1976, seemed to me like walking off a cliff. The terra firma was so firm. I'd always fancied myself as a good teacher, and I'd achieved tenure. After eight years, choosing to go full-time into pottery really seemed like walking off a cliff. Nine years later I think of myself as still being in free-fall, and maybe there is no ground below. It's all something we have conjured up to set ourselves up in some categories.
>
> Those categories, of course, are the measure of our lives, and therefore we can't go beyond them. I think back those nine plus years ago and see a person who wanted to be totally creative. And I was totally terrified that there was no ground on which to stand, be successful, have food to eat, pay the bills, and so on. But I really felt that that was the way to go. Somehow in March of 1976, I chose not to come back. I've been a potter ever since.
>
> When I come to see myself in 1985, I see there is some higher self, some spirit or way that has opened. The

universe responded to allow this kind of activity to take place, and I'm totally grateful every day.

What I found in those early years while doing pottery was that people wanted to buy my pottery, and I won prizes. As I look back I see that the universe was responding to my intention. I was ignorant of these (spiritual laws) and just felt that I was getting some real good strokes artistically, financially as being a potter, which gave me more feedback about doing pottery and the psychological support to keep going.

What impresses me about this person's comments is his admission that he felt as if he were stepping into an abyss. This is a feeling expressed by many people I have talked to about deliberately choosing to cut ourselves off from everything that seems so important to us and defined us in the past. This choice is only possible when we feel strong enough to deal with the ramifications and consequences of our separation from the things that we have heretofore clung to and felt important, such as security, certain relationships, community standing and so on.

Many things can be sacrificed—not just economic stability—when we leave one vocational/work form for another. We give up the support of others. We may have to give up working relationships that we enjoy and even need, as did the woman who left a large organization to go out on her own. And, of course, we are giving up economic security. What makes one person able to give up and let go, and another unable to do so? My thought is that the need to do the new work—especially when this need is ignited by our innate talent—and our inner sense that we will be able to carry it off successfully are important motivators.

In terms of a need to do the work, no doubt the more talent we have and the more we love the work, the easier it will be to pull away from the familiar and move into the unknown. Also, each has a differing need to express some aspect of the unlived life. Some say, "I didn't want to come to the end of my life and see there were important things I'd never tried." Others don't see themselves as lacking in self-expressive channels, or if they see their lack, they prefer to sacrifice themselves, their talent, their need to express something new in favor of previously made commitments. Ultimately, each must evaluate his own decision.

The ability to move into the unknown is related to high self-esteem, as is the ability to risk successfully—that is, to risk so as not to lose all. Let us look first at the relationship between high self-esteem and the ability to tolerate the unknown.

Risk-takers fall into three categories: those who take no risks, those who take poorly calculated risks, and those who take well-planned risks that usually succeed. People who have high levels of self-esteem generally plan their risks correctly, and typically they produce beneficial outcomes. The same potter who was quoted above suggested this "formula" for knowing when to let go and when not to:

> First I began selling to friends, and they encouraged me to sell in the stores. I had success. I think unless the universe feeds back some positive "go" signals, no matter how faint, that it would be the utmost folly to proceed along that direction.
>
> The reverse is equally valid: if I get "stop" signals, then it's time to stop. . . . If I don't, the universe knocks harder, gives me a signal that even a dummy like me can recognize. Because I have enjoyed abundant health since quitting teaching in the public school and I have had some success in creating a reality of teaching, selling, making pottery, then so far it is a "go." So, you ask, "What gave you the strength to let go of teaching and move into full-time pottery?" I would answer that the bolstering for making the change came from outside, not from within.

Usually, people who take successful risks have a memory bank of risk-taking episodes. Perhaps the individual was on his own early in life and thus learned how to gauge uncertainty. Perhaps his parents worked with him as a child, training and teaching him how to take risks. Such was the case with a client of mine, known for his excellent judgment.

My father was an excellent risk-taker. He taught me how to be one, too. He likened risk-taking to passing a car on the road. If you can see just a little bit ahead of you that the road is clear, it usually is safe to go ahead. He preferred to wait until he could see more than just that little bit: that way, he believed, the odds against a car or anything else getting in his way were in his favor. But if there is even a suspicion that another car is coming, or that the bank is too steep, or that the curve is too sharp or you haven't enough room or visibility, then it is best to wait until the correct opening comes along. Be patient. It will come. My dad never had an accident, and he also was a real success—in life and business.

People who have this intuitive understanding of the "correct opening" for risks are those who have fully analyzed the consequences beforehand. When they start their project or make their decision, they have already mentally rehearsed and visualized what might happen. They have seen their options and are ready to put one hundred percent attention and energy into making their decision or action successful.

On the other hand, those with low self-esteem usually lack the mental gamesmanship to do such rehearsing. They have had little training in taking risks, and so they doubt their ability to perform successfully. This doubt cripples their decision-making ability as well as their follow-through. As suggested in earlier chapters, it is foolish to start practicing risk-taking in major areas of life, but probably essential to gain a memory and mental image of oneself as a good chooser. There are areas of life which, however minor, may be better places to get our practice.

As we have said before, given the choice between safety and growth, humans will choose safety. Because of this inclination and need, it is essential to make our risk-taking "safe." A woman I know wanted to start her own business, but she had two children to support and needed a lot of savings in order to embark on her goal. She waited three years, saving money all the while, until she had a year's income in the bank to draw from for her family's needs. Only then did she feel ready to let go of her full time job.

Another person, a man who also had a family to support, used real-estate sales as a way to finance his career-change. Knowing that he was going to make the change, he invested in two single-family dwellings, putting very little money down on each. Then he fixed up each house as nicely as he could with paint, elbow grease and as few cash-intensive expenditures as possible. Finally he sold one house and rented the other at a healthy monthly rent so that he would have positive cash flow coming in. In this way he secured his and his family's basic needs for at least a year and a half. And he also gave himself the courage and permission to do what he wanted to do.

These are creative solutions. To be creative means to bring something into existence that did not exist before. In our working lives, it often means tolerating ambiguity long enough to experiment with different options. While the insecure person is usually blocked in terms of inner images, ideas and imaginative solutions to his problems, the more confident person knows, "No matter what comes along, I can figure out a solution."

The second action (really a non-action or series of acts) which needs to be taken is waiting for the money, which is almost as difficult as letting go. While we wait for our income to match our needs and as we dream of accomplishing the goals that are so important to us, we also evaluate ourselves and our talent. This evaluation process can be very difficult to bear when we are feeling frightened or when things don't go our way.

I recall, when I was just starting my own practice, I knew that in addition to working with corporate leaders I also wanted to write. I wanted to teach and communicate with others via books, articles and tapes. How disastrous it seemed when I received rejection letters from publishers. True, I was buoyed up by the fact that my first article sold immediately, and several articles sold after that, but laced in with these happy events were the inevitable rejection letters, form letters at that, which I grew to recognize even in the envelope! The personal rejection letters were even worse. One New York editor of a slick executive magazine wrote me a scathing personal letter, upbraiding me for the abstract ideas contained in my article, and scornfully telling me that I obviously didn't know a thing about business writing.

To this day I don't know what provoked her to take her own time to write me such a letter.

This "waiting" period is when we must become good readers of our own situation. This is made even more difficult because we are not objective when it comes to our financial affairs.

A friend of mine has worked many years to become an actress, and her work has grown steadily—in terms of both material success and personal satisfaction. She says that she read her situation not only by the money she received from her performances, but by the level of what she terms "movement" and by her own artistic measures:

> In this business you never have a clear feeling of success. There are moments of glorious feelings. But this builds so slowly that you cannot see it happening. You're as good as your last show, and what are you doing next? You try to give the ambiguity a structure, make it as concrete as possible. I did that by making lists, looking at my goals, looking back at each year. I take "it"—my success—by the year, and look to see what I've done. That gives me structure. Unfortunately, there is none for me now in the forward direction, so I look backward to get my structure.
>
> At a certain point it comes down to money: Can I afford to do this anymore? So far, I've been able to increase my income each year. There were a couple of years in the beginning where I had nothing. Then there were a couple of good years, then nothing. Then this year was my best year financially.
>
> As an artist, I hate to measure my track record by money, but it does allow me to remain in the field. If I call myself an artist though, I have to use another standard to measure success. As an artist I have to look at what I have created. With that, I'm not yet satisfied. So I continue, because by the feedback from the external world, I am being paid well enough to continue. And I continue to want to grow as an artist because from my internal measure, my own artistic standards, I must create something better if I am to stay in the field.

One thing I will say: stay away from negative people. Avoid them at all costs. There is always a reason for not doing something, and often a very good reason for not doing it. But just as often there is a reason, and a good one, for doing something. And it is easier than overcoming negative thoughts that you have to wrestle with. Who has the energy for that?

I suppose, in the beginning, my only conscious decision was to begin moving—backward, forward or sideways, it didn't really matter, as long as I could get unstuck. Now my advice to someone who wants to achieve something is: get out of bed in the morning, and it's probably best to get out of bed early in the morning.

Another woman, who made the transition from a lucrative executive secretary's position at a major Beverly Hills brokerage firm to a trades profession, told me she "knew" she was in the wrong work in her old job. She found herself unhappy every day with what she had to do and with the amount of money she was earning. By ordinary standards, she was in a good profession, but she had to answer to someone else all the time. She felt that she could only build a proper future for herself if she went to work for herself. She wanted to have a trade and make the kind of money she saw men making.

I actually went to the library and researched the various trades open to someone with my interests. I used to work in Hawaii as a jewelry designer, and I studied art in school. I came up with the idea of wallcovering which appealed to me for several reasons: It's creative, I could use my art interests, and I could earn as much as any man at it. I liked the idea of working for myself, and I thought I'd be good at it. The problem was that I had to get about five hundred hours of schooling in wallcovering so that I could eventually get into the union. That was hard to do, because women were not allowed to join in the past. I am small, too, and I faced a lot of criticism about my size.

But even though I was scared at the start, I lived

day to day and tried not to worry. I have a lot of faith, I suppose—a sense that some positive energy will get me by. I'm also willing to pay my dues. Of course, this might be easier if I were married, had someone to fall back on when the finances got tight, but I realize I don't need that. I'd also have to say that my father was a really great person in my eyes. He brought up all of us to think that no matter how bad things get, something good comes out of it. If I go back to that lesson when things get rough for me, I see that all I have to do is hang in there and things will ease up eventually.

Why did I want to change careers? I had wanted my old career, but once you accomplish what you set out to do, it's often not what it was cut out to be—so you just let go of it.

I think I've given up some significant things to have the life I have now, but I see that I'm my own person. Since I've done this, I can see that I can do anything. I wouldn't want to go through some things again. But I see that I have had courage, and I know that I can use that same courage to make anything happen correctly for me in my life.

We see embodied in this woman's remarks many of the characteristics we have discussed throughout this book. First, there is her obvious memory of success, which she feels she can apply to other difficulties. It is as if by succeeding in one area and seeing herself courageous at one time, she can leverage that experience into other challenges that life places in front of her.

Next, there is her tremendous capacity to wait—through five hundred hours of schooling. She deals with criticisms about her size and sex and has the ability to sustain a period of little income to gain the long-term reward of having a trade that will allow her to earn as much money as a man. Also, I liked the way this individual thought through her vocational options: she researched her field by herself, she analyzed her strengths, interests and goals and put all of these together to come up with the ingenious trade of wallpapering. Finally, her remark "I'm willing to pay my dues" really sums up nicely the characteristics of all successful people: their ability to choose the consequences, and hardships of their professions, and to act, despite unpleasantness.

As was true for "letting go," self-esteem also plays a role in our ability to wait. From the comments above, we see that wholesome, healthfully striving persons want to do better, study more and achieve some worthwhile goal—and to put in the time and effort it takes to get there. They are willing to work hard and benefit others, not only themselves.

By contrast, people who are tied up with self-doubt, negative feelings or resentments are unwilling to take risks. Moreover, they are unwilling to extend themselves for others in the services they render or the products they create. Because they have impoverished self-esteem, they feel that they must always be outstanding. They feel that they must always be performing at the "significant" company or attending only the best schools in order to have value in their own eyes. I recall one highly capable young information systems client of mine who was unhappy with the lack of recognition he was getting in his company. When I suggested that he write an article for one of the many computer trade journals in his area of expertise, he cringed, saying that the only journal he would want to be published in would be *Harvard Business Review*. This young man did not have an MBA (Master's of Business Administration), nor had he ever written anything before and he expected to start at the top. He could not satisfy himself with mundane success, such as publishing somewhere else, because for him that would mean he is mediocre, which in some ways he is. He is not mediocre as a person or as a thinker, but as an achiever. His reluctance to stretch into new areas and pay his dues—do the "dog work," as Julia Childs calls chopping onions for the stew—is bound to keep him in an average position where he will continue to crave, but not receive, recognition.

Perhaps no one understands this issue better than psychotherapist Samuel Warner who in his book *Self-Realization and Self-Defeat* describes it thusly:

> To the man who harbors chronic resentment toward authority, who inwardly nurses an injured self-concept, and who renders each day bearable by dosage with the opiate

of future grandiosity, there is little or no pride in being an "average success." . . . There is rather for this man a sense of significance only in extremes, in the actual achievement of outstanding success, or in chronic—albeit self-engineered—outstanding failure (p. 158).

Warner continues to outline a predictable pattern in those who have low self-esteem: they repeatedly begin their projects by energetically striving for a huge, flashy success, and, missing that, they turn aside from whatever success might be theirs, experiencing themselves instead as utter failures.

I mention this pattern because in the critical months and years of "waiting" for the money to follow the person who ventures into the loved, not-yet-successful work area faces the risk that not only will the money be delayed, but also that he will feel he has experienced a failure when, in fact, he only lacks a flashy, grandiose victory. This is, in the final analysis, a very personal judgment call, and no book can give the formula for when to stay or quit. As the champion basketball star Bill Russell once said during his radio call-in show in Los Angeles, "It takes a winner to know when to change directions."

The third point I want to touch on in this chapter is inner wealth. There is a sad psychic relationship between our self-worth and our monetary worth. In our society, where people and institutions are measured by their net worth, individuals often make the mistake of appraising themselves by the amount of money they make per year. Upper management jobs are valued by some persons not because of the responsibility they offer, but because of the higher salaries. For example, scientists who are not right for management jobs often leave their technical specialties—where they may be nationally known figures—for a "people position" that pays more, has more visibility, yet doesn't satisfy them at all.

Housewives, by the same token, often feel worthless because they are not earning a salary while their career women neighbors earn handsome sums to contribute to their families' budgets. A friend of mine, home for a short period of time after years of working side-by-side with her husband, admitted feeling hampered and self-condemned because she wasn't adding to the household income.

Women in our society often say they want to marry men who earn a good living, and men often receive more than their deserved measure of recognition and accolades because they are wealthy. The fact that they may be dull-witted, unethical or unattractively aggressive matters less than the fact that they are rich.

Even parents desiring only the best for their children hope— not too secretly usually—that their offspring will select a profession that pays well. Fulfillment on the job and satisfaction as an intrinsic benefit to the work seem to come second.

I have no quarrel with making money. The reason I deliberately put the word money into the title of this book is so that readers could be assured that part of my definition of a successful life involves having the means to provide for ourselves and those who depend upon us.

However, I have seen too many people defeat themselves unnecessarily because their emphasis was wrongly placed. Either they concentrated too much on the monetary gain they wanted from a job or service—and by doing so short-changed the recipient of the job/service—or they believed that if they were to do what they really wanted, they could not earn money. Each person has the ability to produce something that someone else wants, and in so doing to produce at least enough wealth and reward to support himself and his family. Whether he or she will use that ability is another matter. Money "problems" are usually a part of other problems, many of which we have discussed already. Many individuals are not willing to discipline themselves sufficiently to take responsibility for their money "problems." I recall once hearing a psychologist say that people who couldn't manage their money couldn't manage their minds.

I do not remember where I heard this statement, but I have thought about it for a long time. From watching myself overcome certain unproductive attitudes and habits, and from working with many people who have either overcome similar patterns or who have such excellent work habits that they are almost assured material success, my sense is that we have a lot of control over our incomes, expenditures and livelihoods—much more control than we give ourselves credit for—and that there may indeed be a connection between our mental control and focus and our ability to make money.

As long as we have a clear idea of our goals and properly use the inclinations and in-born talents that we already have, I believe that the money will follow. However, while we wait it is essential that we protect ourselves from the cultural consciousness that says we are what we earn. We certainly are not.

Only the individual with a healthy, wholesome self-view will feel inwardly rich when he or she is outwardly broke. This point came home to me strongly when I was interviewing people for my first book. One of the young men that I interviewed, an environmentalist who lived on less than $5,000 per year, had so much adoration and such an ecstatic response for life that I was stirred to try to see what he had that wealthier persons lacked. Essentially, what he possessed was a peaceful, full heart, a spiritually complete nature, and an ability to see beauty all around him instead of lack.

Most people earning less than $5,000 per year would be worrying about their bills and payments and rationalizing why they didn't have more money. Money would be an overriding concern in their life. But this individual, having deliberately chosen his life's work knowing that the consequences of living as he chose would mean his income would be limited for a time, didn't come from that position. Actually, he was secure within himself and so needed very little material wealth to "make" him feel secure.

One of the largest enemies we need to deal with (notice I do not say fight, because this is an inward enemy, and we do not need to become an adversary to ourselves) is our own expectations and attitudes toward money. A gift anyone can give himself is that of expecting to be paid a decent, fair amount of money for his labors. If we are not earning a sufficient amount for our efforts, then it is up to each of us to find out why. Usually, all other things being equal, the problem lies in our own expectations or in the level of energy we are willing to put into the job at hand. A Japanese church I once visited had a saying that went something like this: we should put the other person's interests into our efforts during our work, and we should try to create something valuable for the other person through our concentrated energies.

My sense is that many who are not earning a decent livelihood are hoping to get something for nothing. The people I hire to do work for me are people who not only can be trusted with the technical aspects of the job, but also are trustworthy in terms of the energy they expend. One such person is a carpenter who has been helping me remodel my home.

After many false starts with other workmen—some who weren't really qualified, others who promised to show up for the job and didn't, or who came late and left early—I finally found one who is meticulous and careful with everything he does. He always shows up, always takes his time with the projects, always cleans up carefully after each step of the building or dismantling. In other words, he is dependable and thorough and knows what he is doing. True, he does take a little longer, but I trust his work. Because I trust his work, I had a hunch he was someone who trusted that "the money would follow." I asked him about his work and whether it had been difficult for him to work at something that basically has no guarantees.

I have a master's degree in English. When it was time to continue for my doctorate, my advisor told me that I would have to become a scholar, that I'd have to publish on a regular basis, that I would essentially have very little freedom with the type of academic ladder I'd have to climb in the university setting. I decided that wasn't for me. Instead, I chose to move north and take my chances as a carpenter. I've never regretted it. I cannot say that I chose this work because I loved it. It's more like I chose to live in a place I loved and had to find something to do. I'm good at this work, and it turns out to have been the right choice for me.

He went on to say that he began in the early seventies at $3 per hour as a carpenter's assistant, learning the trade, and finally getting some jobs on his own.

What I especially like is that I call my own shots. I only work at jobs that suit me and only for those people who are on my wavelength. I can honestly say that I love my work and my life and that the two are interrelated. I guess, to answer your question, I trust myself to be able to earn all the money I need, because I've done it. That's all the security I need.

This is a familiar refrain. Rather than allowing the dictates and definitions of society to define them, people who are self-trusting, who know and believe in the value of the service or product they are providing, define themselves. They are not intimidated by a culture that equates high monetary worth with worth as a person. Nor are they intimidated by fluctuating social conditions or economic ups and downs.

In sum, as Emerson once wrote, we are born to grow rich through the use of our faculties. Money does not automatically follow someone who simply decides to embark upon a different career or job path. As we have seen, it is more complicated than that.

But money is more likely to follow the person with determination, talent and the high self-esteem that allows him to be a healthy chooser, so that his risk-taking, judgment skills and sense of timing are sound. Money is also more likely to follow the person who has tapped into the vitality hidden in the things he loves. As we do what we were born to do, as we love the things we are required to do—even the mundane, even the "dog work"—we stimulate a qualitatively superior energy within us. Anyone who has ever been mesmerized listening to someone describe an exciting experience knows how difficult it is to break our attention away from the person who is keenly excited about his own involvements.

The salesman who loves his products sells these to us with a superior level of interest than the one who is half-heartedly involved with the product. The housewife preparing her family's meal, or the one who is excited about the party-table she is setting, puts something special from within herself into the meal or into the celebration.

The potter whose remarks I quoted earlier in this chapter said of his pottery, "When I sell a piece of pottery I've placed some sort of little beacon of intelligence in it which is blinking on and off in the homes of people who have my work. Well, maybe it isn't blinking off and on, it's totally DC current: on all the time. That's the extent of myself that is in the work."

The vitality he puts into his work ("I can get totally mystical about it," he said on tape) adds up to be the happiness and vitality he gets back from it. Vitality stems from expressing the special light in ourselves. Vitality helps us earn money, and perhaps it is the vitality we have for our work that ultimately provides us with the monetary support to continue. Perhaps it is the diligence and perseverance we give our efforts that results in money.

I rather think it is a combination of all the things we have discussed, certainly not the least of which is the enjoyment we get from the work. Our enjoyment predisposes us to create more and better works and enables others to see value in it. Thereby they value us—with the trust, respect, and money to support our efforts.

8

The Three Laws
of Resourcefulness

**Prosperity is living easily and happily in the real world,
whether you have money or not.**

Jerry Gillies

Resourcefulness is the trait we must develop in ourselves if we
want control over our working lives. Whether we plan to create
our own job, or wish only to "retire" early to do other things we
enjoy, or want to combine an "ideal" life-style or place of
residence with work that appeals to us, our own innovation will
be a needed ally. If we examine the definition of the word
resourceful we see that it is little more than creativity: the ability
to bring something into existence that does not yet exist, the skill
of dealing with any kind of situation.

When we examine the personalities of people who do what
they love, we find that they are usually highly resourceful
persons. They are innovative types who dare to try something
new, even when people around them do not support their efforts,
even when they have other responsibilities (such as families to
support).

Again, when we look at the roots of resourcefulness, we see
that the trait is intertwined with high self-esteem: that feeling
that makes a person confident he can figure out what to do—even
when he doesn't have a ready-made blueprint or someone to tell
him "how."

Such a person is my friend Paul who started his own design
and architectural firm when he graduated from college. Although

126

he had worked part-time during college for a variety of architectural firms, he felt that he had to start his own business.

> The pure frustration of not getting credit for my ideas, watching others get acknowledged for things I had created, knowing that I was capable of doing things on a much more elegant scale than others around me—all these frustrations really hurt me. This forced me to say to myself, "Listen, it's time to do it."
>
> Also, deep within me I must have always known I was going to be in business for myself: the way I studied other small businesses, collected catalogues and just thought about the ins and outs of having my own firm must have been a subconscious building up for this time.
>
> There is something strong within me that directs me—I'm not sure if I should call it destiny or what. But I do know that when I have a need or a sense to do something, I just go ahead and do it. Or I think about it in such a way and for so long that eventually it comes to pass.

Paul had not counted on financial difficulties and delays in getting his business on its feet. Although he had put aside several months' worth of income before starting his firm, it was not long before he had used that up.

> In order to make this business succeed, I've changed my life-style completely. I have re-evaluated all of my spending habits. For one thing I don't eat out anymore. I can't buy the clothes I want. I moved into a tiny apartment—if I can call it that. Sometimes I have hot water.
>
> I've made do with a lot less than I ever thought I could, and have even found fulfillment and satisfaction in a simpler life. It's been hard, but in some ways it's also been a blessing. It's allowed me to focus completely on the larger goal of producing good architecture and making this business survive. I would add that I still don't have a desire for "big" financial success. What I really want is to

make a go of this business and produce beautiful architecture.

Paul also admits to enjoying the loneliness of his work and solitary practice.

I have learned not to expect others to understand what I'm about. I'm more intense than most of my friends, and I consciously hold myself back with most people. They don't bring a response or an understanding to the topics I want to talk about. Primarily they are not as involved with architecture as I am. The wonderful thing about having to think things through for myself is that I can then solve problems on my own.

Resourcefulness may mean the ability to deal with any kind of situation, but it is based upon the individual's faith that he can solve his own problems. As we have seen, people who feel competent and powerful also feel that their brains are able to untangle complex, difficult-to-solve life-puzzles. Many even prefer difficulties, because this is how they test themselves fully against the demands that life puts in their path.

The roots of resourcefulness lie in the person's experience with solving problems. Indeed resourcefulness demands problem-solving as a means to develop. Three "laws" or requisites of this important characteristic seem to be consistent. First, the person must have faith in his or her ability to solve problems. Whether we call this self-trust or high self-regard matters less than that we understand how the person learns to depend on his own brain's ability to solve problems. The second law or requisite of resourcefulness would seem to be to practice independent thinking and decision-making—practice that puts the individual at considerable risk if he does not solve his own problems. The third "law" or requisite is determination: the individual must decide deep in himself that somehow he is going to discover the answer to the puzzles he faces.

One seventy-five year old—a general contractor, photographer, husband, father, grandfather and self-made man—

has a lot to tell us about two of these three "laws": determination and faith in the ability of the mind. This man (I will call him Wayne) was born in middle America in 1911. He became a trapper at age six in order to help feed his starving family. Wayne ran away from home at age nine after a serious misunderstanding with his father. Even though Wayne only learned to read a few years ago, he has much to teach us all—perhaps especially those of us who work in affluent corporate environments and believe that degrees, pension plans and a dress-for-success image are necessary before we can reach any real measure of success.

At seventeen, at the start of the Depression, while sitting and looking into the flame of an old wood-burning stove, Wayne decided what he was going to do with his life.

> It was then I laid out my life. I looked at myself and saw that I had no education, no "raising," little association with other people. I began to see other young men, running into town, drinking, gambling, playing around, and I decided I had to have something different. I determined right then and there that I'd make something of myself, despite my background, despite the fact that I had nothing and was all alone in the world. And that's exactly what I've done.

Wayne has that extra measure of motivation that inspires others. He has lived his life pretty much the way he wanted. Of his ability to earn a fine living, without anxiety about where new business will come from, Wayne says, "I never work on anything I don't want to work at. I listen carefully to everything my customer wants because he's got to be satisfied. I recently looked at a job where it was obvious that the man wouldn't be happy unless I cut a few corners and did things so that the building wasn't up to code. That's a job I'll turn down quickly. . . ."

In the heart of the Depression, Wayne was working. Wayne believes, to this day, that a person never has to worry about not working or not having enough money:

> I've always made a living because of me. Not because I can build. During the Depression, with twenty people want-

ing every job, I was working. I'd just go into a place and convince them I could give them excellent service. They not only paid me, they fed me, too. I saw a man stab himself to death out of sadness because he couldn't support his family—that's how bad it can get. But it has nothing to do with what you do. It has to do with what you are. I earned one hundred dollars a day, during the heart of the Depression, cleaning roofs. It didn't have anything to do with the fact that I can do construction. It has to do with me.

Wayne's determination may have preceded his confidence and high self-esteem, but he developed his overall resourcefulness and capabilities during his first decade of life. The problem-solving skills he gained from having to make a life for himself without any schooling, without family, without even so much as shelter, have enabled him to see possibilities where others cannot. This is the option-spotting aptitude that I was speaking about in earlier chapters.

Some people say they are "too old" to do what they really want, or that they cannot find the right job or move into a better position because it's too late, or that they have too many responsibilities. To such comments, Wayne responds with this story:

A while back, my wife bought me $10 worth of tropical fish for a Christmas present. A year later, in addition to my regular work, I was earning $700 a month off that present—just doing it on the side. Later, I sold that business to a man I know who had been an aircraft worker but who had had a heart attack and thought he couldn't work anymore. I showed him exactly what to do, and today that man is the largest dealer in tropical fish in the area.

Recently, I met a man who has become paralyzed and is taking walks around the block just because he needs something to do. He thinks he can't work. I've been talking to him about starting a hobby. I'm going to set him up in business, too—probably tropical fish. Or maybe I'll teach him how to carve wood toys. He can just do this hobby at home and earn all the money he wants. All you have to do is see a need in terms of a service or a product and then get on with it. But first you have to stop feeling sorry for yourself, and use your mind. And that's just about all there is to it.

I think it was a terrific blessing that I had no schooling. What happens to kids when they go to school? All those years under that system, they lose their way once they go there. The one thing I kept hold of was my individuality. I'm an individual if there ever was one. There are many people like me . . . but there is no other me.

Sounding much like Wayne, only some fifty years younger, is my architect friend, Paul, who admits to having little resistance within himself that would hold him back.

I don't experience myself as having very much resistance toward the things I say I want or feel moved to accomplish. In fact, it bothers me that people say, "I want to do this thing or I want that thing," but they don't do anything to get it. Go do it, for God's sake—or stop wanting to do it!

This type of attitude makes resourcefulness possible. The resourceful, active person, such as Paul, feels that if he doesn't risk anything, he will never gain anything. On the other hand, the blocked individual handicapped by low self-esteem feels that if he never tries anything he will be safe, and thus will not fail. Thus, at least one difference between persons with strong or weak inner resources to handle life is the level of self-trust. The resourceful person believes that if he risks just a little, experiments with the elements of the problem or situation, and explores a bit into the unknown, something good will come out of it. He trusts his brain to figure things out because he has experienced his brain as helpful to him in the past. (In later paragraphs we will see how someone who has no previous experience with problem-solving and risk-taking earned her self-confidence.)

Dr. William Glasser, a Los Angeles psychiatrist, whose work

has been important to my own, made a study of long-term meditators and long-distance, regular runners—persons who had engaged in a discipline of one kind or another for a regular, lengthy period of time. Glasser described the many pluses experienced by these people in his book *Positive Addiction*. He found that those who practiced a personal, solitary, regular discipline for at least one hour per day for several months gained many psychological benefits. One of these seemed to be an increase in resourcefulness. Glasser tells us that creativity is "intimately tied to strength, not weakness." The kind of strength Glasser is talking about is the same strength I call high self-esteem. His research showed that people who felt the inner strength to reach for what they wanted—in Glasser's terminology "love and worth"—were more likely to be resilient when faced with problems and setbacks. They did not suffer from spirit-breaking anxiety or worry when difficulties came up in their life.

> Unlike the weak, the strong neither give up nor are driven by pain into rash or stupid behavior. They don't like pain any more than anyone else, but they are not willing to settle for short-term relief if it means reducing their options . . . While most of their strength has been gained through learning how to handle rough situations competently, it is also characteristic of the very strong that they have the strength to take care of themselves in situations where they have neither experience nor support. It almost seems as if they are endowed with the strength to figure out by themselves, with little or no help, what to do in new and completely strange situations. I believe this strength comes from the fact that they have implicit faith in the power of their brains (p. 63).

In his book, Glasser described at length why a solitary discipline, done religiously, helps create inner strength. In my first book, *Ordinary People as Monks and Mystics*, I also traced the factors that seem to be inherent to personality growth and strength. Suffice it to say at this point that it is possible, regardless of our age, to learn how to be resourceful. However, this learning, unlike the success-tips offered in many self-help books, is not "instant." Resourcefulness is learnable, because the human mind can learn to improve the way it solves problems— including difficult ones. But (and this is where the learning lacks an instant, quick-fix appeal) the brain/mind learns to solve problems by having problems to solve. In other words, if we want to become more resourceful, we will have to put ourselves into a sort of Catch-22 position. We need to have a real-life problem upon which to strengthen the muscles of our brain. Because success breeds success, the more we see ourselves as able to solve our most relevant concerns and get what we need for ourselves, the more trust we will have in our own brains and the more resourceful we will become.

We probably all have experienced ourselves as feeling capable of experimentation and using our inner inclinations. This usually happens on those days when we feel strong, healthy and attractive. On those really "good days" we may even attempt something new and untried: a new outfit, talking to someone we don't know because the person simply appeals to us, eating at a different cafe for lunch. In other words, our ability to play with our environment and with situations and people in the environment, to try things out in a novel way, to participate more boldly and fully in life, is enhanced as we are undergirded by our own inner energy or idea that "We are all right and all's well with the world."

People with high self-esteem possess this sense of capability and power almost all of the time, even when they are fearful and anxious. Despite insecurities, they act as if they were operating from an optimistic, powerful position. Before we examine how we can learn this behavior, it might be instructive to study the response of another person: a plucky entrepreneur and successful business woman who talked with me about her way of solving problems.

This woman, now in her early forties, began her career as a secretary. She worked her way into financial independence by a series of assertive, creative moves. Each move was designed to give her financial freedom and more leverage for forming new businesses, which was her original love and her main goal. She currently owns a secretarial/executive suite service that leases offices and support services to professionals in private practice. The woman, whom I will call Gail, is a genius at putting together viable businesses from a seed idea. She is totally self-made in the classic American "Horatio Alger" tradition, and thus serves as an ideal role-model for those of us who have some hope of becoming financially independent, but no plan for getting there. Gail comes from a financially impoverished family, is one of many children and had no financial backing for her accomplishments. She became successful on her own. Of herself she said:

> Basically, my skills were in the secretarial and administrative fields. I was a secretary who had "graduated" into administration. When I arrived in California I realized that I didn't want to work for anyone else. So I began to ask myself, "What is it that I can do? What is it that I enjoy doing?" First I thought of opening a dress shop, because I really do like clothes. But I wanted a business that would eventually allow me some free time. When I thought of this type of business (executive suite service), I began to do some research—nothing very fancy—just talked to business friends, some marketing people. I knew I had to enter a field that I felt competent in.
>
> Also, with this type of service I knew I already had some support in terms of clients. When some computer marketing consultants I knew expressed an interest in what I proposed, I decided the time was right: I plowed right in. We've now been in this building for about nine years. When I started, I had four rentable offices. A year later, we went to eight offices, and then to fifteen–twenty offices for several years. About four years ago, I doubled that size. Also, during that time I started another business, built it up, made it profitable, and then sold it.

Gail's resourcefulness was demonstrated throughout this early start-up period, and actually during her whole business career. She refused to use her husband's support or credit and decided right from the start (even though this was before the women's liberation movement encouraged banks to give fair credit to women) to approach her bank and talk with them about what she was doing.

You have to be persistent, and I was. People need to feel secure about lending you their money or their services when you're starting. For example the bank would never have loaned me the money to begin had I not set it up so that they would: I wanted them to know me, not my husband. So about two years before starting my business, I went in to introduce myself to them. About a year later, in addition to the account I was keeping there and the several visits I'd made to the manager, I went to them and said that I had no credit, and that even though I kept my account with them, there were no business advantages in terms of borrowing power. So they gave me a small signature loan. Now if I need it, I can go down and get quite a large sum of money on my signature alone.

I'm still dealing with the same furniture business that I did when I started. They were great, they took a chance on me—they gambled.

Also, when I started I went to each stationery store and established a relationship with them. I went to IBM for the typewriters I needed. They were fantastic. They said they liked to see women in business, and they really helped me out. They even gave me literature about secretarial performance, which I used with my staff. Of course, in the long run they got my business, so they also knew exactly what they were doing.

Another obstacle was that I was in business in what was truly a man's world. When I needed to introduce our secretarial companies to other firms to get their overflow work, or when I ran ads for occupants for the office space, men would want to finish our business "over dinner." I wasn't naive, but I believed in people. I went to dinner a couple of times, and it was a big mistake. It was uncomfortable. I had a difficult time with that for a while. First, I got angry with the men. I wanted to tell them off, tell them to just forget the business. Then, I wanted to just walk away. But I soon realized that I could conduct myself in such a manner that I concluded the necessary business before we ever discussed dinner. Today, I might have a drink with someone, but I can handle it.

Practice in resourcefulness is often hard to come by because the types of problems that are helpful in training us to use our brains are exactly what risk-averse people avoid. A creative response to problems is needed, yet that is the very attitude some people cannot bring themselves to demonstrate, because all problems frighten them. One of the people I interviewed told me an amazing story about how she learned to face her dominant fears—in her case, the fear of being poor—and gained high, robust self-esteem in the process.

The woman whom I will call Beth is in her late thirties. Beth realized that she needed help from a therapist during a painful separation and divorce. Not only did she experience great bouts of depression and grief during her divorce, but she also felt overwhelming anxiety about separating from her husband. As soon as she began therapy, Beth "remembered" that her decision to marry her husband was based not on a deep man/ woman love, but rather on her deeper need to be taken care of financially.

In her early life Beth had been abandoned by her parents (one parent had died suddenly before her twelfth birthday, the other was institutionalized for mental illness). She managed, at a severe emotional cost, to fend for herself. However, she was so traumatized by the shock of being on her own from the age of twelve that all she remembered was that money—or the lack of it—was her primary adolescent concern. She didn't realize that she had grown inordinately resourceful in the process of taking care of herself, as if she were her own parent. In fact, she showed remarkable prowess in earning an income from part-time jobs, making arrangements with relatives to send her to a boarding school to prepare for college, and getting a scholarship at age sixteen to a fine college.

Beth's one driving thought at the time, however, was to find a man who would replace her father, and this she did just after graduating from college. All that mattered to her was that she was, in her mind, desperately in need of a strong, protective, financially stable mate. Of course, in time, the relationship suffered at its core, having been founded on logical, but not very lasting, motives. Beth and her husband both came to see that their marriage would not last.

The anxiety Beth faced at the time of separation was the same grief and anxiety she felt when her father died. These were feelings that she had buried deep within herself when she avoided her own strength and talent and decided to marry for protection and financial support.

Her therapist, a true maverick and rebel in his field, believed that "the time to kick people is when they're down." By that he meant that the best time to push people to stand up and face themselves was when they were in their habitual avoidance pattern. Under his "tough love" stance, although it was not called that at the time, he gave Beth an assignment that would stop her charade of helplessness.

He asked her to go away by herself for a weekend, to a place where she knew no one, a place at least one hundred miles from home, taking nothing with her but a dime for an emergency call to him should she get into real trouble. She was to use nothing but her own intuitive, native skill to "figure out" how to survive. He told her that, in his opinion, she was as creative a person as he'd ever met and that her only task was to remove the blinders she wore so that she could believe in her own worth and abilities to take care of herself.

"My doctor told me," Beth reported with obvious satisfaction, "that he wanted me to realize I had vast reserves of creative intelligence and that even my decision to marry the type of man I chose was a winning decision, given my background. At the time, I thought he was crazy. But I agreed to do what he asked because I had total faith in him and also because the idea, however bizarre, excited me a little."

Her unusual weekend trip had one other condition: she was not to do anything illegal or—in her own opinion—immoral to help herself "survive," and she was only to call her therapist if she landed in jail—or worse.

When I left the doctor's office, I was shocked with myself for agreeing to go on this weekend venture. It seemed like madness. But even though it brought up all my latent fears—the dread of being alone, penniless, in drab or impoverished surroundings—I was also excited. I knew it would be fun because it was a sort of game and also because, deep down, I knew I was in control. This amazing feeling was not new to me, and this was the biggest surprise of all: *that I enjoyed the thought of having to figure out what to do!*

On my way home that same night, I realized that much of what I was feeling was not fear—it was *excitement*. For the first time in a long time, my mind was not on the catastrophic things I feared, but on how I was going to solve this problem. I experienced a kind of exhilaration that is hard to describe. For one thing, once I got home, I began to feverishly plan my trip. I'd decided to drive to San Diego, where I didn't know anyone. I made some advance phone calls and found out where a youth hostel was located. I wrote down very meticulous directions so that I wouldn't get lost and waste gas. One other requirement was that I only would have enough gas to get there and back. I had no credit card with me so I had to make sure I wouldn't waste any fuel! And I made sure that my therapist knew where I was going so that at least someone would know where I was in case I got into trouble.

I saw myself behaving responsibly and cautiously in my own behalf, and that observation began a process which, for me, has never stopped filling me with self-respect. During the entire weekend—I'm happy to say I survived it completely—I observed myself at my most resourceful and effective best.

When I got to the youth hostel, to my horror I found out the entry fee was fifty cents per night. I only had a dime. I heard myself ask the kid next to me for money, and to my delight—he was a hitchhiker and backpacker who'd come all the way from Canada—he loaned me fifty cents. A girl next to him took pity on me and gave me another fifty cents. I was rich!

I saw myself size up the overnight residents of the facility. Some of them were seedy drug-abusers, others were wholesome college kids just out on an adventurous exploration. My political acumen was such that I made friends with both groups, but decided to sleep next to the college kids, who were sprawled on the floor and on cots in their sleeping bags. There was one frightening episode in the middle of the night when the police came into the place, looking for a young woman who fit my description. She was wanted on suspicion of murder! My breathing stopped, as I tried to respond in my most upright, good-citizen fashion. Somehow, the police bought my story that I was only here for the weekend, and they left without further questioning.

The next day I again realized how capable I was: trying to sell blood (but being ten pounds underweight), and giving rides to the blood bank for fifty cents (there were six people in my car, so I received three dollars). Now I had about four dollars. I took the kids back to the hostel, dropped them off, and took myself to Saks Fifth Avenue, where I knew the restroom was clean (it had been atrocious in the hostel, and I couldn't use it), washed up and put on fresh makeup and then went into the personnel office to apply for a job. Don't ask me how, but I managed to survive a quick interview. I think they were desperate for help, and because I'd had some experience in makeup sales, I was told that I could start Monday morning. Even though my weekend was not over, I realized that I'd "made it" on my own. I had a job, a place to stay and a way to "survive." I learned that it was not necessary for me to marry someone to take care of me. I have all the skills to do that. When I marry again, it will be for other, more lasting reasons.

Beth's experiment in resourcefulness occurred almost five years ago. "Since then, I have returned to graduate school, have started my own research business, and have begun seeing someone whom I really care for—someone who is my best friend, my confidant and my romantic love interest as well. My feelings for him have nothing to do with money, or with being taken care of. I just like being with him."

By remembering how important safety is to each of us, we can also keep in mind that when our security is at stake, it is entirely natural to feel anxious—as if we are losing control, as if we need someone strong to lean on emotionally. Of course, there are times for all of us when leaning on another is perfectly natural: the death or loss of a loved one, a time of illness, the times we want others around to share our joy and our heartaches. But as a life-style, as a pattern of response, the best mechanism for reducing helplessness resides within us. We truly evolve and grow only when we take control of our circumstances and fears. While most people tend to regress to a state of feeling inadequacy when they get anxious and scared, the truly resourceful person uses this as yet another opportunity to take charge of circumstances or events.

And periods of anxiousness are exactly the time to take hold. This is when we most need to see ourselves shaping circumstances in the same way we would a sculpting: first by visualizing what the ideal outcome would be, next by imagining how we would feel if we handled things well, finally by right action. The actions that flow out of these subjective impressions and emotions are usually the spontaneous actions that would bring about our desired solutions.

By conquering our fears one by one and by learning to stand up for ourselves and make decisions, we learn that we can count on ourselves. We learn that what we possess within ourselves provides us with what it takes to be truly secure in a long-term, substantive sense. We learn that this sort of security has little to do with money. This goes back to an issue discussed in the early chapters: we must believe in ourselves, knowing that we have all the skill, intelligence and wit to meet our every need.

For some people this means using their skills to meet financial needs. For others it means learning how to reach out to other people, how to make friends, how to ask for what they want, and how to speak plainly and honestly to another about what they are feeling.

Many people, unable to muster humility in these circumstances, suffer needless loneliness and try to bolster themselves with outward support systems (e.g., money in the bank; proper, if unfulfilling, personal contacts; a secure job; community contacts) which would be unnecessary if they could open up truthfully to the people they really love and respect.

Others must learn that their brains do function under stress, that their intelligence—even if they are not supremely gifted—is designed to serve their survival and happiness. All these lessons are learnable when people take responsibility for functioning effectively each and every day, regardless of feelings that say "I cannot function, I don't know how, I'm too scared, too old, too ill, etc."

This does not mean we don't make mistakes, nor does it mean we should each run away for an adventurous weekend with nothing but a dime in our pockets, to see how ingenious we can be in a strange city. The woman who did that was an unusual case, who was under the supervision of a therapist and who had years of background in solving unusual, complex problems. Although she felt she was a novice in such matters, in fact she was a pro. And that was the point of her weekend adventure. It is certainly not a prescription for everyone!

A fortunate few learn at a young age to function effectively and ingeniously—despite setbacks, obstacles or feelings that they "can't." But all can learn the art of "skillful means" at any age.

The term "skillful means" is the phrase Tarthang Tulku, a lama from Eastern Tibet, uses to describe the spontaneous, flowing energy that is always present to help us meet each need and every goal. He says, "By using skillful means to enrich our lives and bring our creative potential into everything we do, we can penetrate to the heart of our true nature. We then gain an understanding of the basic purpose of life, and appreciate the joy of making good use of our precious time and energy" (p. 80).

Resourcefulness and skillful means are but one and the same thing. We can have faith in the power of our own minds and talents to take us through life. We can practice—again and again—this self-trust and independent thinking/acting in the meeting of life's demands and complexities, sometimes just by stepping back and saying, "What does my best thinking tell me I should do here?" or "What do the people I admire most seem to do in situations like these?"

When we are determined to meet life's challenges, we come to see all problems as opportunities for creativity, growth and new answers. In this way, we tap a source of knowledge within us that carries us through all difficulties and helps us transcend them—in practical ways that actually bring us to the places, people and things we need. In this way we can eventually be resourceful and let go of the false idea that we cannot live fruitfully in the world.

9

Work as Play or Addiction?

The majority work to make a living; some work to acquire
wealth or fame, while a few work because there is something
within them which demands expression. . . . Only a few truly
love it.

Edmond Boreaux Szekely

Supremely well developed personalities, expressing themselves
through work, can be misunderstood. Their way is not without
problems. The individual might feel subjective exaltation and
joyousness in doing his chosen vocation. He may see himself
growing stronger as a distinctive personality. His fearfulness,
timidity, and self-consciousness may gradually disappear in the
process of his work and life. And his perceptual field may grow
whole from his new, unitive understanding of himself in
relationship to his work and to others. But still there are
difficulties along the path, such as the negative reactions of other
people, the lack of time in a given day to do all that needs to be
done, and the desire to give oneself fully to the work, yet meet
all other responsibilities.

In examining the actualizing person at work, we find
attitudes and values that contradict much of what our majority
Western culture holds as "normal." We are cautioned not to work
too hard, or too much. Today people view work as something set
apart, something done from Monday through Friday—a
compartmentalized bit of life, with most of the "fun" times, the
"best times," reserved for weekends, holidays and vacations. The
phrases "Thank God it's Friday," and "It's a blue Monday," have

emerged from the ideas that the week is filled with drudgery and
hard, thankless toil, and that the weekends are the most—or the
only—refreshing times of life. Sadly, for many people this is true
not only at the idea level, but at the level of their direct
experience.

Perhaps these ideas evolved out of the Puritan ethic, which
kept people's noses to the grindstone, grimly slaving away from
sunrise till sunset. A respite was needed—not so much from the
work, as from the attitudes behind the work, which were based
on a deep antipathy to joy and playfulness. The Western concept
of controlling nature, our love and fascination with "progress," our
admiration of material success and victory over obstacles have
helped us equate work with those tasks and activities by which
we shape and control external things: nature, time and the
enemies of life—poverty, blight, a ferocious landscape, illness,
the limitations of geographic distance and space. It would be
natural to want to rest after channeling one's anger and anxieties
toward work projects such as these. Viewed in this way, work
becomes something cut off from the self, a survival vehicle and an
avenue of activity that can make a person bitter, tired or cynical.
Work then fragments and splits the personality, instead of
integrating it.

But this is certainly a far cry from the actualizing person's
view of work. He sees work as a joyful exercise, a calling that is
almost effortless. For him, work becomes a way in which to
understand life around him, a resolver of paradoxes and a path for
personal development. For him, work is a creative, graceful,
present-moment experience. This is in line with the Buddhist
perspective, which uses simple, daily routines as a way to grow,
as a way to maintain an elegant concentrated connection with the
world, and as a way to see the self as having a place in the
scheme of things.

The utter sincerity of this position—almost childlike in its
manifestations—turns work into a deeply valuable, pleasurable
pursuit, despite the hardships and absolute irritations and
frustrations of some of the tasks. No matter how impersonal, dull
or tedious the job might seem to others, for the individual whose
work is like play, daily life is expressed as a lucky or blessed

experience. "I'm so lucky to be able to be doing this" and "I'm so happy to have found something I love to do" are expressions which people frequently make when they have resolved the work/play split.

Any job—telephone operator, bank clerk, office administrator, librarian, carpenter, physician, auto mechanic, sales—is enlivened when performed by an actualizing adult. This individual, working at what he or she really enjoys—even when working at something unappealing on a short-term basis—has a different inward posture than we are used to hearing about in the media or from others.

One man, for example, a mathematician turned stock market investor, has used his love of math to understand the ebb and flow of the market. In talking about how his work was like play, he said:

> It's like the kid who knows Christmas is coming; his excitement builds as Christmas gets closer. Only with the holiday, it only comes once a year. For me, as I get closer to my goal of understanding the way the market works, the excitement builds all the time. Another way I would describe it is by saying that it's like being on a treasure hunt, like following a rainbow for the pot of gold. For me, the prize is big enough to keep me following it.
>
> In mastering the stock and commodity market, I already have achieved a bigger piece of the pot of gold than anyone else I know. But there's much more to do—There is never a perfection level, fortunately. Otherwise, I'd have to find something else to do.

He went on to say that he never thinks about work vs. play, that although he loves to do other things—such as play tennis, run on the beach, or go to parties—these are done when he schedules them into his day.

> I enjoy other things, and I have many other activities in my life. But these are done almost by appointment. With my work, I naturally gravitate to it. Of course sometimes it

is "work." I have to sit there, no ideas come up and I know I have to keep at it even though I don't feel like it. But as I stay with it a little burst of insight or a new thought comes and I'm off again into the most fascinating world there could be.

The actualizing individual is intrinsically involved with his work and uses it to help him understand the world around him. The mathematician quoted above said, "I have a keener understanding of the world as a result of my staying with this work. I am discovering many truths about investing, truths which help me understand and penetrate other aspects of life. For example, I've realized that all the news and superstitious thinking which others say affects the stock market is really worthless. The news, all the superstitions, get in the way. They confuse things. I used to resist that realization as I resisted other things. Now I accept my own perceptions. I just ignore the media and all the 'experts.' I believe this holds true for other things in life like health matters or choices we want to make. It's important to listen to ourselves and close out the noise from outside."

The whole individual has a different posture about his work, a posture which includes these patterns:

● Work itself is playful and fun, an activity that permits the individual to tune in to deeper, more truthful parts of himself. Work becomes something fulfilling—even with its frustrations and irritations—a joyous event, and an integral part of one's self, expressing itself as naturally as the bird sings its song. In this framework, work is not something upon which to "force" one's control. Rather it is another exercise of "mindfulness," which we spoke about in an earlier chapter—an activity that allows the person to be more aware of himself, and of what is happening, reality, the present moment here-and-now.

● Work is experienced as one of the "best times," as the weekend is the best time, as this moment now is the best time, even as this or that "problem" is the best thing upon which to put one's mind at this given moment. In other words, the self-actualizing person (i.e., integrated, whole, healed, known-to-himself) functions fully in every moment, rather than reserving a special category for some moments as "good" and others as "not good." He does not inhibit, reserve or withdraw attention, participation, enthusiasm and energy in order to save these for "better times," such as weekends, holidays, the Monday night ballgame, etc. The individual is fully there at work and makes use of all his energy and concentrative/ creative abilities.

- Work thus becomes a natural element, a fulfilling expression of the life-force within the person. Even with its ups and downs, time-demands, pressures or conflicts, work is experienced as pleasurable and something to be done both as personal calling/ destiny and as the activity that helps one grow into a better, more enlightened, perfected, capable, trustworthy, committed human being.

- Work is something connected to the self, a part of the spirit, mind, body and senses—a mirror of the person. It is neither good nor bad in the judgmental sense of one job being better than another, but rather is "right," "correct," non-materialistically, in that it is simply what makes sense to that particular person's life in an organic, synergistic context.

- This person's work allows his weaknesses to be worked on, while his strengths and talents grow into full use, while he is linked to others. As work opens him up to himself, creating more angles, edges and distinctiveness in the individual, it simultaneously teaches him to be more like others. It teaches him to be a compassionate, functioning, contributive, disciplined part of the whole—a better "servant" who dies daily to his "larger self."

- Work is not something to apply oneself to aggressively, as if it were an enemy. Nor is it something upon which to vent hostile, unresolved feelings of anxiety or resentment. Rather it is an avenue by which to further express the positive, caring, energized, all-present, committed, staying-with-it, standing-in-for aspects of the individual's developing personality. These traits push to be expressed—a push from within which comes to be the "is-ness" of being, the more responsible parts of self-urging to be used in the individual's daily reality.

Without exception, the people I have interviewed who fit this profile describe their work as a key vehicle for expressing their most positive emotions. They describe their efforts as a way to demonstrate their affection for others and to grow in respect for themselves. At the same time, these persons are capable of behaving in what seem to be the most extreme forms of "selfishness." For example, they protect their time, say "no" to unrewarding social invitations, recoil—naturally and without much guilt—from toxic people, situations, jobs and responsibilities. It is as if they instinctively know what they must do with their time and energy, and then determine to do only that.

It is in this connection that the subject of workaholism invariably comes up and I am asked: What is the difference between being a "workaholic" and someone who loves his work. While it is true that, on the surface, there often seem to be similarities, at the heart of each work style resides a completely different set of attitudes and motivations.

First, the person who loves his work is drawn magnetically to that work, as if there were a pull or a perfect "fit" between it and himself. The individual develops what I call a committed heart with respect to all the demands, difficulties and undesirable qualities of the tasks—just as a mother gives no second thought to the unpleasant tasks in caring for her sick child. Indeed, this is the crux of it: the motivation that ignites the individual is positive, loving, devotional and earnestly sincere.

On the other hand, the motivation of a "workaholic" is usually fear. This person is an alienated, anxious, aggressive, stressed individual who typically uses work to stave off buried hostility, maladaptive social attitudes, and feelings of inadequacy.

For the workaholic, work provides the addictive high similar to a narcotic. It frees him from having to face unresolved personal problems—say a bad marriage or unhealthy relationships with his children. His work with its time-pressures and responsibilities protects him from seeing and dealing with his inability to be intimate with family or friends, and also perhaps the inability to play, relax, and just live life fluidly. In other words, he cannot "enjoy." His capacity for joy, for creative, effortless, spontaneous expression, is blocked by his own tension. As an easy example, his sensitivity for the changing of the seasons might be dulled by thoughts of what he must do. He is one who cannot take time out to "smell the roses." He cannot, because he is not free to choose. His anxiety and gnawing sense that he may lose control (over self, schedules, problems, etc.) continually pull him back to his office, paperwork, time, calendar, schedules and demands. He cannot follow the example of Chinese writer Chin Shengt'an and list—for himself and for posterity—his truly happy moments of life. If he did, they would all be working moments. Chin Shengt'an listed thirty-three such moments, none of which had anything to do with formal work. Here are two examples:

> I am drinking with some romantic friends on a spring night and am just half-intoxicated, finding it difficult to stop drinking and equally difficult to go on. An understanding boy servant at the side suddenly brings in a package of bit fire-crackers, about a dozen in number, and I rise from the table and go and fire them off. The smell of sulphur assails my nostrils and enters my brain and I feel comfortable all over my body. Ah, is this not happiness?
>
> To hear our children recite the classics so fluently, like the sound of pouring water from a vase. Ah, is this not happiness? (p. 132).

Psychiatrist Jay Rohrlick defines the workaholic and his addiction to work in this way.

> The critical factor in defining work addiction is the level of choice and free will in a person's work habits. An addiction is measured not by what an individual does, but by what he or she cannot do. . . . Only if a person cannot do *with-*

out the excitement of work when such excitement is not appropriate or consciously desirable can we call him or her an addict. . . . When a person must work while sleeping or instead of sleeping, while eating, while making love or reading a novel, while talking to friends or playing with his children . . . he is revealing what he cannot do. The work addict has no choice in the matter, even when he wants to change. He cannot stop working (pp. 165–66).

As Rohrlick states, the critical issue here is free will. The workaholic's deliberate choice is hampered by his constricted development.

The one who loves his work, the actualizing person, has progressed as a personality despite his fears or angers. He is one who "has light" in himself, to use Schweitzer's apt phrase. He is an attractive, wholesome, luminous personality who does not require approval, status symbols and rewards from others. He does not—unlike the workaholic—crave outward shows of respect and rank (e.g., titles, large offices, special parking spaces, top floor suites) in order to continue manifesting, striving, "playing," and enjoying what he does. He strives, he does the work because he loves it, because in doing it he develops himself more completely, draws upon hidden inner reserves and abilities and creates from the depths of his being and imagination.

However, on the surface he may appear to be driven, just like the workaholic. And this is where onlookers, family, friends and co-workers may need to reserve their judgment and grow in their own understanding. The number of hours worked, the intensity of the work drive, the immersion in work and preoccupation with the ideas, details and future of the work may look identical to that of the workaholic.

Only the individual knows and can ultimately say whether he is a workaholic or not. I want to stress that we not judge ourselves or others by the appearance of work habits and that we not judge ourselves by the definitions of others—especially those whom we inconvenience or displease by our non-conforming, non-cooperative work schedules. As one woman put it, "It's not a matter of being a workaholic; it's a matter of pursuing the energy that the work itself generates."

Such committed attitudes, however fulfilling to the individual, can be hard on family and friends who do not understand the person's preoccupation. Others often feel left out. For example, a young professional said that money was not his main interest and that moreover his friends found him hard to understand. "They see me turning down some business because it is not what I most enjoy doing. They laugh at me and say that I'm foolish. But really I think they are uncomfortable because we cannot truly relate or share our interests on this point. Money is simply not my big-ticket item. What turns me on is the type of work I know I must do. That is the fork in the road—the place where I find it difficult to communicate to most of the people I know. Also, I spend more time thinking about my work. My intensity is greater than that of my friends. I have learned to keep to myself on the subject of my work because my attitude is definitely hard for people to understand."

Another, a business woman, said of her family's opinions about her workdrive: "They are simply in another place. They would like to see me successful, yes. But in the popular conception of the word. You know, nice clothes, good title, 'balanced' life—which to them means time for socializing, marriage, children. What amazes me is that even though they are family and want to see me happy, they don't know me. They don't see that I *am* happy. Not only that, but I'm probably a genius in my field and they won't grasp the extent to which this fact is true until the media, the world and a host of other outsiders whose voices they respect start acknowledging the validity of my ideas."

Almost anyone who devotes himself to a given vocation, and who pours his love and energy into that activity, develops a certain genius in the field: the vocation opens itself up to him in terms of its truths and principles, it bends itself to his imagery and ideas, it becomes his friend and most able co-creator, building up the person as he invests himself in the work. And any work can serve this purpose, so that whatever it is one chooses to do—done with the right attitude and proper affection—becomes a graceful, joyful activity as well as an ally in life.

In connection with this research, I received a dual letter from a husband and wife team of apple pickers. They each wrote a letter extolling the virtues of apple picking. An introductory note on the wife's letter instructed me to read the husband's letter first, so I quote him first in deference to their wishes:

> We heard of your research and feel we have something to offer you. We both do agricultural work. For thirteen years we've picked apples. Twelve of these years were at the same orchard . . . We don't love apple picking, but I really enjoy it plus it enables us to live our lives as we choose, and we have not found any other job that suits us better.
>
> Eighty to ninety percent of our income is from four months of employment. I like to maximize opportunities to be outside, so employment outside fits in very well. Spring and fall are great times to be outside. Using my picking requires use of the whole body, bending, squatting, stretching—all of which I like. How hard you work is up to you, and payment is by the bushel, so you get reinforced for working faster. Usually I feel no pressure from a boss, so a good level of independence exists for me. We work with a crew of pickers which necessitates a certain amount of cooperation and an opportunity to make friends. Picking is a job we can leave behind when we go home, and . . . it is very important to us to earn money locally in order to maintain a sense of stability and community.

His wife added the following comments about her work in the letter she wrote:

> Being able to work with my husband is important to me. . . . Work is a large part of most people's lives and I am glad I can share this with someone I love. Also, I want to repeat my husband's emphasis on being able to work outside. I feel people in the U.S. are not connected to the

land, and this is a part of the source of our problems as a
society.

Both of these individuals contradict the popular
misconceptions about "non-professional" work, showing us why
their work is so well suited to them. Both also disclosed a good
understanding of what they needed from life, as well as from
work, and certainly expressed a strong sense of identity and self-
knowledge:

The man described himself in this way:

> I am on the borderline between being an extrovert and an
> introvert. I enjoy quiet and doing one thing at a time. Spiri-
> tual growth has become increasingly important. I enjoy
> life, and I have a positive attitude. I am not ambitious. I
> am probably less assertive than is healthy. Playing the pi-
> ano is an integral part of my emotional health. I do not
> strive for "perfection."

His wife described herself in similarly sophisticated terms
calling herself "extroverted, on the Myers-Briggs personality
test . . . but moving, over the last five years, toward the middle
of the scale. I know a good number of people, but am really close
to about ten beyond my family of mother and three sisters with
whom I keep in close contact, although the closest one is five
hundred miles away. I have attended church for twenty years,
and have held a variety of positions. Generally, I would have to
say I am quite happy with my life."

Moreover, this woman gives us a good example of the
learning, personal growth and pure fun that people can
experience through doing work that is right for them:

> I am not easy with heights. When we started picking ap-
> ples, the ladder work was very difficult for me. My friends
> helped me survive the first five years or so until I could
> feel more confident. By the eighth year I actually began to
> enjoy the ladder work. Now I will miss it as more and
> more of the trees are dwarfs and semi-dwarfs. This has

been very helpful to me, to realize I can outgrow a fear by using the work I do each day to help me in this growth.

Another individual, a woman who had worked for many years as a librarian assistant, said that hers was "the most perfect job" she'd ever had. She told me at length what it felt like to be both playful and dedicated, committed yet open to the unknown during one's working day. Her remarks underscore the fusion of childlike playfulness and intense commitment inherent in the actualizing person's experience of work:

> At the close of my first day on the job, I came home and told my husband, "You know, I think I can use all that I have ever known and can possibly remember in this work." There truly are no words to express what a tremendous feeling of wonder overwhelmed me. From then on, it was all excitement.
>
> If a week came by when they didn't need me at work, I would go in as a volunteer. I can't think why it didn't occur to me in college to do this type of work. But honestly, it didn't. I liked this work so much it seemed perfect—seemed really pointless to do anything else.
>
> I had to be able to take the place of anyone, working in any capacity, in any of the seven libraries we had in the county. There always seemed to be a crisis somewhere. People would come in with all kinds of questions, such as the woman who asked what she should do about her husband who disappeared for days at a time, or the little boy with a bug in a bottle who needed to know what kind it was. The main fun of it all was the challenge.

She went on to describe how her job had stretched her as a person, taught her about herself, and introduced her to a larger aspect of life:

> My co-workers were a grand crew, many of them women who had lost their husbands and were raising families on their own. I would never have had the chance to know peo-

ple like these in my own, rather isolated situation. The youngsters who did the shelving were the top students from the surrounding high schools and colleges, and I have always claimed that they were the brightest of any of us. At one time we had four Phi Beta Kappa's working in one library. People who used the libraries regularly were in a class by themselves, too, and their particular interests began to rub off on me.

My reading spread out more widely than it had before. Who could resist, for instance, a title such as *The Lives of a Cell* or *The Double Helix*. They sound like great mysteries, and of course they are. After that, I was amazed how interesting a good textbook could be. I began to feel more aware, sensitized and open.

Now, ten years later, my hands still stretch out toward books as if magnetized. I love the feel of them in my grasp, three or four at a time. It is as if they are alive with all the years and thinking that went into their making. And I know that they are just waiting to speak to me.

I read in one of Elisabeth Kübler-Ross' books that if you can find and do work that you love, you probably have an excellent chance of being able to accomplish what you were sent here for. I relate to that and thought you would, too. It makes complete sense, doesn't it?

This woman speaks in the past tense because she is now retired from her job as library assistant. Her current preoccupation and pastime is helping her community art center establish a library, turning what was just a random assortment of books into an organized collection. Workaholic? Not likely.

Other people also spoke of their work's influence on their growth and how it allowed them to demonstrate their most cherished values on a daily basis. This is a devotional aspect of work that we will examine more fully in the next chapter, especially as it relates to spirituality. For the present, some of the remarks of the people interviewed will help us understand the close link between personal growth and vocational excellence.

Certainly it would seem that when motivated by positive

emotions, when performed by the actualizing adult, working outcomes are elevated to a qualitatively superior level. For example, the headmaster of a private school said that he was finally able—after many years of frustration in a variety of academic settings—to utilize his philosophy and leadership to empower young people. His work taxes his time, but is so rewarding to him that it has been worth every personal adjustment and sacrifice he has had to make:

> If I had a million dollars to design a school, ninety percent of it would be like this one. Certainly it is humbling to me to have seen [another side] of life, to have had to ask myself what my priorities were, and now to see that I have the chance to make a difference in the lives of others through my leadership style and heartfelt values. This is a great, rich reward to me. I feel privileged to be in this work.
>
> When I was a young man I dropped out of college twice and took myself "up to the mountain top" to see what was truly important for me to do with my life. I asked myself what my priorities and values were, and the two most important ones were, first, honesty, and, second, compassion. This is a situation where I can use myself fully as a human being and where my values come into expression every day.
>
> My wife and I have also arrived at a point where we want to demonstrate our authenticity. One way I do that is to have a completely single-minded intention to put the needs of children first. This means I have an "open-door" policy so that all can come in and talk, as need be. But it also means the door is shut whenever conferences are of a sensitive or confidential nature. So the paperwork gets left to the end of the day. Translated into realistic terms, I work late into the night sometimes. But I have two youngsters still at home, and I want to be an in-home father. So I also take time to spend my evenings with them as much as is possible.
>
> Also, after twenty-three years of marriage, my wife

and I still work at our marriage. We do this by taking long walks, by talking things out, by asking ourselves what is important to us and by making a concerted effort to act upon what we decide has worth. Yes, it is demanding. Yes, it is time-consuming. But it's worth it. This is the very stuff that makes life meaningful to me.

A woman who is the director of volunteers for a large 1,500-bed hospital in the midwest also talked about the balancing act required of her, given the fact that she is also a wife and a mother of a ten year old son. She described how she had learned to do the things that were important to her and her family and how this learning helped her stretch and grow as a person.

I enjoy this work so much. I started working at the age of fourteen through the American Friends Committee, which had a format for putting young people together to work on community problems. Our work ethic was developed at that time, and I can still see much of it in me today.

In terms of wholeness, there is no question that being able to work as I do helps me—allows me—to use parts of myself that being a mother doesn't call for, that being a wife doesn't draw out. The way I was taught to work as a youngster set a trend for me and for most of us in that program: we are all participating in the human experience as fully as we can. I remember someone wrote in my high school yearbook, "Kahlil Gibran said, 'Work is love made visible,' so work like hell." I guess that's what I'm doing—showing my love.

I'm learning all the time. I'm working with people (doctors, nurses, volunteers) who choose to be here. This is such a fine experience and in some ways—given my previous work experiences—new for me. They are not desperate about their need to work. This is euphoric for me. Of course, the hospital itself is very innovative and advanced. It is like being in a super graduate course. I'm learning all the time.

I spent six years being a single parent, so that

taught me ways to juggle things so that I could protect my time with my son. This was important to both of us. We did things together. I trained myself to work until five, then to spend time with him until he went to bed, then to work at home after that. The Army has that motto, "Be All You Can Be . . ." If they didn't have it, I'd take it.

The way these people speak of their work indicates that they are at one with it—that their work allows them a great range of responses and allows them to use many sides of themselves. Another person, an accountant, described the dichotomies of her job in this way:

> I really do love what I do, despite the occasional tedious parts and time pressures. I find satisfaction both cognitively—in not only doing needed tasks but in presenting complete financial pictures and preparing budgets essential to the operations—and emotionally, because I am in close touch (with people) and share their triumphs and discouragements. . . . My whole value system is expressed in my working life.

As we have seen, any work (either part-time or full-time) can provide an individual's life with so much enjoyment that it begins to be experienced as "play." But prior to experiencing work in this exuberant, almost effortless sense, the person must first know himself well enough to consciously choose that work—whatever it is. Either he consciously chooses the work because he genuinely loves it, and can think of nothing better to do with his time, or he consciously chooses to do that which is placed before him because being mindful, staying awake and connected to his task at every moment is a way of experiencing a larger part of himself. This latter condition is precisely the meditative, integrative and connective approach to work which precedes a transcendent mind, a Zen mind, an openness of awareness, and which elevates the individual into fully functioning, fully conscious awareness.

This manner of working demands not only courage, but a type of "whole-seeing," in which the individual separates himself from society's expectations, as well as from its definition of success. In the case of the person who, needing to work at something less than his ideal—as with a sculptor who must work part-time in order to pay the bills—the conscious choice to stay with the unappealing part-time job goes against all cultural programming to do as little as possible when that work goes against our grain.

The person who chooses to work at something which society doesn't value, or who works at a job which his friends and family say is not worthwhile, must transcend whatever biases others put in his way and stay with the job anyway. In either case, each must define the word "success" in his own way and consciously choose to do what is there to be done, doing it with full attention.

The apple-picker, for example, realizing that he needs to work outdoors and that he likes to use his body in his work, and his wife who knows that it is essential for her to work beside her husband, and who also enjoys the outdoor working conditions, and who—with her husband—wants a certain degree of freedom and stability from work, are persons who consciously chose agricultural work. They chose this work even though our present-day society does not place as high a premium on this type of work as it does, say, on a white-collar professional job.

Another person, a part-time hospital worker, admitted that she could not sustain a healthful, happy life while working full-time:

> I do not have a traditional job in the 9 to 5 sense, but rather a balance of part-time experiences. I work at a psychiatric hospital fifteen to twenty hours a week, doing vocational counseling. In addition, I teach one section of a career development course at the community college, and then I see independent clients one evening a week for career counseling. I find this situation rewarding because it allows me to function in different formats with varied populations. Also it gives me freedom and flexibility to put time into my children, my garden, and other activities which are important to me. (When) I tried to

work forty hours a week, I found life too chaotic; I didn't have enough time for the activities I really enjoyed.

Another, a friend of mine, has considered going to work in an office or returning to graduate school to study a profession. But she has finally come to see herself as she really is—as an artist: In a letter, which I paraphrase, she writes:

> I am painting fairly regularly now. It may never be my bread and butter, but I dearly love it and it is my one passion . . . and we all need that. Doing all the work I "should" be doing—the work with logic and numbers and detail— has been a real challenge for me, and for that I am glad. It was always scary to me, and once the mystery cleared up I saw it for what it is. But I definitely view the world through "artistic" eyes, as opposed to "scientific." . . . It is this final realization that makes me know that a more graceful, home- maker's life is probably for me, perhaps something with an artistic flair.
>
> I plant beans and lettuce in my garden, and when I stand at the sink I can see my darling little sprouts. Isn't it all so wonderful . . . the whole plan, that is? These little seeds turn into plants and give life and are activated by the sun and water which fall out of the sky. These are the things that fill me with wonder, and move me. Not the idea of going back to graduate school.

And yet another, an entrepreneur, says of himself:

> As a youngster (at twenty) I was in the Army. I found it so stultifying, so regimented. The communica- tions there, in the purest sense, are horrible—even thought it is enormously efficient. I learned there that Hewlett Packard or IBM or one of those other large compa- nies is not for me. I can't be happy there. I have to be my own boss and do things in my own way and in my own time. I just know that about myself, so to do anything else—no matter how materially successful or secure I would be—would be self-defeating.

What we see in each of these comments is that in order to have a positive, mature and personally helpful attitude about doing work the individual must first be aware of having a *distinct self*, a self that is able to choose, a self whose reality is clearly understood and appreciated and worth making some sacrifices for. It is this understanding of the self as distinctive (as well as having the developmental readiness as a personality which allows one to choose, which permits one to take the consequences for conscious choices) that precedes and produces life's constructive actions.

A certain detachment is involved at this level of personality development—a detachment which makes one able to be objective to one's self as well as to the dictates and expectations of society. As I have described in my other works, only the person who acts and chooses authentically brings a vitality, a uniqueness and a spontaneous richness to his activities. It is through this energy—for want of a better word—through his essential connectedness to self that the individual serves the other. And, ultimately, it is through services to self and others that we become fully human.

10

Vocational Integration:
Work as Love, Work as Devotion

**It is no use walking anywhere to preach unless our walking is
our preaching.**

St. Francis of Assisi

Work is one of the ways that the mature person cares for himself
and others. Through his work and relationships the individual
finds a place in the world, belongs to it, takes responsibility for
himself and for others. Work becomes his way of giving of
himself. His work (perhaps because of the way in which I am
meaning it here, the term "vocation" is a more accurate word)
provides him with a way of dedicating himself to life. Through it,
or—if he is retired or if he doesn't work in the formal sense—
through his hobbies and community involvements, he cultivates
his talents, stands in for others, exhibits his involvement and
connection to the world. Through work this individual at the
same time both loses himself yet becomes more distinctive.

It is this radical transformation of duty into love, fascination
or pleasure which allows the individual to feel that he is at play.
This is because he is fully present, as a personality, fully there in
the moment. And because he has committed his heart, attention
and intention to doing the work (and doing it with a kind of
narrowed, intense focus which transcends ordinary consciousness)
he heightens his energies and intelligence, and thus is able to
give his all to the job at hand. This is the type of person
sufficiently developed to be able to say, as did one man, "Yes,

you can say I love my work. I always say that when you can't tell the difference between work and play, you are happy."

In all cases, the by-product of a fully present, involved, concentrated and committed mind is a special type of imperative. This intrinsic urgency, felt especially keenly during those times in which the person is involved with something vitally interesting to him, is the result of an "inner push" to self-express, to understand the work, to make something happen, to create. It involves a kind of surrender of self in that the person becomes at-one with the work, fuses with it, is it, and—in this way, through this absorption and identification—disappears.

It was Shunryu Suzuki, a deeply respected Zen master, who wrote of this phenomenon in the classic Zen understanding of the issue. He described the Buddha as being more concerned about how he made bread than with metaphysical subjects. The Buddha discovered that the actual practice of making bread, repeating the bread-making over and over and over again, was the way to find out how to "become" bread, the way to fuse himself with the action and thereby transcend himself. The Buddha became the bread when he baked it—to that extent did he put himself into his task. Suzuki describes this state further by analogizing it to the act of painting.

> A wonderful painting is the result of the feeling in your fingers. If you have the feeling of the thickness of the ink in your brush, the painting is already there before you paint. When you dip your brush into the ink, you already know the result of your drawing or else you cannot paint. So before you do something, "being" is already there. . . . All the activity is included within you. That is your being (p. 106).

This is an ecstatic condition, not available to the closed or contracted personality. As we shall see, this state or condition—which exists regardless of the physical or environmental condition of the person—produces a sense of wonder, awe and fascination. In the actualizing person it gives rise to love, in the sense that the work itself is somehow sacred—although not necessarily directly tied to religious concepts or dogma. The individual feels that the work is part of something universal, special, sacred. He feels this way in part because a part of his being is in the work, as Suzuki has so beautifully put it. Also, he experiences the sacredness of the moment because in this moment he lives in full consciousness, surrendering his attention totally into the moment. Even though he may come to his work with quite an ordinary attitude, just his knowledge that the work has special relevance and meaning for him can transport him to an elevated, open awareness so that he becomes completely at one with the task. Or he may be so concentrated and involved, so wholeheartedly absorbed in the work, that he experiences himself to be a part of something bigger than himself. However it happens, his full focus and commitment lifts him out of an ordinary self-conscious condition, leaving him fully functioning in the moment. This is not so much a feeling as it is a state of being. I would go so far as to say that this condition itself gives rise to love, and perhaps I should also add that this is the primary face of love.

Love reveals many of its faces through us during work. Interviews with successful people show that they realize this in one way or another. One of love's faces may simply be the continuing, ardent desire within a person to produce something unique and beautiful. The young architect, quoted earlier, who admitted that money was not his main goal, but that producing good architecture was his chief ambition in life, illustrates this aspect of love. His positive emotion, his heart's direction is given force and life through his involvement with forms, through his service to others, through his ability to translate into substantive functional structures the hidden inexpressible images of beauty which his clients carry about inside their heads.

Another significant aspect of love displays itself when we concentrate on what we are doing. Being *is* love. And when someone is positively and wholly present in the moment, he exists completely as Being, at the level of, and through the "play" of, his specific functioning.

Many others have tried to explain this ecstatic instance, for truly this is an immensely euphoric state. This high, steady focus produces experiences, insights and creative outcomes which are beyond words, time and logical understanding. This is the moment of mystery which provides us with the sense of having an inner nucleus of uniqueness and, at the same time, connects us to all else. This is the all-consuming, all-powerful instance in which miracles can and do happen, the "no-mind" state of being which Laotzu called the state of the True man who transcended both joy and resistance to death. Countless others throughout history have attempted to put this experience into words.

Hagakure: The Book of the Samuri, for example, instructs that this state of concentration precedes and is the cause of victory. Three such lessons, among a host of others, outline the value of entering fully into the moment:

> How should a person respond when he is asked, "As a human being, what is essential in terms of purpose and discipline?" First, let us say, "It is to become of the mind that is right now pure and lacking complications. . . . This is very difficult to discover. Once discovered, it is again difficult to keep in effect. There is nothing outside the thought of the immediate moment."
>
> According to what one of the elders said, taking an enemy on the battlefield is like a hawk taking a bird. Even though it enters into the midst of a thousand of them, it gives no attention to any bird other than the one that it has first marked.
>
> [A man said], "When I have faced the enemy, of course it is like being in the dark. But if at that time I tranquilize my mind, it becomes like a night lit by a pale moon. If I begin my attack from that point, I feel as though I will not be wounded." This is the situation at the moment of truth (pp. 32, 46, 147).

In an almost identical vein, in an exquisitely written little article titled "Stalking the Snow Leopard," professor of theology Belden Lane writes that concentration upon one's job even, or especially, during ordinary, boring times brings one into "full awareness of the unnoteworthy but immediate moment [which] is

the grandest and hardest of all spiritual exercises. . . ." He quotes
author Peter Matthiessen's words from that author's book *The
Snow Leopard* to further develop his point:

> In the mountains of Nepal, Peter Matthiessen learned that
> "the purpose of meditation practice is not enlightenment; it
> is to pay attention even at unextraordinary times, to be of
> the present, nothing-but-in-the-present, to bear this mind-
> fulness of now into each event of ordinary life" (p. 15).

Perhaps this state of mind is what is meant by the biblical
passage instructing us to "have the mind of Christ," or the
reassuring words that teach that "perfect love casteth out fear." It
is certain, this I know, that when we are fully present,
concentrated, completely involved with what we are doing, fear's
chilling touch cannot reach us. Here-and-now we are perfectly
safe.

Testimonies of soldiers or professional athletes (or even the
would-be victims of criminal attack who live to tell about their
survival) reveal that they functioned spontaneously and
victoriously despite and through both fear and pain. They were
successful because their attention was rooted firmly in the
moment. In the same way, persons who manage to forget their
self-consciousness during a public speaking presentation (which
they may otherwise fear and dread) report that they triumph over
the activity and actually enjoy it. Also, those who, forgetting
themselves, manage to save the lives of people in danger say that
because they were concentrated with full power on what they had
to do, they and the other were ultimately safe. These stories add
weight to the truth that when we focus completely on a given
point, on a task or an idea, we are transformed and transported to
another state—a higher, liberated, more masterful state.
Concentration of this sort can even help us through our grief.

In a valuable passage of an equally valuable book, author
John Cantwell Kiley reminds us that even in the deepest grief we
can rescue ourselves by focusing on the moment:

The how of going on must be in things—it cannot be in your thoughts, for they offer only desolation and despair. You must surround yourself with things, and as you turn to this task, you discover it is not difficult. . . . These, properly experienced . . . will anchor you in the now and defend you from the thoughts which would keep you continuously informed about your tragedy . . .(p. 45).

Surveying the working habits of the accomplished in any field, we see that they work in exactly this way. They are more likely to be preoccupied to an extreme degree with the job in front of them than with distractions which bother others. Largely because they love the work and are fascinated by its challenges and secrets, they remain transfixed in the now, protected from thoughts of rewards or losses or the trivialized details which bar others from full and satisfying personal success.

Surely, this is what Thomas Merton's translation of the classical poem of Chuang Tzu, that most spiritual of Chinese philosophers, is about:

When an archer is shooting for nothing he has all his skills.
If he shoots for a brass buckle, he is already nervous. . . .
The prize divides him.
He cares.
He thinks more of winning than of shooting—and the need
   to win
Drains him of power (p. 107).

Interestingly, an article in a recent science section of the *New York Times* likens this state to euphoria. In his article, journalist and author Daniel Goldman writes:

New research is leading to the conclusion that these instances of absorption are . . . altered states in which the mind functions at its peak, time is often distorted and a sense of happiness seems to pervade the moment. Such states, the new research suggests, are accompanied by mental efficiency as a feeling of effortlessness. One team of researchers describes these moments of absorption as "flow states."... A psychologist at the University of Chicago [says], "flow" refers to those times when things seem to go just right, when you feel alive and fully attentive to what you are doing.

But of course, with due respect to Daniel Goldman and the *Times'* prestigious and honorable journalistic tradition, this is not "new research," unless it is the packaging and the description which is new. Poets, such as William Blake, have always known of flow states. For this is the state in which they often write at their best. Thankfully poets are able to describe these times in much more tender ways than researchers. Blake's now immortal words, "If the doors of perception were cleansed, everything would appear to man as it is, infinite," allow us to glimpse at yet another dimension of the "flow state," namely its relationship to and ability to link us to that ineffable non-dualistic reality in which physical and spiritual merge and become one.

The writings of the legendary mystic Meister Eckhart were saturated with this very issue, indicating that he himself was immersed in this state of being:

Who are those who honor God? Those who have wholly gone out of themselves, and who do not seek for what is theirs in anything, whatever it may be great or little, who are not looking beneath themselves or above themselves or beside themselves or at themselves, who are not desiring possessions or honors or ease or pleasure or profit or inwardness or holiness or reward or the kingdom of heaven, and who have gone out from all this, from everything that is theirs; these people pay honor to God, and they honor God properly, and they give him what is his (p. 183).

Of course, Eckhart is describing that identical condition of mind which now, generations later, mind-experts and researchers try to codify and make their own. However this domain belongs to all who would have it, and is in fact the birthright of anyone who would lift himself out of the mediocre posture of an unconscious existence and discipline himself to a life of loving, stewardly and focused conduct.

Whatever love's particular manifestations, I stress that it is always beyond mere forms, formulas or predictable, always-observable behaviors. Love is communicated through a person's appropriate and responsible actions, through his alertness to the moment, through his tenacious self-affirmation. In its highest and most elevated moments, love comes to, and appears through, the one who has lost all self-consciousness, all self-serving desires, as the various quotes above have helped us understand. But I maintain that it manifests itself throughout eternity in countless other ways: even through the self-consciously, weakly focused individual who timidly—to cite but one example—tiptoes into some new, untried behaviors that serve and prosper self-and-other. No matter how timid or awkward the act, no matter how fragile and slight its influence, love always heals the one who dedicates himself to act upon its directives.

In this connection again I quote Thomas Merton who, in discussing the phrase "experience of love," made it clear that he was talking about a total awakening of the person, a renunciation of self which is made in order to live functionally in relationship with others: "Such love is beyond . . . all restrictions of a desiring and self-centered self. Such love begins only when the ego renounces its claim to absolute autonomy and ceases to live in a little kingdom of desires in which it is its own end and reason for existing" (p. 86).

Merton, like Suzuki, and as I am meaning it here, is defining love as a condition of a liberated, non-self-conscious self, a self which has so totally entered the moment as to have dissolved into it, disappeared.

This may have been what Christ meant, at least in part, when he said that he who would try to save his life would lose it and that he who abandoned it would preserve it—in other words, that each one's salvation comes from losing his egocentric self and giving himself over entirely to life, as a choice, as a conscious response to the demands of the moment.

When such love manifests itself through someone's work, the individual experiences himself as called, committed, even devoted. This quality of devotion exists whether or not the individual is "religious" by self-definition. It is the attitude of loyalty, zeal and ardent interest which makes me call the individual "devoted." Sometimes these feelings start early in life. A woman working as a special needs teacher in a public school system says that she read *Heidi* in the third grade and wanted to be like her and has never changed her desire.

> I would do this work in one form or another in whatever I do. . . . My husband and I are also volunteers (with Asian refugee families), so in this way, too, we are committed. There is a Buddhist saying about not being able to enter the kingdom of heaven unless you bring one person along. I may be just helping to enable that one other person in the journey. My work is my life, and my life is my work.

A man working for the United Nations describes how he found entry into his work. He too recalls having had an early desire to do the work, even though in early adulthood he forgot his teenaged fascination with the field:

> I needed a job in New York for family reasons, and while I chose the U.N. for idealistic reasons, the job I landed there was pure accident—the only one that happened to be open the day I walked in. . . . My wife, however, reminds me of a high school essay of mine, written when I was fifteen, mentioning a desire to work for the U.N. So I guess my war experience, after which I swore "Never Again," and saw the U.N. as on the cutting edge of the next chapter in history, was a way to be in on that, in however small a way. I supposed the war merely reinforced an aim that was already there five years before the U.N. was formally founded.

A seventy-five year old poet told me that although for the first thirty-eight years of his life he lived on the family farm, later holding a variety of other jobs, he merely used these activities to earn money. He found himself after realizing that he had always liked to read, that he was interested in words and in devising a better alphabet (as well as a more handy number system), and he put these interests to use as "hobbies." Eventually, relatively late in his life, in connection with printing up some booklets of poetry, he discovered that these "hobbies"—namely printing, writing poetry, playing with words, the number system—could be used to "help make civilization more peaceful and useful."

A librarian wrote me a letter in which she outlined the way in which she came into her profession.

Nothing really "called me" to being a librarian. Before I took my degree in Library/Information Science, I had been an assistant professor in education. And I quickly learned that I wasn't of academic ilk. But librarianship offered me a chance to stay in contact with students and still teach and go home feeling like I'd done something constructive and helpful. God personally didn't speak to me about being a librarian, if that's what you mean by a calling. And I didn't dream I saw myself standing in a field of bound volumes or anything like that. But when I started working in a library I'd felt like I'd "come home."

In whatever way the individual is able, in whatever way he finds personally meaningful, through paid or unpaid activity, through his relationships, his community service, his formal or informal work, to the extent he becomes functional and steadfast in his efforts, mature in his personal development, his activity invariably grows into a loyal, persistent avenue of giving to himself and to others.

To the degree his giving stems from his love for the activity, to the degree he honors that which is best and most generous within himself and "forgets" himself, to the degree his motives are spontaneously expressive, creative, faithful (i.e., to himself, the task, the demands of the job, the other, etc.), his giving is experienced by him as sacred, sublime, devotional.

We generally use the term "devotion" to mean a religious worship of some sort. I repeat, before developing this theme further, that in talking about work-as-devotion, I am describing a state or condition of being, not a type of person—not, as I said earlier, for example, merely a formally religious individual or someone who attends church every Sunday and feels, in this way that he has paid homage to God. Nor am I speaking about people who are merely dogmatically inclined. However, the state I am describing is likelier to be found in the self-actualizing individual.

What I observe in such persons is a giving up of self, as manifested by the dedication of one's entire attention and being to some activity, relationship, or pursuit, or to the requirements of the here-and-now—whatever these may happen to be. This quality of being, absolutely essential to the integrity and health of the personality, wherein the individual is, in his awareness, as pure, innocent and spontaneous so as to be empty of ego concerns and of all self-consciousness, is what I define as devotional. In this state, the person is liberated from the confines of cultural, parental or personal programming. He transcends these, and thus he is free to enter into the work in a wholly different, fresh non-ordinary way. In this state he himself is morally elevated and experiences himself as one with others, with the work, with the cosmos.

Only now can he give up all that he has within to what he is doing. Only now does the task become as if sacred. Now he possesses a firm sense of himself from which to give something unique and substantive to others. Of course, for the naturally religious, devout personality, this experience adds to his opportunity to put his beliefs, his training and his religious understandings or inclinations into practice. The one with a religious temperament will find any task worthy of dedication to God. And it is likely that such persons will not resist the term "devoted" when describing themselves. A cook and housekeeper says of her vocation:

> For me, preparing food is really an act of worship. Being aware of what goes into raising crops, the people involved in making it possible for me to go to the store and buy it, is sort of a background against which I work, and in back of it all is a loving God who has made it possible for growth and life and my part in this service.

Others, especially those who are not religiously inclined (i.e., by their own or others' definition), may experience devotion in their act of creation, as did one man who created an electricity system for rural homes using solar-powered generators. Of his work and himself he says:

> This work was selected from personal need, but also because I have been playing with electronics since the age of six, and my second interest is philosophy (along with conservation, ecology, vegetarianism, religion, psychology, etc.). I found this work to be the meeting point of it all . . . except when the business goes too fast and I become trapped into (a repetition) which sometimes crowds out creativity.

Both religious and non-religious persons come to know themselves as devoted through their work. Most actualizing persons do, in fact, speak in reverential tones about what they do. They express a yearning to reach out further in their work than perhaps they have. They express themselves as dedicated to something larger than themselves—whether this be to God, to universal values, to the needs of others, or to the future.

If they have had a peak experience it is also likely that their work will be further transformed. Such is the case of a therapist from Illinois who, after a mystical experience, came to see a divine quality in his patients:

> Last fall I experienced a spiritual awakening. This was highlighted by meditative experiences in accord with what Aldous Huxley called the "Perennial Philosophy" . . . Now I yearn to be more in touch with the Inner Light, the Divine Spark in my clients, and want to use this energy, or dynamic, in the healing process. . . . This inspires me to want to help other clients get in touch with the divine within them.

The man working for the United Nations, for example, speaks in a classical yet "non-religious" way about the devotional aspects of his work, and through his comments we can better understand that when one listens to self-actualizing persons talk about their work, one hears a selfless, passionate and generous attitude which is also highly practical in its application, indicating that the person is committed to something beyond himself which then benefits others in a way which surpasses "form," techniques or artificiality:

> The devotional element came in and never left me. The stated aims of the U.N. organizations add up to the closest thing we have to a charter for the self-actualization of people. For those aims to be realized, we need men and women who can break out of their racial, sectarian, nationalist boxes and work together for the good of the global village. In this way they help create an international civil service which may be one of this (and the next) century's paths to salvation, comparable to the copying of manuscripts, the draining of swamps and the building of cathedrals in past ages—that humankind may have life and have it more abundantly.
>
> Of course, on most days during my thirty-three years in the U.N. bureaucracy, such thoughts were submerged. But those other days, when your weight tips the balance away from tired or rigid or cynical habit toward openness, imagination or love, or when you see little acts of integrity that people are capable of, those days make up for all the rest.

He continues to say that he believes there is a close connection between life-styles and integrity and that if one's style is simple enough not to need superficial egocentric "boosts," this itself does wonders for one's integrity. And certainly this is much the issue: that only the egoless, self-sacrificing moment affords the individual complete integrity, and that only the authentic, actualizing individual, having known such moments, can then perform this work in a selfless, functional and devoted fashion. More than that, his life—in all its variation—is marked by a progressively frequent number of such moments, and ultimately marked by a vivid stamp of realness which penetrates the work, regardless of the type of work the person elects to do.

This stamp of realness, this ecstatic confrontation with the simplest requirements (as well as the most complex) of life, is so marked as to exist only in the person who has reached what I call vocational integration. I use this term because it designates an individual who has committed himself to his vocation so wholeheartedly as to embody its qualities in his being and so that he does not have to wonder at every turn whether or not he wishes to continue to direct his commitment and energy to it or not.

I also choose this term because it suggests a kind of completeness and thus relates nicely to what Merton (albeit through the work of the psychoanalyst Arasteh) called the "final integration."

Also, in corresponding with and personally interviewing actualizing people I heard them repeatedly refer to themselves as having a kind of integrity in the doing of their work. People meant different things by this word. Some referred to themselves as having integrity because they saw themselves acting out of what they felt was best in themselves. They saw themselves as honest, as trustworthy, as reliable or courageous because they had had the good fortune or tenacity or the risk-taking skill to do the work they loved. Others used the term "integrity" to mean the values which they found inherently in the work. They saw a certain tightness or beauty or truth in the work, or they sensed that their work had meaning in relation to the whole of mankind and helped them understand the whole world or the universe better, even though they knew it was just a part of that whole. Still others spoke of an integrity which they felt they had achieved by virtue of the fact that in doing the work they were being truthful about what they wanted to do and that they did it in a way that suited them.

Thomas Merton's discussion of the phenomenon of "final integration," in which he describes the monk who has passed through numerous vocational problems and conflicts and who finally resolves the critical, existential crisis of his life, speaks more fully of the integration process I am describing here.

This integration, this resolution of oneself to one's life work, the taking-on of the work responsibility, is both psychological and spiritual accomplishment in that the person comes into his own as a specific, distinct individual. Because of this he achieves a kind of spiritual health or wholeness which is a direct result of his own truthfulness, courage and conscious choices. First the achievement, if I can call it that, is psychological because in choosing his work, he takes a conscious, responsible life-direction and acts in such a way as to be psychologically "there," all of a piece, understandable, unique as an individual. He knows, as the saying goes, "what he wants to be when he grows up." Knowing, he grows up.

Second, it is a spiritual achievement because his life is thereafter dedicated to a conscious, intentional manner of living; rather than withdrawing or contracting himself from life, his "livingness," or steadfast functional effectiveness, as I have already said, is his devotional act and consecrates everything it touches because through the faculty of being he is present, in the moment, *as life*.

Before elaborating upon Merton's discussion of final integration and prior to returning to the issue of work as a devotional act, I want to cite a common illustration of the kind of thing I am describing as "a psycho-spiritual achievement," so as to merge an everyday, concrete example of the phrase "coming into one's own" with that of Merton's more heady, transpersonal account of "final integration."

A neighbor of mine and I meet frequently for lunch. We meet—as if by accident—almost every day at a nearby deli, situated in a lovely rural spot. While we warm ourselves, eating outside on the deck in the sun, we also casually talk. Lunch for me is a time away from my writing, and I like to leave my house and spend some time with friends. I rarely talk about my work and look forward to these lunches as a way to take a breather from the intensity of my work. My friend similarly avoids talking of his work, and so we usually discuss the weather, local politics or the food.

However, one day not long ago, he happened to ask me what I was working on and I said I was writing the last chapter of a book about people who love their work. Upon hearing this, he became visibly animated and emotional and launched into a personal story about how he had been struggling for the last few months with wanting to leave work he didn't really like. "I've always been the kind of person who would leave work when it wasn't fulfilling. As a result I've never been in a situation like the one I find myself now. I'm involved in something I don't enjoy, where I have many responsibilities to others. I've made promises and commitments, and it is going to be a while before I can extricate myself from this work. I've always been used to having a job which was enjoyable despite its ups and downs. But now I'm not having any fun. I've put on weight. I've become impossible to talk to at home. I know what I have to do, but so far I haven't done it. When you write your chapter, don't forget to tell people that if they don't like what they are doing, they should figure out what to do about it, take a risk and get out. Better to be true to yourself than to spend your time worrying about whether you should or shouldn't make the move. Life's just too short for that."

I use his comments to illustrate a part of the psychological process of vocational integration. Certainly for most people it does involve a struggle to be "true to themselves," at least in the beginning. Often the desire to stay and the pull to leave are equally intense. The Should I?/Shouldn't I? struggle can be a lengthy, emotional and bitterly anxious one. One woman, a writer who left a secure position in the publishing field to go on her own as a free-lance writer, said of her leap of faith (which she knew would be required in order to make the move) that she faced what amounted to a vocational crisis.

This is a scary period for me, and a wonderful and exciting one too. I've known for a long time that I have a book in me, that I want to write about something that is stirring around in me. More than that, I don't like the stance my magazine has been taking. I'm certain that I can return to this position if I want to. I'm certain that I can do a good job if I want to. But honestly I don't know if I want to.

I wonder if I really want to spend the rest of my life writing "how-to" advice for people about their electronic work-stations. If I answer honestly I would have to admit there'd be little relevance for my life doing that. I want and need something more. Still, I have to say, I'm unclear about how I'm going to support myself, and about what the future will hold for me.

This is the same type of vocational crisis which prompted my lunchtime friend to become so heatedly insistent that I include his experience in my chapter. He too wanted to have relevance in his life and in his work, but didn't know how he could extricate himself from his responsibilities. He too was unsure of what the future held for him if he left his present position. This is the sort of crisis which precedes the full and wholehearted investment of self, the mature choice-making which actualizing personalities are willing to make in their work.

The reason that the culminating resolution is both psychological and spiritually healing to the personality (resulting in what Merton spoke of as a "final integration") is precisely because the individual has chosen, consciously, to commit himself to his vocational choice.

This commitment necessitates his surrendering his egocentric, often infantile, grasping and "secure" way of being. This conscious surrender, or sacrifice, is the beginning of his ability to love, to serve, to be wholly present, and to be a responsible person. The choice, if it is made, is preceded by a fearful crisis because the person's limited idea-of-self, his ego, senses that it is about to die. Of course, it will—in a way—die, but only to a larger part of itself. In fact, there is no such thing as "an ego," although it is often helpful to use this term as a way of communicating certain psychological attitudes and phenomena. The renowned spiritual teacher Sri Ramana Maharishi used to teach that the surest way to strengthen the ego was to ask the question, "How is the ego to be destroyed?" He meant that only the ego ponders such issues, looking for formulas and logical solutions. In actuality, such an entity does not exist, and is simply a fiction devised by the human mind to help explain its own functioning.

As an individual transcends his limited self-idea, as he grows into a larger self by surrendering even some aspect of the fear which grips and cripples him, he gradually discovers that he can do what he previously believed he could not do. Such a discovery comes slowly for some, and in a burst of freeing insight for others. In all cases, this discovery—and the behaviors which ensue—amounts to an awakening.

Thomas Merton, in describing this predictable developmental issue, leans on the work of the Persian psychoanalyst Dr. Reza Arasteh, who studied the complete maturing of the personality on a transcultural level and likened it to the individual becoming "fully born."

> The man who is "fully born" has an entirely inner experience of life. He apprehends his life fully and wholly from an inner ground that is at once more universal than the empirical ego and yet entirely his own. He is in a certain sense "cosmic" and "universal man." He has attained a deeper, fuller identity than that of his limited ego-self which is only a fragment of his being. He is in a certain sense identified with everybody. . . . He is guided not just by will and reason, but by "spontaneous behavior subject to dynamic insight" (p. 163).

The individual who achieves vocational integration is thus able to fully focus on what he is at the core. Moreover he is able to be that unique, distinctive personality in and through his work because he has gained a specific, vital, unobstructed strength which empowers him, which is life-giving, energizing, creative, loving. This added power is gained when the individual sees himself as he really is, understands what drives him, what motivates him to act—or to back away from things—when he knows what he wants to live for (perhaps even to die for), and then consciously chooses to enact that knowledge in everything he does. Naturally, his work falls into place as the correct thing for him to be doing (or, when he senses it is not appropriate for him, the incorrect thing).

The vocationally integrated person is able to choose to risk all and surrender to the truth of himself as he exists within himself in that most private and sacred core of self, and this choice—as I have indicated—is the beginning of the dissolution of his limited, egocentric former life. However, it is this choice which initially produces the profound risk and death-related images and emotions that are so troubling. Happily, once the initial steps are taken by him to settle for nothing less than living out the truth and reality of his life, other lesser choices become easier and the actualization process (and with it vocational integration) is freed to accelerate.

The initial "letting-go" steps can appear in a variety of decisions, not just through vocational ones. The individual may feel impelled to leave long-time friends or loved ones or move away from the community where he has grown up. Whatever these separations are, as mentioned, the first such step is usually the most anxiety-provoking one, where the person feels as if he were abandoning all that is important to his life and to his well-being. If (as in the case of the writer who—despite her anxiety—chose in the direction of her true yearning) he can resist the temptation to run from this difficult choice, if he can manage whatever risks are there so as not to do himself in, if he can live out his life-choice instead of his death-choice, he will usually be liberated from the obstructions of his lesser self in many other areas of life as well.

Merton also speaks of this in his discussion of "final integration" and says that there exists a state of insight which is an openness, an emptiness, a poverty. He too, like the Zen masters and so many Christian mystics (such as St. John of the Cross, Meister Eckhart and others), uses these types of words to help describe the way an individual's perceptions and consciousness are radically altered as he becomes whole.

The individual who has reached "vocational integration" is not just momentarily transported into more creative, spontaneous and healthy performance. His integration marks his entire manner of being and creates in him the ability to function responsibly in daily life. Quite possibly this is because fear no longer has the same powerful hold on him as it did previously, and thus its opposite—love—begins to govern his awareness, his emotions, his relational life, his choices, his work.

Insofar as the individual allows himself to develop, to become integrated (and some would say this is a grace and not entirely as a result of anything he "does"), he gains a bonded, ecstatic identification with the moment—ecstatic because all his energies, intelligence and attention become fully merged with and in the present.

This is, in fact, one of the conditions, and also a by-product, of actualization. The more actualized the person, the more total his concentrative abilities and his willingness to make choices that serve himself and others. But it should be noted that the type of intensified energies and focus I am speaking about, by themselves, are probably not the triggers which transform the individual's way of being. If this were the case, people could become actualized simply by taking some chemicals. Even though some researchers, including Maslow, have felt that, for example, selected drugs (like LSD) could move an individual in this general developmental direction, I am speaking about a complex of attributes which stem from the individual's lastingly living in such a way that he loves, rather than fears, life and which allow him to consciously choose life over death.

The more actualized the individual, the more his vocational life will be "poor," egoless, without blocks, spontaneous; the more the person can choose, act, and be wholly present in his work, exhibiting that which is most noble, truthful and generous within himself, the more he insures further growth and development.

However one understands this high state (e.g., as the ultimate objective of Karma Yoga, in which "right action" is a goal; as the attainment of the Satori state in the Zen philosophy; as the Christian ideal, in which each is to do God's will if one hopes to achieve his full potential) does not seem to be the key issue, since one particular cultural understanding of "how" to reach perfected state may differ from another in imagery and vocabulary; all essentially point to the same goal.

The point seems more accurately to be that all major cultures have, somewhere within their instructive tradition, grasped this central truth: that work, done rightly, affords the individual an understanding of the key principles of life and of the universe, and—moreover—that work is a critical avenue and a discipline for personality health and optimum, responsible functioning. If the individual will but use his work for this end, then whatever his role in life, his work can become an immediate and practical way of developing his highest motives and transforming him in such a way that he reaches completeness as a personality.

The vocationally integrated person centers himself in his tasks, is responsible in his relational life, and creates with great force and vitality. He gives all he has to the thing at hand because this giving is the way in which he exists. His life becomes rooted in a condition of giving; he cannot "not" give—to put it another way. In a concrete and specific way, his is a dynamic and expressive personality, and his energy increases, is satisfied, only by being put to purposeful use. Also, because he must discipline himself in order to act in this way, he develops his own virtuousness as well. His patience grows. His ability to listen to others is cultivated. His understanding expands, in terms of what he needs, wants and must have in order to be a complete person—in order to be responsible to the values he believes in. Through his daily efforts he becomes more tenacious. He learns to care properly for people and things entrusted to him so that lives, projects and property are well managed. He is able to see things through to completion.

All these hard-to-control aspects of self are improved, while simultaneously his idiosyncratic mannerisms and work style may become more defined, as I suggested in an earlier chapter. The individual may be brusque with those who interrupt his thinking; he may overindulge at times as a way to give his mind rest; he may disappear for days at a time in order to think things through alone, or he may display any number of what others might feel are "odd" traits primarily because he knows what he needs and is not afraid of providing this for himself. The more boldness he exhibits in his workstyle, the likelier his idiosyncratic work habits will serve his overall purpose, strengthening his contribution, rather than weakening it.

Whatever his style of working, we can be assured that this is an individual who will grow as a person. In part this is because he is totally committed to his chosen work and—ironically—because his dreams, values and inner condition "grow" him. By this I mean that he is stretched through what he does and he is developed because of what he chooses to be, because of what he is and what he is becoming.

Of course, there are many degrees and levels of vocational integration. Certainly a first level is to simply move in the direction of what one loves to do: whether the movement is through non-work, unrelated acts (as discussed in a previous chapter) or vocational means, the essential point is that people benefit from seeing themselves do what they feel they ought to do.

The ability to feel happy and enthused at the opportunities presented in anything we are given to do is another level of "movement." One man said to himself, "I like working. My work, prior to obtaining my undergraduate degree, was as warehouseman, delivery driver, pizza cook, forklift driver and steel mill worker. I found something in each of these jobs that brought me joy and a sense of accomplishment." This attitude may simply be a sign of emotional health. Thus it is a natural precursor to finding one's right livelihood since the individual who enjoys working, who has a cheerful disposition, is also one whose resistance is minimal and who is more likely to be self-determining.

Another, perhaps higher level of work (in keeping with the issues raised previously) is the totally committed individual who, upon finding himself on the right vocational path, devotes himself more and more completely to it. A mother wrote me about her parental role, describing the satisfaction she finds in motherhood:

> My work is a full-time commitment to bringing up three children. I have been doing this since 1972. I find it totally satisfying. As time has gone on, this work has evolved into work with other families as a breastfeeding counselor. First, I worked with the La Leche League in the U.S., and since 1978, with the breastfeeding information group in Kenya, where we now live. At this point I am spending 30 hours a week for various organizations. . . . Neither raising the family nor my other work carries any remuneration.
>
> My husband provides the family income. I hope

you do not subscribe to the common fallacy that a woman
is not working unless she is getting a salary; I have got to
the point where my hackles rise when someone asks me,
"Do you work?" meaning "Is somebody paying you
money?" . . . If you have done it, you know that bringing
up small children to be secure and useful people requires
"full focus" . . . and also constant presence. . . . I wonder
if you will hear from anyone else who has found that total
commitment to meeting the needs of their children forms
the basis for their working life, and who find vocational satisfaction in this very demanding occupation.

This woman's comments reinforce points made earlier,
namely that her commitment of energy, attention and service to
her chosen vocation are strong because she loves the work,
because she has made conscious choices to live the values she
believes in, because she has an underpinning of inner strength to
give to what she does. As we have seen, high self-esteem,
confidence that we can make a difference, the ability to be
present as a person, the courage to behave in ways that others
may not understand or approve of, are all factors which go into
the capacity to commit fully to something. These traits, like the
ability to be happy with one's lot and with whatever one must do,
are also components of emotional health.

People who merely conform to the working norms and the
expectations of parents, community or culture have a thousand
ways of withdrawing themselves from a serious commitment and
from relationship. Whether that relationship is with their work,
with people or with themselves, the immature, under-developed
personality is always tentative, wavering, dependent, grasping
and outer-directed. Ever craving comfort, security, approval,
reassurance, applause, he or she works so as to get something out
of the other rather than to give.

That "something" might be a striving to hold another's
attention so as to feed a starved and deficient ego. That
"something" might be striving to guarantee for oneself a fixed
secure salary so as to fight off anxious feelings about an unstable,
ambiguous world. For instance, one manager in a very ethical,

sophisticated corporation found herself sorely out of place. She had come from a plant facility where she had been able to dominate and control her subordinates and extract enormously servile behaviors from them.

In her new environment, however, people had been encouraged to move along more stewardly lines, such as those I have been describing. All levels of personnel had participated in workshops which taught them how to give to others through their working efforts. They responded positively to the concept, not only during the course of the workshops, but long after, in their daily functional responsibilities where they practiced some of the techniques and ideas they had been exposed to. They expected to work with giving, stewardly managers, and also wanted to give of themselves to their new supervisor. Give they did: they came into her office, as a group, and told her in straightforward, non-abusive but plain-spoken terms what kind of a work climate they had previously enjoyed and what type of climate they wanted to have. They told her what they needed from her in order for them to do their jobs responsibly, and shared with her openly and compassionately what she was doing that didn't work. In a way, they acted out the role of teachers, helping her adjust to the corporate values. They did this in a manner that helped develop her understanding, rather than in a way that threatened and demeaned her. The episode was traumatic for this manager, but—because of it and the way it was carried out—she ultimately succeeded in her job. Later she said that she could feel their concern for her and that this concern, or friendly interest, made it possible for her to hear them out.

I bring up this example because once people have begun to act out of a responsible and mature base, they are less willing to tolerate the more infantile aspects of their own and others' personality. Their awareness is opened up to the possibilities of serving the other in countless areas of life; they are not only able to correct themselves as they work, but they are also able to firmly and appropriately assert their needs and values so that others grow into more responsible behaviors as well.

I also like the example of an employee-group helping their manager become more responsible because it teaches us another lesson. There is a myth in our country—perhaps all over the world—that only "experts" or gurus or specially appointed, titled persons (e.g., with advanced degrees and certificates, etc.) can be actualizing or that these types of people are the ones to model enlightened behaviors for the rest of us. Nothing could be further from the truth. Sometimes, in fact, the individual in authority is so enamored with himself, so driven by egocentric ambition, so out of touch with himself as a human being, that he is immature, pompous and exploitive. My own experience is that within each organization are numbers of able, expanded, responsible beings, each one of whom—were he to have confidence in his own goodness and in the power of his own "voice"—could elevate the quality of working life and of the relationships within the place.

I mention this point because one mature, whole and balanced individual has incredible power. In him, greed, egocentricity and self-involvement are diminishing traits; concern for the other, patience for the tedium and demands of the work, kindliness and a disciplined will (just to name a few characteristics) are ever increasing. Also increasing in him are moments and periods of intensely satisfying experiences with the work—so satisfying that this is reward and motive enough to try to make a difference to others.

While the actualizing person may also receive status, adulation, power or security from his working life, these are not his main concerns nor are they his primary reasons for working. He works, as I have said, because he is in love with what he does and because he senses in an intuitive, strange way that the work loves him too, opens itself up to him, shows him its special rules and secrets and requirements. Perhaps, as the man working for the United Nations said, the individual demonstrates his love in some small, consistent integrities. Perhaps, as a client of mine once told me, he demonstrates his love by telling the truth in a meeting—even when things go against him as a result. Maybe, as with the mother now living in Kenya, the individual's love is shown by his full focus, by his constant, responsible presence, or even by his continuing ardent wish to produce something worthwhile and lovely as was the case with the potter quoted in a previous chapter.

The point is that a vocationally integrated person shows active, continual and predictable indications of his service to himself and to others. He does this in countless, repetitious ways (not always understandable or noticeable to onlookers since many things he might do go unnoticed) that establish him more firmly in his faithfulness to himself and his chosen vocation.

There is a story I recently heard in this connection about Mother Teresa which epitomizes the attitude of faithfulness I am describing. It seems that Mother Teresa was in Ethiopia, around the time of the worst droughts and famine. She was caring for the needy, blessing dying children, although people were dying around her at alarming rates. A reporter who happened on the scene asked her if she didn't get discouraged seeing, day after day, so many people die despite her efforts to help them. She briskly replied, "We are not here to be successful. We are here to be faithful."

Her total commitment was enough to keep her on the path, and she did not need outward signs of approval or achievement to keep her energies and love flowing. This, of course, is exactly the quality of love which I am suggesting is shown in a myriad of ways in vocationally integrated people, in all walks of life, even though their actions might not be so dramatic. The dramatizable aspects of love are deceptive, and are not good indications of the quality of faithfulness behind them. Whenever the individual is constant to the law of his own being, whenever he passes beyond his limitations—his negative or fearful or grasping self—whenever he draws something new, vital, living, compassionate, truthful from within himself, he honors himself and the other. I call these acts of love.

In this connection, an artist describes her "way of being," and helps us see more clearly how our being truthful to our inner self is linked to outer, loving acts:

Ever since I was a child I was considered to be "different," artistic and creative. I'm not sure why, since I can't recall any particular example of that ability—only that "doing art" and leading other people to it has been the steady way of being for me. The only other "theme" of my life has been religion. Again, whatever I do or have done has been just that—variations on a theme.

At this time, I feel that even if I never painted again, I would still consider myself as an artist—because I'm sure that it would mean that I've only changed my "medium" or means of expression. I'm open to the leading of the Spirit . . . I always feel directed.

Her constancy as a person becomes her relational life and naturally allows her to "do art," as she herself puts it, which others can enjoy. Had she tried to conform as a child, tried to be more like others, her art would have suffered because she, herself, would have been thwarted, constricted, unable to function freely as an artist.

Another person, in this case a decidedly spiritual woman, the wife of a partially handicapped husband who also cares for her mother in a nursing home and an eighty-eight year old father who lives alone, describes her vocation in these terms:

I feel my work is devotional because, at my best, I want to do it to please God alone. This is a most satisfying aspiration, which I try to renew each day by thoughtfully considering how I have managed my affairs in regard to my highest understanding. I conscientiously, and hopefully as honestly as possible, write down problems I have in my daily tasks, when my experience is difficult, my attitude poor, my failure evident.

I also write God's directive and guidance down, that which he aspires for me to do in my situation, especially regarding my attitude and spirit and will. Thus, I bring into God's light my daily tasks for his leading and my healing. . . . It is easy to forget to "do for God's sake whatever we would commonly do for our own," or that it is not the greatness of the work, but the love with which it is performed. But I do aspire to make all the moments of my day, whether peeling potatoes or calling my congressman, an offering of love to God.

A less religious person has this to say of the way his work is a loving act:

I cannot say I am a religious person. At least I do not attend church. But I try, within the confines of my work and life, to make all my decisions fit the Golden Rule. I strive to make my word mean something, to have my life in balance, so that I can listen to people and not be absorbed in my own thoughts or cut them out.

As a lawyer, I was trained to live by logic. But I have found that poetry and literature and my own intuition are enormously good guides in situations where logic doesn't serve me. My job, as I see it, is to give something of myself to my clients, and to do it in a way that helps the community too. When I am at my best I experience myself as loving, even though I don't always feel love as an emotion: I choose to do or say something because it is true, or right, rather than because I love the person who is involved.

Still another person talked about how she had struggled with the most positive, affirming parts of herself, and found that in order to express these aspects of being she had to go against her own family:

When I realized that my parents were abusive, really sick people, I knew that if my life was ever going to amount to anything I was going to have to protest by setting a standard for my life and turning my back on anything that went against that.

First, I spoke about what I wanted and needed from them. That didn't work. Then I said that if I didn't receive the privacy, respect and dignity from them that I required in order to survive as a person, I would not have a relationship with them. That didn't work either. It was as if they discounted my words, my very right to exist. So I left, and I have never looked back.

This action, which seemed to be so unloving, was

actually an unequivocal act of faith in the dignity, potential and worth of my own life. Since then, as a result of that single, completely conscious choice, I have had the clarity of mind and the reservoir of energy to complete my education, marry and live as a positive force in this community. To me, we honor our parents when we honor the life that they gave us, the life in us. If I had to describe my life's work I'd say it was just that: honoring the life in me through my moment-to-moment conduct and choices.

However people define their work, however they speak about it, whether they are a mother, an executive, a carpenter or an apple picker, makes little difference. The traits found in common in the vocationally integrated, actualizing personality are much the same:

● The individual possesses a firm sense of identity, can "stand alone," be alone; he is fully present in the moment and in his work.

● The individual is able to and willing to consciously choose to do his work, and this very ability to make conscious choices, to take the consequences for the choice, is precisely the mark of his maturity, his inward strength, his independent, whole personality and at the same time is one of the elements which activates his future growth.

● His choices are prerequisite to his feeling that he has power, that he can "create," that he has options, that he can make a difference, that his actions—however slight—matter, if only in his eyes. Again, it is from these attitudes and from his values that the individual gains the strength to contribute stability and something from within himself to the world.

● At his best, the individual is truly himself, more completely authentic and integrated as a personality and thus is able to bring the complex of his full, entire self (i.e., all his energies, talents, courage, attention, sub-selves, etc.) to the work at hand. As a result he has more to give through his working efforts than the one who withholds attention, talents or loyalty or who is working "just to earn a living," or merely to make ends meet. He has more to give because he has a completely integrated self to give.

● Work becomes a devotion, a labor of love, and indeed— whatever the person himself might call it—a spiritual exercise because the individual's concentrative powers, his choices, actions and values, are motivated, prompted and fueled by love, and his service, as it were, is simply the enactment of this positive life-force. His being or essential self lives in all he does.

The vocationally integrated person does not long for love: he has it. He does not yearn for happiness: he has it. He does not strive for completion, finality, satisfaction: he has these, and he has qualities in the very act and process of doing the work he enjoys. The healthier the personality, the more likely it is that the individual experiences his entire life (including his vocational life) in this abundant manner.

Of course, this conception of work contains the seeds to alter the way we become "successful" at work. Instead of just working for things, we can learn to work so as to create more vitality for ourselves. We can start to work so as to create and express something whole, distinctive, beautiful, truthful and positive for ourselves and others. As we learn to do this *we* become more distinctive, whole, beautiful, truthful and positive.

Instead of withholding our energy and concentration, we can use our work to grow in functional effectiveness—if for no other reason than it feels good to do so, and that by our growth in this area we are expanded, opened up inside, fueled in some mysterious way. As Erich Fromm once wrote when talking about active listening, to be concentrated in anything makes us more awake, while every unconcentrated, unconscious activity fatigues us, makes us more tired. When we learn to function with full concentration and purposefulness, we are the ones who are energized, activated, alert.

We can practice consciously choosing to do those things which elevate our self-respect. In this way we develop our ability to choose, to know what we want and need, to stand up for ourselves and the actions we value.

We can practice love through our work. Through this worthy discipline we grow in our capacity to love—both ourselves and others.

And finally, we can start to do more of the things we love and let go of our debilitating, toxic or spirit-breaking choices and relationships. Truly these do not belong in a healthy life. In this way we learn what it is we love, discover what it is that has meaning and elegance for us.

As we grow in this knowledge and in these abilities we will find it easier to put more of what we value into our own life. Through these acts and attitudes, we grow to see that our work is more than something by which to "earn a living"; it is that which helps us build our life.

References

Cousins, Norman. *Anatomy of an Illness*. New York: W.W. Norton & Co., 1979.

Meister Eckhart. *The Essential Sermons, Commentaries, Treatises and Defense*. Translated by E. Colledge and B. McGinn. New York: Paulist Press, 1961.

Gillies, Jerry. *Money-Love*. New York: Warner Books, 1978.

Glasser, William. *Positive Addiction*. New York: Harper & Row, 1976.

Golas, Thaddeus. *The Lazy Man's Guide to Enlightenment*. New York: Bantam Books, 1980.

Goldberg, Herb. *The Hazards of Being Male*. New York: Signet Classics, 1977.

Goldman, Daniel. "Concentration Is Likened to Euphoric States of Mind," *New York Times*, Tuesday, March 4, 1986.

Hagakure: The Book of the Samurai. Translated by William Scott Wilson. New York: Avon Books, 1979.

Jung, Carl. *The Archetypes and the Collective Unconscious*, Vol. 9, Part 1, Bollingen Series XX. Translated by R.F.C. Hull. New York: Pantheon Books.

Kiley, John Cantwell. *Self-Rescue*. New York: Fawcett-Crest, 1977.

Lane, Belden. "Stalking the Snow Leopard," *The Christian Century*, Vol. 101, January 4–11, 1984.

Levinson, Harry. "When Executives Burn Out," *Harvard Business Review*, May-June, 1981.

Lindner, Robert. *Prescription for Rebellion*. New York: Grove Press, 1952.

Maslow, Abraham. *Toward a Psychology of Being*. New Jersey: D. Van Nostrand Inc., 1962.

Merton, Thomas. *Contemplation in a World of Action*. New York: Doubleday & Co., Inc., 1971.

Merton, Thomas. *The Way of Chuang Tzu*. New York: New Directions, 1965.

Merton, Thomas. *Zen and the Birds of Appetite*. New York: New Directions, 1965.

Needleman, Carla. *Work of Craft*. New York: Alfred A. Knopf, 1979.

Rohrlick, Jay. *Work and Love*. New York: Summit Book, 1980.

Sanford, John and Paula. *Transformation of the Inner Man*. New Jersey: Bridge Publishing, Inc., 1982.

Sinetar, Marsha. *Ordinary People as Monks and Mystics*. Mahwah, N.J.: Paulist Press, 1986.

Steiner, Claude. *Scripts People Live*. New York: Random House, 1975.

Suzuki, Shunryu. *Zen Mind, Beginner's Mind*. New York: Weatherhill, 1975.

Szasz, Thomas. *The Second Sin*. New York: Anchor, 1975.

Szekely, Edmond Boreaux. *Creative Work*. USA: International Biogenic Society, 1973.

Teutsch, Champion. *From Here to Happiness*. Los Angeles: Price, Stern, Sloan, 1975.

Tulku, Tarthung. *Skillful Means*. Emeryville, Cal.: Dharma Publications, 1978.

Viscott, David. *Language of Feelings*. New York: Pocket Books, 1976.

Warner, Samuel. *Self-Realization and Self-Defeat*. New York: Grove Press, 1966.

Youtang, Lin. *The Importance of Living*. New York: Capricorn Books, 1974.

Do What You Love, The Money Will Follow

"This is 'how-to' writing at its best. Marsha Sinetar has earned something that few writers of how-to books do: she has earned the title of a true path-finder who points the way to an understanding of the legitimate place that work has in the natural order of adult life."
— New Families

"Exceptionally insightful...powerful and enlightening. It highlights an important realm of possibilities in our life in the Spirit."
— Quaker Life

"Offers objective advice on a subject that many of us regard as an idealistic dream: to do what you love, and love what you do."
— Wholistic Living News

Do What You Love, The Money Will Follow

"The book's great strength is its insistence on patience and that money and recognition *follow* doing what you love. It provides an important challenge for individuals to find their way back to the Garden, where work is no longer toil and each soul hears God calling."
— *The Common Boundary*

"The title says it all. Buy this book!"
— *Clout*

"Provides a much needed spiritual, yet practical, approach to following your heart and making a living."
— *Spectrum*

Do What You Love, The Money Will Follow

"Gently reassuring guide to all who yearn for work that will express their particular creative abilities."

— *Library Journal*

"Very helpful to people who want to integrate their work more meaningfully with who they are."

— *Praying*

"A very inspiring and positive book about a subject that is more important to us than we sometimes care to think about."

— *Critique*